Standards for Instructional Supervision

Enhancing Teaching and Learning

Stephen P. Gordon, Editor

EYE ON EDUCATION
6 DEPOT WAY WEST, SUITE 106
LARCHMONT, NY 10538
(914) 833–0551
(914) 833–0761 fax
www.eyeoneducation.com

Library of Congress Cataloging-in-Publication Data

Standards for instructional supervision : enhancing teaching and learning / edited by Stephen P. Gordon.
        p. cm.
Includes index.
ISBN 1-59667-011-8
1. School supervision. 2. Education—Standards. I. Gordon, Stephen P., 1948-
LB2806.4.S73 2006
371.2'03—dc22

                                        2005016661

10 9 8 7 6 5 4 3 2 1

Editorial and production services provided by
Richard H. Adin Freelance Editorial Services
52 Oakwood Blvd., Poughkeepsie, NY 12603-4112
(845-471-3566)

Foreword

Standards for Instructional Supervision will soon be one of the most popular books published on the topic of supervision. No doubt timing will be one reason for this book's success. We are, after all, in the midst of a standards movement that seems to be here to stay.

Editor Stephen Gordon and the authors who contributed to this book are the second reason this book will be successful. The authors write with restraint, thoughtfulness, care, and good sense. This group of authors is the best that supervision has to offer and their work in this volume shows it.

The third and most important reason this book will be successful is the commitment the authors have to the idea that supervision and teaching can have quality standards without unduly standardizing things. For standards to work in supervision they must increase, not decrease, the amount of discretion that teachers and supervisors have. Quality standards can help us to focus our work by supporting a purposeful and coherent strategy for teaching and learning. Sometimes standards should be common and should be shared by teachers and supervisors. At other times standards should differ. In seeking balance, schools have a responsibility to choose standards wisely. When successful, they avoid still another "one best list" of standards and of practices to implement.

While all of the authors are in one way or another committed to the ideas in this book, not all of the authors share the same level of commitment and this is a good thing. The standards conversation in supervision is just warming up and the reasoned debate that I imagine will take place as this book is published will only help sharpen our thinking and help move things along.

Editor Gordon invites readers to join the conversation by visiting the website of the National Center for School Improvement at Texas State University. Not only will the standards be available at the website but readers will have an opportunity to discuss, to debate, to accept, to challenge, to reject, and hopefully to offer alternatives to the standards as now configured. If we get the standards piece right, we will have taken a giant step toward professionalizing the art and science of supervision.

Thomas J. Sergiovanni

Lillian Radford Professor of Education, Trinity University, San Antonio, TX
August 2005

Preface

It might seem strange that someone opposed to mandatory standards for instructional supervision would edit a book about supervision standards, yet this is the situation in which I find myself. In assuming the editing task, I brought a set of nontraditional beliefs with me, at least in comparison to many educators in the "standards movement." "These include the beliefs that our profession can have model standards without standardization, standards should be educative rather than controlling, and districts and schools should have the freedom to modify and adapt standards to local contexts and goals. I'm not sure if all of the authors in this book share these beliefs with me, but I am most impressed with the standards they have proposed and with the discussions that accompany those standards. Each set of standards is built on a platform that was shared with the authors before they agreed to write chapters for the book. This framework also should be shared with the reader. Four key planks in the platform follow.

1. For the purpose of developing the standards, instructional supervision is defined as leadership for the enhancement of teaching and learning. Thus, it assumes that supervision may be provided by not only formally designated supervisors but also any and all instructional leaders, including principals, department chairs, team leaders, lead teachers, specialists, and regular classroom teachers.

2. The standards proposed in this book are standards for school-based supervision programs. Because everyone in a successful school is responsible to some extent for instructional supervision, standards need to be developed for the school's *supervision system*, not just for individual leaders or the graduate programs that prepare them. Standards adopted by the school should be agreed upon by the school's entire professional community, with all members of the school community accepting responsibility for helping to meet the standards. Also, schools should be able to revise and adapt standards so they are relevant to local school contexts and goals.

   Although the standards are intended for school supervision programs they also have implications for the development of supervisor preparation programs and the improved performance of individual supervisors.

3. If standards are to be truly educative, they must be closely linked to professional development for supervisors and other instructional leaders. To provide examples of connecting standards to professional development, each author describes a professional development activity designed to assist leaders and programs to meet one or more standards. Most authors also include criteria to assess the effectiveness of the professional development activity.

4. The proposed standards are intended as a starting point rather than an end point in the development of supervision standards. With the publication of this book, the authors invite scholars and practitioners across the nation to begin a broader discussion of standards for instructional supervision. To facilitate dialogue on supervision standards, the National Center for School Improvement, located at Texas State University, has established a Web site **(www.txstate.edu/ncsi)** inviting comments on the proposals in this book as well as the submission of proposals for new standards and professional development activities. New proposals will be reviewed by a national commission on supervision standards composed of scholars and practitioners representing various stakeholders, and new standards and professional development activities that are approved will be posted on the Web site for public review. Hopefully the Web site will eventually house a large selection of standards and professional development activities available for adoption or adaptation by districts and schools.

Part one, the introduction, places the proposed standards in context. Henry St. Maurice and Perry Cook provide a genealogy of standards in chapter 1, and eight questions and issues on standards are discussed in chapter 2 by Judy Castles-Bentley, Sharon Fillion, David Allen, Jane Ross, and Stephen Gordon.

Part two addresses cultural standards for supervision. Duncan Waite (chapter 3) proposes standards of democratic supervision that he considers "difficult to attain, but worth pursuing." Robert Starratt (chapter 4) describes standards of ethical learning and teaching "intended to support the cultivation and enhancement of moral character of *all* forms of learning." Sally Zepeda (chapter 5) presents standards of collegiality and collaboration that foster learning communities. Daisy Arredondo Rucinski (chapter 6) suggests standards of reflective practice that lead to expert and ethical practice. John Smyth (chapter 7) argues for standards of critical inquiry intended to foster a new "pedagogical imagination." Finally, Geneva Gay (chapter 8) offers standards of diversity intended to bridge the gap between theoretical conceptualization of multicultural education and school practice.

Part three is focused on supervision processes. Elaine Stotko, Edward Pajak, and Lee Goldsberry (chapter 9) propose standards for clinical supervision aimed at helping teachers reflect on and improve their own practice. Patricia Holland (chapter 10) offers standards for teacher evaluation that inform and guide rather than prescribe the teacher's practice. Stephen Gordon (chapter 11) presents standards for supervision of professional development that integrate school and teacher development. Bernard Badiali (chapter 12) suggests curriculum development standards that promote the collaboration of all stakeholders in curriculum planning and implementation. Jeffery Glanz (chapter 13) describes standards for action research that foster instructional dialogue, self-assessment, and professional problem solving. In the concluding chapter (chapter 14), James Nolan discusses standards for program evaluation that encourage stakeholder participation, valid and reliable data, and balanced reporting.

I am most thankful to the authors for their innovative and thoughtful approaches to proposing standards for instructional supervision. I am grateful for the assistance of Megan Dvorsky in organizing the overall manuscript and to Julie Diehl, my graduate assistant, for her research and editing.. Finally, I salute Eye On Education's Bob Sickles for having the foresight to call for a book on standards for instructional supervision, and the courage to publish a book that presents an alternative approach to developing standards.

Stephen P. Gordon
San Marcos, Texas

Table of Contents

Part I

Introduction

1

Toward Standards for Instructional Supervision: A Genealogy of Standards

Henry St. Maurice and Perry Cook

Meet the Authors

Henry St. Maurice

Henry St. Maurice is Director of Field Experiences and Professor at the University of Wisconsin-Stevens Point. He has also taught in elementary, secondary and rehabilitation programs. His research interests include rhetorical, philosophical, and historical studies of instructional supervision.

Perry Cook

Perry A. Cook, Professor of Science and Adolescent Education, earned his Ph.D. from the University of Wisconsin—Madison in 1992. After working two years as an assistant professor of science education at the University of North Dakota he came to the University of Wisconsin—Stevens Point, his undergraduate alma mater. His teaching career began in Redlands, California where he taught science and served as science department chairperson for four years at Arrowhead Christian Academy. Dr. Cook's research interests include the use of virtual supervision for science student teachers, interdisciplinary approaches to pre-service elementary methods preparation and the process of teacher socialization.

In this chapter, we ask where standards come from and whether their provenance offers a means of analyzing prospects for the development and promulgation of new standards in the field of instructional supervision. Our method of inquiry is genealogy, as described by Foucault (1980):

> Let us give the term "genealogy" to the union of erudite knowledge and local memories, which allows us to establish a historical knowledge of struggles and to make use of this knowledge tactically today. (p. 83)

Briefly, a genealogical method combines analyses of scholarly texts with analyses of local and tacit knowledge to show contradictions and discontinuities, and points of struggle over how official discourses and practices are constituted, and by whom.

The aim of this method is to show how words and ideas have changed and how they can change. As Fendler (1999) said, "The purpose of genealogical critique is to render events and circumstances historically contingent, and therefore changeable" (p. 185). This is not to imply there are no shared meanings of terms or to lessen the value of social constructions. By this method we analyze standards as constructions, which institutionalize what people say and do. This sets limits and possibilities for what is, is not, and will be appropriate discourse and practice.

In the following sections, we trace a genealogy of standards by specifying etymological, historical, and conceptual aspects of instructional supervision in the words and conventions that have been built and inhabited by educators since mass public schooling began in Europe and North America. This expounded, contextual understanding of standards may serve as a basis for instructional supervision reform.

Etymology

Etymologies of the word *standard* indicate a transition from military to civilian and scientific denotations of the word, maintaining strong moral overtones (*The Concise Oxford Dictionary of Current English 1990*). *Whether in a battle, a counting house, a factory, or a laboratory, a standard is more than a neutral point of reference, it is a paragon of rectitude. Williams (1985) captured these moral connotations in his definition:*

> Instead of referring back to a source of authority, or taking a current measurable state, a standard is set, projected, from ideas about conditions which we have not yet realized but which we think should be realized. There is an active social history in the development of this phrase. (p. 299)

Another historically social understanding of the word standard is rooted in finance and, by analogy, medicine. The often-cited term *gold standard* represents a shared meaning that implies not only inherent value but also a projection of hierarchy (Michaels, 1986). Literally, a gold standard transubstantiates a lesser element (e.g., paper) into a greater one. In practice, paper representations were exchangeable for gold. In professional fields like law and medicine, an analogous gold standard is assigned to practices generally agreed as best, but nonetheless open to challenge and change, much as monetary standards have changed at regular intervals. The image of immutability and the presence of mutation seem to inhere in every standard.

Historical Background

Processes of making and changing standards were crucial in the development of Western science and the expansion of European nations and empires (Crosby, 1997; Lindberg, 1992). For our genealogy, we will summarize some of the social history of standards since the mid-19th century. That is when a gradual process of weights and measures standardization, as indicated in the above etymologies, rapidly underwent major changes in Europe and North America over a short period of time. Railways, ship lines, and telegraph networks coalesced into something new in human affairs: a network of social, political, and economic systems larger than any single empire. Within a single decade, from 1840 to 1850, a patchwork of local markets merged into a global web tending to form monopolies (Hobsbawm, 1975). As information, goods, and services sped around the globe at unprecedented speeds, uniform standards emerged for quantities such as measurement (Alder, 2002), finance (Michaels, 1986), production (Hughes, 1990), time (Landes, 2000), and quality.

Environmental historian William Cronon (1991) described the origins of quality grading in Chicago in the 1850s: as elevators commingled separate crops, farmers were given receipts showing quantity in pounds and quality on a three-part scale. These receipts became commodities to be traded. Soon, derivative instruments such as futures contracts were traded as well. In a world of mass marketing and standardization, anything that could be measured was graded and traded. If a wagonload of wheat could be assigned a grade, so could a can of milk or a portfolio of stocks and bonds.

The first standards for quantities established simple benchmarks but science and industry soon required more complex systems. Most notably, the synchronization of clocks raised many questions. For example, how could noon as measured by the sun directly overhead be replaced by standardized numbers? And, should standards be set requiring timepieces to run together in zones or over the whole globe? If so, how could a signal that takes time to travel ever accomplish perfect synchronization? Before Einstein's special theory of relativity established the speed of light as a constant, scientists searched for a physical invariant. One of the foremost, Pierre Poincaré of France, proposed that geometric laws offered the best model of standardization but with an inherent contradiction: nature is rarely straight or round. As Galison (2003) summarized,

> In differential equations or in the physical systems they represented, there were always many ways of choosing variables—to describe, for instance, the flow lines of water down a stream. What was significant were the underlying relations that remained unchanged even after such changes in description: the vortices in a flow of water, the knots, saddle points, or spiral endpoints of geometrical lines. Similarly, the length of a line remains fixed when we rotate coordinates. These two aspects of Poincaré's work—the variable and the fixed—emerged together and can only be understood together. He says, in different ways over many years: Manipulate the flexible aspects of knowledge as tools; choose the form that makes the problem at hand simple. Then seize those relations that stand fast despite the choices made. Those fixed relations stand for knowledge that endures. Together the variant and invariant make scientific progress possible. (p. 79)

Standards make certain kinds of science possible, in short, by projecting invariance onto variance.

In the United States, philosophers of science also struggled with antinomies between precision and indeterminacy. Pragmatists such as Chauncey Wright, Charles Pierce, and William James stated that natural phenomena like the weather could be accurately measured but not perfectly predicted. Peirce, Marquand, Franklin, Mitchell, and Gilman (1883) asked whether laws of nature were themselves subject to laws. As Menand (2001) summarized, "Does the principle that everything can be explained have an explanation? Or…does the law of causality (which is another name for the principle that everything can be explained) have a cause?" (p. 275). Philosophers of quantitative science used their inquiries to install their discourses and practices at the top of hierarchies in academia, industry, and the military. Further down the ladders, in qualitative experience, these questions were addressed in everyday routines. Weather forecasts that people saw in their newspapers might be wrong as they walked out their doors, and clocks they saw in their train stations might vary from the ones they carried on their persons, but these standards had as much precision as needed; no more and no less.

The biological sciences give us an example of the development of genetic standards derived from research and from which practices emanate. The Office of Health and Environmental Research in the U.S. Department of Energy developed a plan to map the entire human genome (National Institutes of Health, 1990), now known as the Human Genome Project (HGP). This large-scale process led to standardized medical research and development that not only promised breakthroughs in health care but also had potential for bioethical, legal, and social malfeasance, as Paabo (2001) discussed:

> From a medical standpoint, improved predictive capabilities provided by the identification of disease-associated alleles harbor great potential benefits but also problems. The benefits will come from using individualized risk assessment to modify the environmental and behavioral components of common diseases…[but] increased medical predictive power obviously represents a societal challenge in terms of medical insurance, especially in countries that, unlike most Western European countries, are not blessed with health insurance systems that share risks in an equitable fashion among the whole population. (p. 1220)

Standardization does not diminish the consequences of science and technology and may instead intensify them.

The processes by which scientists and policy makers determine whether a standard was sufficient came to be known as conventions, which, as Galison (2003) says, are

> likened to terms in language [e.g., French or German] that can be freely chosen and also to the freedom the mathematician or physicist has to choose a coordinate system [e.g., Euclidean or non-Euclidean] as well as a choice between the arbitrary system of meters and kilograms and the arbitrary system of feet and pounds. (p. 82)

As linguistic devices, standards and conventions harbor ambiguities, despite the rhetoric of precision and accuracy in which they are couched. In short, standards are formed by consensus among an elite, who decide which sets of quantities and qualities are most suited to their uses while tacitly agreeing that no one set of standards can be definitive (e.g., American National Standards Institute [ANSI], 2004; International Standards Organization [ISO], 2004; National Institute of Standards and Technology [NIST], 2004).

In the alchemy of modernity, standards, despite their artifice and ambiguity, become dominant facts of life for masses who toil by the hour and whose labors are measured, graded, bought, and sold. No one has said it better than Marx and Engels (1848/1998): "All that is solid melts into air, all that is holy is profaned, and man is at last compelled to face with sober senses his real condition of life and his relations with his kind" (p. 5). The solid fact of the sun in the sky gave way to the ephemera of standard time. The solid fact of a bag of grain was first commodified as a contract, then abstracted into a number on a tote board. By the beginning of the 20th century, standards and conventions, despite their limitations as ambiguous projections, became dominant in human life.

Standards for Supervision

There is an active social history of standardization in the field of instructional supervision. Mass public schooling grew in industrially developed nation-states during the 19th century with the explicit purpose of fostering more and better industrial workers and national citizens (Green, 1990). From the beginning, mass public schooling in the United States. was instrumental in industrial development. To run schools that Mann (1849) said were the "the balance-wheel of the social machinery" (p. 59), managers were said to occupy a "classless profession" (Mattingly, 1975; Tyack & Hansot, 1982). The first standards for instructional supervisors were simple: either a school had a building with desks, books, and a teacher or it did not (Blumberg, 1985). As supervision became professionalized (Glanz, 1998), it embodied the "cult of efficiency" in industrialized nation-states (Callahan, 1964; Hughes, 1990; Tichi, 1987). There are hosts of examples of the primacy of social efficiency in the United States during two centuries of schooling (Cremin, 1988; Glass, Mason, Eaton, Parker, & Carver, 2004; Kaestle & Foner, 1983; Kliebard, 1986). A concise statement of standards based on efficiency is found in the *Fourth Yearbook of the Department of Supervisors and Directors of Instruction* of the (U.S.) National Education Association (Woody et al., 1931):

Supervision may be evaluated in light of any one or any combination of these three considerations:

1. *Effect.* The degree to which its effect on persons (including pupils, parents, teachers, and the community as a whole) and on educational methods and materials approximates the results desired

2. *Activities.* The degree to which its activities conform to accepted standards for supervisory activities

3. *Supervisor's characteristics.* The degree to which the characteristics of the person doing the supervision conforms to the standards for such traits (p. 15).

The standards invoked in this passage embody "autocratic methods and procedures" (Glanz, 1998, p. 49) derived from religious and military hierarchies, alongside business and government bureaucracies. For generations, this has been familiar to all teachers. One example of these standards in school folklore is the "snoopervisor," described in the following poem by an anonymous author. It was first published in 1929 (quoted in Glanz, 1990):

> *With keenly peering eyes and snooping nose,*
> *From room to room the Snoopervisor goes.*
> *He notes each slip, each fault with lofty frown,*
> *And on his rating card he writes it down.*
> *His duty done, when he has brought to light*
> *The things that teachers do that are not right.*
> *With cheering words and most infectious grin,*
> *The peppy Whoopervisor breezes in.*
> *"Let every boy and girl keep right with me!*
> *"One, two three, four!*
> *"That's fine! Miss Smith I see*
> *These pupils all write well." This his plan*
> *"Keep everybody happy if you can."*
> *The Supervisor enters quietly.*
> *"What do you need? How can I help today?*
> *"John, let me show you. Mary, try this way."*
> *He aims to help, encourage and suggest,*
> *That teachers, pupils, all may do their best.*

Between the male and female figures in the poem are a host of tensions over "standard practices." Specifically, the supervisor's parameters of efficiency are said to occupy neutral space apart from race, class, gender, or politics. To teachers, however, the discourses of social efficiency clash with practices like minatory male supervisors peering through keyholes, seeking "weaknesses" in subjugated female teachers. The supervisor of the poem, left unstated but implied, is far from the norm. The first two caricatures not only predominate in folklore, but in practice, as empirical studies have repeatedly shown (Glanz, 1998; Blass, Mason, Eaton, Parker & Carver, 2004; Tyack & Hansot, 1982).

As Menand (2001) pointed out, social efficiency movements thrive during times of political crisis: civil wars, wars of imperial conquest, the two World Wars, the Cold War, and economic depression. For instance, during the Great Depression of the 1930s, scientists and policy makers were challenged to develop and implement technologies to ameliorate social crises. In their turn, scholars of instructional supervision proposed more scientific analyses of teaching, even as teachers sought greater democratization through their professional organizations, which began to adopt aims and methods from labor unions (Glanz, 1998). One leading proponent of more rigorously quantifiable standards for supervisors, A. S. Barr (1931), declared that "supervisors must possess training in both the science of instructing pupils and the science of instructing teachers" (p. x). Such quests for certainty remain unresolved. At the same time, teachers and teacher educators proposed various other standards based on differing philosophical and political systems, including liberal humanism (Charters & Waples, 1929) and socialism (Counts, 1932). These struggles continued and expanded for decades. Edelfeldt and Raths (1999) listed 10 major standardization proposals put forth by teacher educators and supervisors in the United States since Barr's declaration and concluded that most recommendations for reforming teacher education and supervision are often "totally ahistorical, with no authors wondering why the profession had ignored previous recommendations or adopted them without changing dramatically the practice of teachers or the status of teaching" (p. 27). Decades after Mann and his successors sought utopian solutions for schools, teachers and their supervisors have not come closer to a consensus over the aims and means of instructional improvement. No one has secured a "king's standard" that, as Williams (1987) said, is a projection like the end of a rainbow.

Nevertheless, movements for standardization have not only persisted, but intensified. Following the publication of *A Nation at Risk: The Imperative for Educational Reform* (Bell & United States National Commission on Excellence in Education, 1983) and a series of well-publicized national reports and summit meetings, a highly charged movement for "world-class standards" swept through schools in the United States (Riley and United States Department of Education, 1995). For example, the National Policy Boead for Educational Administration (NPBEA) promulgated national standards for instructional leadership (NPBEA, 2002), and one pertains to supervision: Instructional leaders are exhorted to "utilize a variety of supervisory models to improve teaching and learning (e.g., clinical, developmental, cognitive and peer coaching, as well as applying observation and conferencing skills)" (p. 14).

Most recently, beginning in 1992, a set of six national standards has been developed for school leadership in the United States (Council of Chief State School Officers, 1996), versions of which have been adopted in various states (e.g., Wisconsin Department of Public Instruction, 2004):

- ◆ The administrator leads by facilitating the development, articulation, implementation, and stewardship of a vision of learning that is shared by the school community.

- ◆ The administrator manages by advocating, nurturing, and sustaining a school culture and instructional program conducive to pupil learning and staff professional growth.

- ◆ The administrator ensures management of the organization, operations, finances, and resources for a safe, efficient, and effective learning environment.

- ◆ The administrator models collaboration with families and community members, responding to diverse community interests and needs, and mobilizing community resources.

- ◆ The administrator acts with integrity, fairness, and in an ethical manner.

- ◆ The administrator understands, responds to, and interacts with the larger political, social, economic, legal, and cultural context that affects schooling.

In a similar vein, standards for instructional supervision recently have been proposed (Allen, Fillion, Butters, Gordon, & Bentley, 2004), some based on the U.S. National Board for Professional Teaching Standards (Bernstein, 2004).

These recent standards and their ancestors, beginning with the pioneer educator's visions of stable social order, followed by the progressive reformer's quests for efficiency and scientific validity, and leading up to contemporary visions of democratization and empowerment, all share discourses and practices, which disperse power relations with multiple points of authority and therefore a myriad of points of contestation. When thousands of instructional leaders in schools and agencies implement different models of improvement for millions of teachers, a net of power relations is strung, without a center, but no less pervasive. Such relations enact what Foucault (1988) called "technologies of power, which determine the conduct of individuals and submit them to certain ends or domination, an objectivizing of the subject" (p. 18). In short, the discourse of standards and the practices of instructional supervision remain in conflict. For example, under U.S. federal rules implemented since 2001, instructional supervisors must now make educational decisions that are determined by the outcomes of standardized testing, not the processes of deliberation and communication indicated in the standards in the above list. As Glanz (2004) summarized, "Supervision within a standards-based environment resorts to mechanistic, bureaucratic means, aimed not at instructional improvement, but to implementing narrowly prescribed measures of performance" (p. 3). The technologies of standardization are once more bifurcated into palliative discourses from supervisors and proletarianized processes.

Conclusions

Our genealogical review and analysis of standards for instructional supervision offers five specific points:

1. Standards are discursive constructions for projecting invariance onto variance, usually in quantitative terms.

2. Standardization is a process of projecting invariance through the formation of conventions that are first adopted by elites and then enforced on masses.

3. All movements for standardization are contingent on circumstances and contexts; their rhetoric of continuity sustains a network of power relations.

4. Invariance inheres in standardization, despite whatever anyone says or does otherwise.

5. Movements for standards for instructional supervision have occurred in parallel with increased standardization of life and work for more than 15 decades of rapid industrialization.

In general, for more than a century, standardization of instructional supervision has dispensed rhetoric of continuity at best, and widened disconnections among discourses and practices at worst. Reviews of supervisor discourses and practices during those decades (Glanz, 2004; Glass et al., 2004), show gulfs and "cold wars" among educators, whether in the name of social efficiency, social transformation, or social mobilization (Blumberg, 1980). In particular, standardization has not fostered developmental approaches to instructional supervision, as described by Glickman, Gordon, and Ross-Gordon (2004): "Goodness, purpose and hope for all our students [in a] purposeful school dedicated to teaching and learning" (p.476).

In conclusion, our brief genealogy of explicit and implicit discourses and practices indicates that schools are institutions in which quantities such as time, mass, and distance may be standardized, but qualities such as learning, engagement, and improvement are not yet and probably will not be standardized. Such processes depend on concentrated control over the discourses and practices by an elite, through its conventions. But democratic schools depend on dispersed control over diverse discourses and practices. This antinomy would seem to make impossible standards for supervision. The teachers, leaders, students, and communities that inhabit schools require more complicated tools for instructional leadership toward educational equality and excellence.

References

Alder, K. (2002). *The measure of all things.* New York: Free Press.

Allen, D., Fillion, S., Butters, J., Gordon, S., & Bentley, J. (2004, April). *Considering national standards for instructional supervision: A review of the literature.* Paper presented at the annual meeting of the American Educational Research Association, San Diego, CA.

American National Standards Institute (2004). *ANSI—an historical overview.* Washington DC: Author.

Barr, A. S. (1931). *An introduction to the scientific study of classroom supervision.* New York: Appleton.

Bell, T., & United States National Commission on Excellence in Education. (1983). *A nation at risk : The imperative for educational reform.* United States Department of Education. Washington, DC: Government Printing Office.

Bernstein, E. (2004). What teacher evaluation should know and be able to do: A commentary. *NASSP Bulletin, 88*(639), 80–89.

Blumberg, A. (1980). *Supervisors and teachers: A private cold war.* Berkeley, CA: McCutchan.

Blumberg, A. (1985). Where we came from: Notes on supervision in the 1840s. *Journal of Curriculum and Supervision, 1*(1), 56–65.

Callahan, R. (1964). *Education and the cult of efficiency: A study of the social forces that have shaped the administration of the public schools.* Chicago: University of Chicago Press.

Charters, W., & Waples, D. (1929). *The Commonwealth teacher-training study.* Chicago: University of Chicago Press.

Council of Chief State School Officers. (1996). *Interstate School Leaders Licensure Consortium Standards.* Washington, DC: Author. Retrieved August 29, 2005 from http://www.ccsso. org/projects/Interstate_Consortium_on_School_ Leadership/

Counts, G. (1932). *Dare the school build a new social order?* New York: John Day.

Cremin, L. (1988). *American education: The metropolitan experience, 1876–1980.* New York: Harper & Row.

Cronon, W. (1991). *Nature's metropolis: Chicago and the great West.* New York: W. W. Norton.

Crosby, A. W. (1997). *The measure of reality: Quantification and Western society, 1250–1600.* New York: Cambridge University Press.

Edelfelt, R., & Raths, J. (1999). *A brief history of standards in teacher education*. Reston, VA: Association of Teacher Educators.

Fendler, L. (1999). Making trouble: Prediction, agency and critical intellectuals. In T. Popkewitz, & L. Fendler, (Eds.). *Critical theories in education*. New York: Routledge.

Foucault, M. (1980). *Power/knowledge: Selected interviews and other writings, 1972–1977*. C. Gordon (Ed.). New York: Pantheon.

Foucault, M. (1988). Technologies of the self. In L. Martin, H, Gutman, & P. Hutton, (Eds.) *A seminar with Michel Foucault*. Amherst, MA: University of Massachusetts Press.

Galison, P. (2003). *Einstein's clocks, Poincaré's maps : Empires of time*. New York: W.W. Norton.

Glanz, J. (1990). Beyond bureaucracy: Notes on the professionalization of public school supervision in the early 20th century. *Journal of Curriculum and Supervision* 5(2), 150–170.

Glanz, J. (1998). Histories, antecedents and legacies of school supervision. In G. Firth & E., Pajak (Eds.) *Handbook of research on school supervision* (pp. 39–79). New York: Macmillan.

Glanz, J. (2004 Spring). New York City politics and the demise of instructional supervision. *Supervision and Instructional Leadership SIG Newsletter*.

Glass, T., Mason, R., Eaton, W., Parker, J., & Carver, F. (2004). *The history of educational administration viewed through its textbooks*. Lanham, MD: Scarecrow Press.

Glickman, C., Gordon, S., & Ross-Gordon, J. (2004). *SuperVision & instructional leadership: A developmental approach*, (6th ed.). Boston: Pearson-Allyn Bacon.

Green, A. (1990). *Education and state formation: The rise of education systems in England France, and the U.S.A*. New York: St. Martin's Press.

Hobsbawm, E. J. (1975). *The age of capital: 1848–1875*. London: Vintage.

Hughes, T. P. (1990). *American genesis : A century of invention and technological enthusiasm, 1870–1970*. New York: Penguin.

International Organization for Standardization. (2005). *How it all started*. Geneva: Author. Retrieved August 29, 2005 from http://www.iso.ch/iso/en/aboutiso/introductin/index.html

International Standards Organization.(2004). *How it all started*. Geneva: International Standards Organization. Retrieved month day, year from http://www.iso.ch/iso/en/aboutiso/introduction/index.html#four

Iwanicki, E. (1998). Evaluation in supervision. In G. Firth & E. Pajak (Eds.), *Handbook of research on school supervision* (pp. 138–180). New York: Macmillan.

Kaestle, C. F., & Foner, E. (1983). *Pillars of the republic : Common schools and American society, 1780–1860*. New York: Hill and Wang.

Kliebard, H. (1986). *The struggle for the American curriculum, 1893–1958*. New York: Routledge.

Landes, D. (2000). *Revolution in time : Clocks and the making of the modern world*. Cambridge, MA,: Harvard University Press.

Lindberg, D. C. (1992). *The beginnings of Western science : The European scientific tradition in philosophical, religious, and institutional context, 600 B.C. to A.D. 1450*. Chicago: University of Chicago Press.

Mann, H. (1849). *Twelfth annual report to the Massachusetts Board of Education*. Boston: Dutton & Wentworth.

Marx, K., & Engels, F. (1998). *The Communist manifesto: A modern edition*. London: Verso.

Mattingly, P. (1975). *The classless profession: American schoolmen in the nineteenth century*. New York: New York University Press.

Menand, L. (2001). *The metaphysical club*. New York: Farrar, Straus and Giroux.

Michaels, W. (1986). *The gold standard and the logic of naturalism*. Berkeley: University of California Press.

National Policy Board for Educational Administration. (2002). *Standards for advanced programs in educational leadership*. Washington, DC: AACTE.

National Institute of Health (1990). *Understanding our genetic inheritance: The U.S. human genome project, The First Five Years*. Washington, DC: Author.

National Institute of Standards & Technology (2004). *NIST Information*. Gaithersburg, MD: Author. Retrieved August 29, 2005 from http://www.nist.gov/public_affairs/general2.htm

The Concise Oxford Dictionary of correct English (1990). New York: Oxford University Press.

Paabo, S. (2001). Genomics and society: the human genome and our view of ourselves. *Science, 291*, 1219–1220.

Peirce, C. S., Marquand, A., Franklin, C., Mitchell, O., & Gilman, B. (1883). *Studies in logic*. Boston: Little Brown & Company.

Riley, R., & United States Department of Education. (1995). *Turning the corner: From a nation at risk to a nation with a future*. Washington, DC: U.S. Department of Education.

Tichi, C. (1987). *Shifting gears: Technology, literature, culture in modernist America*. Chapel Hill: University of North Carolina Press.

Tyack, D., & Hansot, E. (1982). *Managers of virtue: Public school leadership in America, 1820–1980*. New York: Basic Books.

Williams, R. (1985). *Keywords: A vocabulary of culture and society*. New York: Oxford University Press.

Woody, C., Kibbe, D., Kyte, G., Lindquist, R., McClure, W., McGaughy, J., Mingo, J., & Rankin, P. (Eds.) (1931). *The Evaluation of Supervision*. New York: Teachers College.

Wisconsin Department of Public Instruction (2004). *PI34 Standards for Administrators*. Madison, WI: Author. Retrieved August 29, 2005 from http://www.dpi.state.wi.us/dpi/dlsis/tel/pi34.html

2

Standards for Instructional Supervision: Questions and Issues

Judy Castles-Bentley, Sharon Fillion, David Allen, Jane Ross, Stephen P. Gordon

Meet the Authors

Sharon Fillion

Sharon Walker Fillion is a Doctoral Candidate in the Ph.D. program in school improvement at Texas State University-San Marcos. She also is an elementary school teacher in the Austin (Texas) Independent School District. Her interests are in teacher education, multicultural education, and culturally responsible pedagogy. Her dissertation, in progress, is a qualitative examination of the phenomena of the culturally responsible teacher in the homogeneous White classroom.

David Allen

David Allen is a doctoral student at Texas State University-San Marcos. He is pursing a Ph.D. in education with a major in school improvement. Mr. Allen has over ten years of teaching experience at the middle school, high school, and junior college levels. He is also a project leader with the Educational Testing Service, Elementary and Secondary Education Division. Mr. Allen has worked with the development of large-scale state assessments for several US states and Puerto Rico.

Jane Ross

Jane Ross serves as curriculum and instruction assistant principal and lead mentor at a predominately minority middle school in Austin, Texas. She has taught seventh-grade mathematics and was voted as campus teacher of the year. Dr. Ross received her Ph.D. in education with a major in school improvement from Texas State University-San Marcos, where she recently accepted an adjunct teaching position in the educational administration department. Her publications and presentations include a focus on culturally responsive education; new teacher development; parent and community involvement; professional development; and teacher voice in educational policymaking.

Stephen P. Gordon

For information about Stephen P. Gordon please see page 156.

This chapter will address questions and issues on professional standards in general and possible standards for instructional supervision in particular. We will present arguments on different sides of the issues, but also discuss the issues within the context of this book, which itself presents a particular orientation toward standards. The questions and issues include:

- What are modern professional standards in education, and where did they come from?
- Should there be standards for instructional supervision?
- Who should develop standards?
- What should be the process for developing standards?
- What should be the scope of supervision standards?
- Should supervision standards be differentiated?
- How should standards be organized?
- What should be the relationship between standards and assessment?

What Are Modern Professional Standards in Education, and Where Did They Come From?

A Nation at Risk: The Imperative for Education Reform was a call to action issued by the National Commission on Excellence in Education (1983). This report is considered by many educators to be the seminal event of the modern standards movement in U.S. education. The report warned that the foundations of our society were "being eroded by a rising tide of mediocrity that threatens our future as a nation and a people…an act of unilateral educational disarmament" (p. 5).

As a result of the challenge of *A Nation at Risk: The Imperative for Educational Reform*, individual states and the profession as a whole were inspired to reorganize and create new standards for students and teachers. Educators began meticulously defining new professional standards for content areas, subject by subject, in the early 1990s. The standards were prepared by associations of educators in academic subjects, ad hoc groups, scientific organizations, and individual states. Content standards were followed by performance standards designed to measure and ensure accountability for the achievement of content standards (Wise & Liebbrand, 2001). Performance standards were intended to define "how good is good enough" (Thurlow, 2000, p. 1).

Standards for teachers were followed by standards for teacher preparation programs. A comprehensive accreditation program establishing rigorous standards for teacher preparation programs was developed by the National Council for Accreditation of Teacher Education (NCATE). In 1993, NCATE outlined a continuum of teacher preparation and development, indicating that linkages among preservice preparation, licensure, and professional development were needed to formulate a more coherent system of quality assurance. Many states adapted the continuum, developing tiered licensing systems. NCATE and the states using NCATE standards held colleges of education accountable for producing candidates with the same knowledge and skills for which the states held individual candidates accountable.

While new standards were being developed for teachers and teacher preparation programs, they also were being developed for school leaders and leadership preparation programs. In 1998, the National Policy Board for Educational Administration (NPBEA) was founded by 10 professional organizations. In 1993, NPBEA adopted a national knowledge and skill base for principals (Wilmore, 2002). A working group of NPBEA representatives, the Educational Leadership Constituent Council, developed a set of guidelines for the accreditation of advanced programs in educational leadership, which were adopted by NCATE in 1996. Also in 1996, standards for individual school administrators were developed by the Interstate School Leaders Licensure Consortium (ISLLC), a program of the Council of Chief State School Officers (CCSSO).

In 2000, NCATE revised its accreditation process, shifting to a performance-based paradigm to ensure that graduates would be prepared to function in real-world settings (National Policy Board for Educational Administration, 2002). In 2002, new standards for advanced programs in educational leadership preparation were developed jointly by the National Policy Board of the Educational Leadership Constituent Council (ELCC) and ISLLC. They were created to align educational leadership preparation standards with the standards for teacher evaluation prepared by NCATE. These standards seek to prepare "educational leaders who have the knowledge and ability to promote the success of all students" (NPBEA, 2002, p. 2)

A serious concern among scholars and practitioners of instructional supervision is that none of the national standards for educational leadership discussed above have seriously addressed standards for supervisors and instructional leaders. Although the national leadership standards acknowledge the importance of instructional leadership, they lack sufficient specificity to guide the development of successful supervisors or supervision programs. The purpose of this book is to initiate and promote the development of a comprehensive set of supervision standards, although it takes a different approach to the development of standards. Rather than focusing on preparation programs or individual supervisors, this book is focused on standards for school supervision programs.

Should There Be Standards for Instructional Supervision?

Proponents of instructional supervision standards argue that standards create criteria for professionalizing instructional supervision (Firth, 1998), require managers and leaders to rethink existing systems and practices (Hess, 2003), and illuminate the best practice in the field (Zepeda, 2003). Pajak (2000, 2001) pointed to standards as a way of addressing the loose coupling between administration and instruction, between universities and schools, and between preservice and in-service expectations, which create inconsistencies in achievement. Standards can bridge gaps and smooth transitions in the aforementioned areas (Pajak, 2000, 2001).

Firth (1997) argued that standards for instructional supervision are necessary for clarity, consistency, specialization, and meaningful accreditation. Firth added, "No common agreement exists on the nature of educational supervision, the role of the school supervisor, or the expectation of performance by a school supervisor.... The field of educational supervision must reach agreement on these matters if there is to be any hope of having a profession of educational supervision" (p. 176). Zepeda (2003) emphasized the critical need for instructional supervisors to understand and be guided by educational standards so students ultimately benefit from the implementation of best practices. Pajak (2000) noted that standards clarify and raise expectations, provide a common set of expectations, define performance, and provide consistent and rational interconnections among the components of educational systems.

Critics cite a variety of reasons against the development and use of standards. Marion (2000) believed that promoters of the standards movement are fueled by political and corporate motivations that gain popular support through deceptive claims about the benefits of standards. Marzano and Kendall (1996) noted that some critics see the standards movement as a source of resource depletion creating inequity among systems. Others claim that previous standards movements have failed, and a resurgence of those efforts will have similarly unsuccessful results. Criticism also comes from those who believe that standards promote behaviorism and objectivity.

Hazi (1997) argued that setting standards is a control strategy that builds on exclusive rather than inclusive practices. She characterized supervision standards as dogmatic and illusory. Hazi stated "The process of articulating standards is problematic. Although it may be described as consensus building, it is a process of control and dominance that gives the illusion of inclusion, objectivity, and collaboration" (p. 192). She believed that standards for instructional supervision promote distrust and their codified knowledge base represents only the consensus of those involved in their development. Hazi did not believe true consensus on standards ever can be reached. Discussing the argument that standards are associated with professionalism, Hazi argued the concept of professionalization itself is problematic, because it is based on a "dysfunctional and hegemonic" (p. 189) trait approach that undermines equity and diversity.

We believe the types of standards proposed in this book address many of the concerns of those opposed to traditional standards. First, these standards are for a supervision program or system—they do not attempt to impose particular traits on individual supervisors. Second, adoption of these standards will be voluntary. Schools that adopt the standards are encouraged to revise and adapt the standards so they are congruent with school contexts and goals. Finally, rather than promoting control and dominance, we believe that the standards in this book promote democracy, inquiry, and critical thinking.

Who Should Develop Standards?

Standards for professions outside of education, such as the legal and medical professions, tend to be generated from within the profession. Sizer and Rogers (1993) argued practitioners should be included in developing standards, and they should be "represented directly and not, as is often the case, through token representation on centrally controlled bodies" (p. 19). Hazi (1997) warned that design efforts that are inclusive and collegial on the surface can be weakened by external mandates on how standards should be written. She also noted that in the past, practitioners have been asked to respond to predrafted standards, rather than becoming actively involved in their development. Hazi concluded that what has been described as consensus building actually is a process of control and dominance that gives the illusion of inclusion, objectivity, and collaboration. Not all authors argue for—or lament the absence of— practitioner involvement in the development of supervision standards. Shoop (2002) called for "recognized educational administration experts" (p. 49) to develop supervision standards. Others have proposed the National Board for Professional Teaching Standards take the lead in developing supervision standards (Archer, 2002).

Although the proposed standards in this book have been developed by professors of instructional supervision, we hope this book will initiate a much wider process, including practitioners from across the nation not only in the review and revision of these standards but also in the development of additional standards, perhaps in whole new domains of supervision. Additionally, we view both the standards in this book and any standards that will emerge from a national dialogue as model standards to be examined and voluntarily adopted or adapted by districts and schools.

What Should Be the Process for Developing Standards?

Hazi (1997) explained the standards development process at its best:

> The process allows its participants to engage in a transformative experience in which they critically examine what they do and come to a different understanding about that when they are through. The process of standard-setting—not the standards—is the key to promoting quality. (p. 193)

A number of recommendations for assuring a participatory and successful process for developing standards are found in the literature (Consortium for Policy and Research in Education, 1993; National Board for Professional Teaching Standards, 2001; O'Day & Smith, 1993). Several suggestions for developing standards follow.

- *Identify stakeholders and invite their representatives to participate in developing standards.* To identify stakeholders, one should ask who will be implementing the standards, who will be expected to meet the standards, and who else will be affected by the standards.

- *Create a timeline for the process, with adequate time provided for research, writing, dissemination, review, feedback, and revision.* Timelines for developing standards vary greatly. Examples of the timelines we reviewed ranged from nine months to 10 years. The Consortium for Policy and Research in Education (1993) has described the process used by the National Council of Teachers of Mathematics (NCTM) as lengthy but successful.

  > One of the keys to NCTM's success was a slow, lengthy developmental process, which took nearly a decade to complete. The association took plenty of time to educate the

community about the need for standards, conduct research before the development committees met, and to solicit review and feedback. (p. 4)

♦ *Examine various viewpoints.* Broad, general standards may be acceptable, but the more specific the standards, the more controversy arises. Part of the process of developing standards should be to examine viewpoints of the various branches of a discipline to achieve a more comprehensive perspective (O'Day & Smith, 1993).

♦ *Provide for feedback on and refinement of standards.* Stakeholder review of standards is an essential part of the development process, but should not be the only type of stakeholder involvement. One way to improve standards prior to full-fledged implementation is to field-test standards. "The principle goals of this field testing phase include the further refinement and development of the standards and protocol, and the discovery of the best means of implementation" (Godfrey, 1997, p. 97). Public forums, focus groups, and questionnaires on draft standards are other ways of gathering feedback to refine standards.

Our hope is that this book will initiate a broader standards development process that will involve representatives of stakeholder groups, follow a timeline that allows a developmental approach, examine various viewpoints (including those that may not be represented in this book), use flexible but meaningful language, and provide for feedback and refinement.

What Should Be the
Scope of Supervision Standards?

Decisions on the scope of instructional supervision standards are related directly to decisions on the scope of instructional supervision itself. Our primary sources for surveying the scope of supervision were over 50 instructional supervision textbooks. Most of the texts selected were written over the last 40 years, but we also selected a small number of "classic" supervision texts published from the 1920s through the early 1960s (for a more comprehensive review and a list of the texts that were reviewed, see Allen, Fillion, Ross, Gordon, & Bentley, 2004).

Supervision Processes

One way to define the scope of supervision is to determine the processes that supervisors engage in, sometimes referred to in the literature as functions, duties, purposes, tasks, or activities. Across the supervision literature, the same processes might be discussed under any of these general terms. One process almost universally considered to be supervision is classroom-based assistance, and the most common structure for classroom-based assistance is clinical supervision (Acheson & Gall, 2003; Cogan, 1972; Goldhammer, 1969; Pajak, 2000). Other structures for classroom-based assistance include peer coaching, classroom-based action research, self-directed teacher growth, teacher portfolio development, and mentoring (Glanz & Sullivan, 2000; Nolan & Hoover, 2003; Zepeda, 2003).

As early as the 1920s, additional processes were described as part of supervision, including professional development, curriculum development, and teacher evaluation (Burton, 1922). By the mid-20th century, group development also was discussed as a supervisory process (Wiles, 1950). Two additional, related processes considered to be part of instructional supervision in several texts include general program evaluation and evaluation of the supervisory program. Supervision processes described in only a few texts include school–community relations, action research, human development, organizational leadership, school improvement, teacher induction, and teacher development.

Knowledge, Skills, and Dispositions

Another way to define the scope of supervision is to identify the knowledge, skills, and dispositions needed by successful supervisors or supervision programs. Figure 2.1 summarizes the knowledge, skills, and dispositions discussed in detail in at least several of the supervision texts that we reviewed (Allen et al., 2004). The various topics listed in Figure 2.1 are classified according to the frequency with which they are discussed across the texts.

Figure 2.1. Examples of Knowledge, Skills, and Dispositions Discussed in Supervision Texts

Frequency of Discussion	Knowledge	Skills	Desired Disposition Toward:
High Frequency	Teaching and learning History of supervision Change process School as organization Human dynamics/ relations Supervision as field of study	Observation Interpersonal/ communication Conferencing Change facilitation	Democratic leadership Collegiality and collaboration Supervision as moral activity
Moderate Frequency	Differentiated supervision School climate and culture Teacher morale and motivation Legal dimension of supervision Philosophy of supervision	Leadership Organizational management	Creativity Flexibility Learning communities
Low Frequency (but still discussed in several texts)	Developmental supervision Trends and issues in supervision Instructional strategies and learning resources Child development	Analysis of teaching Coaching Conflict management Decision making Planning Relationship building Group process	Empathy for others Diversity Inquiry Job-embedded learning Objectivity Reciprocity

Scope of Proposed Standards

This book includes proposed standards for several traditional supervision processes, including clinical supervision (the most popular form of classroom-based instructional assistance), professional development, curriculum development, teacher evaluation, and program evaluation. Because of the discussion of action research in recent supervision texts and its tremendous potential as a supervision process, standards for action research also are proposed. One certainly could argue that other processes be considered part of supervision, and as the movement toward supervision standards continues, we expect that others will propose additional processes for which standards are needed.

The supervision literature has paid some attention to the cultural aspects of improving teaching and learning, but in large part has not addressed cultural topics like diversity, and critical inquiry. The development of supervision standards provides us an opportunity to focus on the intersection of instructional leadership and school culture, a topic that supervision and supervision standards must address if supervision is to effectively foster schoolwide improvement of teaching and learning. Thus, this book includes chapters on standards promoting desired dimensions of school culture, including standards of democratic supervision, authentic and ethical learning, collegiality and collaboration, reflective practice, critical inquiry, and diversity. Meeting both the cultural standards in the second part of this book and the process standards in the third part will ensure a supervision system that fosters schoolwide improvement of teaching and learning.

This book does not have separate chapters on knowledge, skills, and dispositions for successful supervision like those listed in Figure 2.1. Although important, our view is they should be embedded within the cultural and process standards proposed throughout the book.

Should Standards Be Differentiated?

Many current standards in education are generic. For example, The National Board for Professional Teaching Standards, (2001) does not distinguish between content areas and among elementary, middle, or high school levels; and the ISLLC Standards for School Leaders do not differentiate by type of leader, level of leadership, or specialization (CCSSO, 1996). Despite the trend towards generic standards, various experts have argued for differentiating supervision standards by specialization (academics, fine and performing arts, occupational education, special education), academic discipline (math, language arts, and so on), educational entity (school, district, intermediate agency, state department), school level (elementary, middle, high school), central office role (curriculum coordinator, associate superintendent for in-struction, etc.), and whether the supervision is for preservice or in-service teachers. Cook (1998) argued for two levels of standards: general standards that span all areas and reflect broad goals of supervision, and differentiated standards that reflect the unique needs of specialized areas.

The standards proposed in this book—which is intended to encourage di-alogue on supervision standards and the development of additional volun-tary standards—are generic. However, the creation of additional, specialized standards is a path that practitioners and scholars may wish to pursue as the standards development process continues.

How Should Standards Be Organized?

Standards can be based on a set of core beliefs. For example, the ISLLC standards are organized around a set of seven core principles. The first three of these principles are:

1. Standards should reflect the centrality of student learning.
2. Standards should acknowledge the changing role of the school leader.
3. Standards should recognize the collaborative nature of school leadership (CCSSO, 1996, p. 7).

Guided by the seven core principles, six standards were developed, with each standard divided into core knowledge, dispositions, and performances. The guiding principles represent core beliefs about the nature and purpose of standards, and the standards themselves represent the required knowledge, dispositions, and performances of the school leader.

Standards may be organized as subsets of broad categories. For instance, the National Standards for School Counseling Programs are classified under the broad categories of academic development, career development, and per-sonal and social development. Standards may be holistic or discreet, and a particular field may have both holistic and discreet standards. Holistic stan-dards may serve as stems for discreet standards or may be accompanied by discreet standards that apply the holistic standards to subareas. The Council for Exceptional Children (2001) bases its accreditation of special education programs on a conceptual framework of 10 holistic standards, which are the same for all programs, with comprehensive lists of knowledge and skills for core competencies as well as disability-specific areas of specialization.

The level of specificity at which standards should be written is an issue for consideration. If standards are not specific enough, they can take the form of glittering generalities that have little meaning for programs and practitio-ners. If they are too detailed, they may be impossible to achieve within local contexts. Thus, practitioner feedback on the appropriate level of specificity is essential.

The standards proposed in this book are organized under the broad categories of cultural and process standards, and then under subcategories representing desired aspects of school culture (Chapter 3–8) and specific supervision processes (Chapters 9–14). The individual standards are holistic, allowing for adaptation to local school contexts and school goals.

What Should Be the Relationship Between Standards and Assessment?

The relationship between standards and assessment seems clear to many in the standards movement. Standards are written so they can guide practice, and to evaluate the success of practice in relation to standards there must be some sort of assessment. However, not every profession makes the assumption that standards and assessment are two sides of the same coin. For example, the American Medical Association and the American Bar Association generate standards but do not provide assessments. Which standards are to be assessed and how to assess them is decided at the state level. When standards are accompanied by assessment, the assessment can take a variety of forms, including written tests, observations, portfolio review, and surveys of various stakeholders.

Wise and Leibbrand (2001) reviewed 10 criteria for assessment systems developed by NCATE. These criteria are summarized below:

1. Assessments should be driven by a framework that ensures evaluation of both the individual and the program.

2. Assessment should be goal-oriented, linked to both program goals and national standards.

3. Assessment should use multiple measures to provide both formative and summative evaluation.

4. External experts should be involved in the assessment development process.

5. Assessment policies and procedures should be well-defined and available to all stakeholders.

6. Performance levels need to be clearly delineated.

7. Polices and procedures for score reporting and usage should be well defined.

8. Data analysis procedures should be clearly delineated.

9. Assessment instruments should be evaluated in relation to the standards to be measured.

10. Self-assessment procedures should be established as part of the overall assessment.

The standards proposed in the following chapters are not accompanied by assessments. Our philosophy is that local districts and schools should first adopt or adapt supervision standards consistent with local contexts and school goals, and then develop their own assessments consistent with local contexts and school goals. We also believe that districts and schools need the flexibility to change standards and assessments to adapt to changing contexts and goals. Finally, we believe that a critical phase between adapting supervision standards and assessing the supervision program is professional development—for supervisors and other instructional leaders as well as for all staff members. The improvement of the supervision program as well as the improvement of teaching and learning should be viewed as a continuous cycle of standard setting, professional development, improvement efforts, and program assessment.

References

Acheson, K .A., & Gall, M. D. (2003). *Clinical supervision and teacher development* (5th Ed.). New York: Wiley.

Allen, D., Fillion S., Butters, J., Gordon, S. P., & Bentley, K. C. (2004, April) *Considering national standards for instructional supervision: A review of the literature.* Paper presented at the annual meeting of the American Educational Research Association, San Diego, CA.

Archer, J.,(2002). Leadership groups hope to launch advanced certification. *Education Week,* 21(40), 14.

Burton, W. H. (1922). *Supervision and the improvement of teaching.* New York: Appleton.

Cogan, M. L. (1973). *Clinical Supervision.* Boston: Houghton Mifflin.

Consortium for Policy Research in Education (1993). *Policy Brief. Developing content standards: Creating a process for change.* New Brunswick, NJ: Rutgers University.

Cook, G. E. (1998). Supervision in academic disciplines. In G. R. Firth, & E. F. Pajak (Eds.), *Handbook of Research on School Supervision* (pp. 493–505). New York: Simon & Schuster Macmillan.

Council for Exceptional Children. (2001). *Guidelines for the preparation of the special education program report.* Arlington, VA: Author.

Council of Chief State School Officers. (1996). *Interstate School Leaders Licensure Consortium: Standards for school leaders.* Washington, DC: Author.

Firth, G. R. (1998). Governance of school supervision. In G. R. Firth, & E. F. Pajak (Eds.), *Handbook of Research on School Supervision* (pp. 872–943) New York: Simon & Schuster Macmillan.

Firth, G. R. (1997). Should there be national standards for supervisors? Yes. In J. Glanz & R. F. Neville (Eds.), *Educational supervision: Perspectives, issues, and controversies* (pp. 175–186). Norwood, MA: Christopher-Gordon.

Glanz, J., & Sullivan, S. (2000). *Supervision in practice*. Thousand Oaks, CA: Corwin Press.

Godfrey, K. (1997). Performance-based standards: Development of standards will enable facilities to measure progress. *Corrections Today, 59,* 94–97.

Goldhammer, R. (1969). *Clinical supervision: Special methods for the supervision of teachers.* New York: Holt, Rinehart and Winston.

Hazi, H., (1997). Should there be national standards in the preparation of supervisors? No. In J. Glanz & R. F. Neville (Eds.), *Educational supervision: Perspectives, issues and controversies.* (pp. 187–200). Norwood, MA: Christopher-Gordon.

Hess, F. M. (2003). The case for being mean. *Educational Leadership, 61*(3), 22–25.

Marion, B. (2000). The standards juggernaut. *Phi Delta Kappan, 81*(9), pp. 648–651.

Marzano, R. J., Kendall, J. S. (1996). *A comprehensive guide to designing standards-based districts, schools, and classrooms.* Alexandria, VA: Association for Supervision and Curriculum Development.

National Board for Professional Teaching Standards (2001). *What teachers should know and be able to do.* Arlington, VA: Author.

National Commission on Excellence in Education. (1983, April). *A nation at risk: The imperative for educational reform.* Washington, DC: Author.

National Policy Board for Educational Administration. (2002). *Advanced programs in educational leadership for principals, superintendents, curriculum directors and supervisors.* Washington, DC: Author.

Nolan, J., & Hoover, L. A. (2003). *Teacher supervision and evaluation: Theory into practice.* New York: Wiley.

O'Day J., & Smith, M. S., (1993). Systematic reform and educational opportunity. In S. H. Fuhrman (Ed.), *Designing coherent education* (pp. 250–312). San Francisco: Josey-Bass.

Pajak, E. (2000). *Approaches to clinical supervision: Alternatives for improving instruction* (2nd Ed.). Norwood, MA: Christopher-Gordon.

Pajak, E. (2001). Clinical supervision in a standards-based environment. *Journal of Teacher Education, 52*(3), 233–243.

Shoop, R. J. (2002). Identifying a standard of care. *Principal Leadership (Middle School Ed.), 2*(7), 48–52.

Sizer, T. R., & Rogers, B. (1993). *Designing standards: Achieving the delicate balance. Educational Leadership, 50*(5), 24–26.

Wiles, K. (1950). *Supervision for better schools.* New York: Prentice-Hall.

Wise, A. E., & Liebbrand, J. A. (2001). Standards in the new millennium: Where we are, where we're headed. *Journal of Teacher Education, 52*(3), 244–255.

Wilmore, E. L. (2002). *Principal leadership: Applying the new Educational Leadership Constituent Council (ELCC) standards.* Thousand Oaks, CA: Corwin.

Zepeda, S. J. (2003). *Instructional supervision: Applying tools and concepts.* Larchmont, NY: Eye On Education.

Part II

Cultural Standards

3

Standards of Democratic Supervision

Duncan Waite

Meet the Author

Duncan Waite

Duncan Waite is a professor of educational leadership at Texas State University-San Marcos. His academic interests include instructional supervision, educational leadership, anthropology and education, and qualitative research. He is editor of *The International Journal of Leadership in Education* and director of The International Center for Educational Leadership and Social Change. Published works include a book on supervision – *Rethinking Instructional Supervision: Notes on its Language and Culture*, and chapters in numerous edited volumes, including *The Handbook of Research on School Supervision; The International Handbook on Globalization, Education, and Policy Research*; and *The Encyclopedia of Language and Education;* among others. He has published in *The Journal of Curriculum and Supervision,* the *American Educational Research Journal, Teaching and Teacher Education,* and others. Current projects include work on corruption in education and its relation to democracy, an oral-life history of an African-American school principal during and after desegregation, and a model of major social forces and their relationships, especially as concerns education.

Successful supervision:

- Promotes and facilitates students and teachers coming to know themselves and to be themselves
- Helps students and teachers become more self-directed, both individually and collectively
- Promotes and facilitates everyone's transpersonal development
- Promotes and facilitates a voice in policies, practices, and procedures for everyone
- Encourages various types of discourse and communication events
- Promotes and facilitates critical inquiry—of self, context(s), and practices—and fosters critique
- Acts on critical input
- Promotes and facilitates the elimination of coercion and intimidation
- Fosters different kinds of association, in classrooms and throughout the organization
- Buffers the organization and its individuals from undemocratic or antidemocratic forces
- Calls on supervisors to adopt a role as "first among equals"

Achieving sainthood, winning a multimillion-dollar lottery, writing the great American novel, eradicating world hunger, bowling a perfect 300 game, being a better parent, a better teacher, or a better citizen of the world—cynics, skeptics, and defeatists might decide these are impossible, unrealistic goals, and because of that, never undertake their realization. But these people aren't teachers. Teachers—and I count myself among them—by their very nature, disposition, temperament, desire, and choice, embrace the ideal, the nearly impossible goal. That is, they dedicate themselves to the goal of educating each and every child who crosses the threshold of their classrooms, despite the odds against them and the barriers they face. Are they crazy? Have they lost their minds?

Democracy and democratic supervision are ideal goals: difficult to attain, but worth pursuing. Democracy and democratic supervision are made even more difficult to attain because of the present educational and social contexts in which we find ourselves. The challenge for those wishing to practice democratic supervision is how to operate more democratically within decidedly undemocratic structures, contexts, and organizations. Addressing this challenge will be the focus of this chapter.

The Three Sides to Democratic Supervision

There are at least three sides to democratic supervision: the goals and rationales, the immediate objectives, and processes, including tasks and functions. What are the processes and procedures of democratic supervision? What are its objectives and how are these unique to this type of supervision? How might the more democratic supervisor act, and what strategy would be chosen? What is the ultimate goal of democratic supervision? Why even engage in such a difficult task, one likely fraught with setbacks, especially when it is often easier just to go along to get along?

Democratic Supervision: Goals, Contexts, and Rationales

It will perhaps be simpler to begin with a discussion of the rationale for democratic supervision and the part it can and should play in the contexts within which it operates. This should then suggest the functions and roles of such supervision and how a supervisor could enact them.

At its most fundamental level, supervision is concerned with improving instruction. It could be said, stretching just a little, that supervision might concern itself with improving learning, though ultimately, that is the teacher's task. Now, nothing is ever as simple as it seems. There are nuances and different perspectives on what supervision is or should be, and how to go about whatever that is.

But we must be clear that supervision is not administration, just as the standards discussed here and elsewhere in this volume are proposed standards for supervision and not standards for educational administration. Educational administration is more concerned with running a school than with supervision (see Waite & Nelson, in press). Supervision is more concerned with instruction and instructional development, in all its manifestations and with all of its ramifications, than it is with educational administration. It is true that one of the tasks of educational leaders or administrators, be they principals, vice principals or assistant principals, is instructional leadership. But, without wishing to be too simplistic, for the administrator this involves management of instruction, not supervision of instruction. Although, as things are never all that simple, there is bound to be some overlap, some blurring of the boundaries. For example, though formally appointed as a principal, a leader's personality and philosophies, or interests, may incline the leader more toward supervision than to administration. But any leader or administrator would be ill-advised to ignore administrative issues in favor of supervision tasks alone, as judgment is apt to occur based on administration. One of the difficulties for those who wish to perform supervisory tasks is that, in an age characterized by managerialism and instrumentalism (Waite & Nelson, in press), educators of all kinds are under increasing pressure to perform more and more managerial, bureaucratic tasks, and have less and less time and support for supervisory tasks. One must literally struggle against all the pressure and expectations to do supervision. First, raise test scores. Then, and only then, might one have the luxury to attend to supervision in the sense I am speaking of it here. In my opinion, we have our priorities backward. Achievement test scores are a poor proxy for learning, and by extension, teaching (Waite, Boone & McGhee, 2001; Sarason, 2004).

Supervision is concerned with improving teaching and learning. But this begs the question: Learning to what end? And, likewise, supervision to what end? The instruction teachers deliver and that supervisors promote is steeped with implications. Curricularists are familiar with the concept that, as Eisner (1999) put it, "students learn both more and less than we teach." Curricularists were among the first to draw our attention to the existence of the hidden curriculum. It's not just what we teach, but how we teach it that matters. Students learn to read many contextual cues: from how our classrooms are arranged to who gets called upon, to how various students are disciplined or rewarded, to the status hierarchies among both the students and the adults, to the status hierarchies of types of knowledge (i.e., what is valued, what not). For example, when my eldest daughter, Tamara, was about seven years old, she played school like other children. But when she played with her younger sister, *she* took the role of the principal. She gave her younger sister, the teacher, the note shown in Figure 3.1.

**Figure 3.1. A Principal's Note to a Teacher,
by a Seven-Year-Old Girl.**

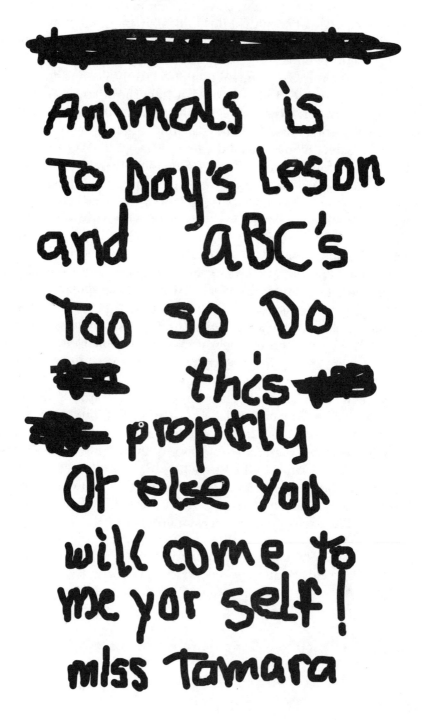

Notice the threat (with exclamation point!) and the implication that the principal can and should tell the teacher what to teach and how (i.e., properly).

Children learn about the wider world through the lessons we provide in school, whether intentional or not. They learn hierarchy. They learn about power and powerlessness. The point was made quite a while ago by John Dewey (1916), who reminded us that school is not simply a preparation for life, it is life. Dewey wrote that "democracy is more than a form of government; it is primarily a mode of associated living, of conjoint communicated experience" and "a democratic society repudiates the principle of external authority" (p. 87). Sarason (1996) taught us that neither schools nor education will change until the fundamental power dynamics in classrooms change.

To enact democratic supervision, the contexts (i.e., the policies, procedures, attitudes, dispositions, and more) must be conducive to its realization. Therefore, democratic supervisors are concerned with more than simply supervising teachers, because teachers also are embedded within multifaceted contexts that influence and perhaps determine what they do. Supervisors must attend to those contexts (Waite, 1992). You might say that democratic supervisors supervise contexts, just as they supervise teachers.

This is a more constructivist approach to supervision, a more interactionist approach. Contexts influence how we act and they permit only a certain degree of freedom. Contexts vary widely among even similar types of organizations, such as schools. Authors in the field write of school climate or school culture (e.g., Alfonso, 1986; Deal & Peterson, 1999; Sergiovanni, 1992). These earlier conceptions of context and culture have been shown to be overly simplistic in terms of recent work done on the anthropology of education (e.g., Varenne & McDermott, 1999; Waite, 1998). Neither context nor culture is as deterministic as portrayed by earlier authors. Contexts are dynamic: They influence us, just as we influence them. They are, after all, human constructions. It's all very complex, especially for adults like teachers and supervisors. It makes little sense within dysfunctional contexts to ask teachers to improve or to try harder. Sometimes, despite the teacher's best effort, the contexts work against being able to teach to the best of one's ability. In cases like this (and there are functional and dysfunctional aspects within nearly every context), the supervisor, sometimes in collaboration with the teacher, must turn his/her attention to the contexts in an effort to ameliorate the negative aspects of an educational context and to attenuate the positive. There are striking similarities among this type of supervision, which I call situational supervision (Waite, 1992, 1995), action research, and organization development. But democratic supervision is more than this.

Contexts—an amalgamation of the forces at play, historical precedents, our mental models, our practices, our policies, and our interpretation and enactment of them—are part of what influence us and the work we are able to accomplish. One aspect of contexts we are often unconscious about or do not usually deal with well comprises the psychological factors that affect teaching, learning, and supervision (Gramston, Lipton, & Kaiser, 1998). Though it is claimed to be one of the foundations of supervision (Lucio & McNeil, 1969), in everyday practice the psychology in and of supervision is often ignored. Perhaps this is human nature. But as our psyches, both individually and collectively, play such an integral part in how we conduct ourselves (Pajak, 2003), this should be addressed as part of the overall contexts that foster or inhibit democratic supervision. This is the transpersonal area (Rothberg, 1999) alluded to in the standards for democratic supervision. Transpersonal development might be thought of as raising consciousness with a psychological twist.

Supervision theorists (e.g., Glickman, Gordon, & Ross-Gordon, 2004) have included group development among the tasks of supervision, but this only scratches the surface of the dynamics involved in a community of people. Transpersonal development (Rothberg, 1999) gets at the personal and spiritual maturation of individuals, groups, and society (Waite, 2000). It is what Rothberg referred to as an integrative approach, one that "connects experiences of nonordinary reality, spiritual insight, and long-term spiritual practices with everyday life...with the life of families, communities, relationships, work, education, institutions, and social issues" (p. 43). As an integrative approach, transpersonal development has as its aim "no less than spiritual transformation, the cultivation of wisdom and love, the opening of the heart and mind, the deep communion with life" (p. 56), all through a process of what Rothberg referred to as "socially engaged spirituality" (p. 56). Rothberg was clear that he used spirituality "as a more specific term referring to a *lived transformation* of the person and/or the community toward a more complete alignment with what is held to be divine or sacred" (pp. 62–63). Such transformation, according to Rothberg, "may (or may not) be supported by religious doctrines, practices, and social organization" (p. 63).

The personality of the designated leader (principal, supervisor, or superintendent) has a profound impact on an organization like a school. If, for example, the principal is mature, secure, and self-assured, the school is healthier than if the principal is dealing with personal issues. If the principal or other leader is insecure, egotistical, or immature, the school suffers. The same can be said of the other personalities involved. It takes only one extremely difficult personality to hamper a group's efforts. The image I have of such sabotage is of those juveniles who throw rocks or chunks of concrete off freeway overpasses at the windshields of the cars passing underneath. The act is juvenile, but the result is often devastating. The level of development (or lack thereof) of the supervisor or administrator along several different continua can seriously affect a school's progress toward the realization of more democratic ends (Grimmett & Housego, 1983; Schommer, 1994; Waite, 2002a), just as the leader's personality or psyche affects individual teachers.

Other concerns for supervisors who seek to foster more democratic schools and supervision have to do with the psychological and micropolitical processes involved in coercion and intimidation (Waite & Allen, 2003). Each of these inhibits democratic forms of association and retards the development of individuals and groups. W. Edwards Deming (1986), in developing his concept of total quality management, recognized how coercion and intimidation would inhibit organizations from fulfilling their goals and called on managers to drive out fear.

All of this is by way of saying that supervisors must lay the groundwork for democratic supervision. It doesn't just happen. This is an altogether different way of operating than undertaking supervision from a technicist orientation. It's messier and more complex. When operating within a technicist mindset or paradigm (e.g., Acheson & Gall, 1992; Hunter, 1973), the supervisor simply walks into a teacher's room and supervises. A more responsive and more inclusive model of supervision attends to all the conditions that influence instruction. This is where inquiry enters into the process of democratic supervision (see chapter 7); for, from a holistic perspective, everything influences teaching and learning, to a degree. To work to improve every condition that influences instruction would be maddening, for there is a universe of possibilities. Critical inquiry, whether through action research or some other vehicle, helps supervisors, teachers, and other leaders direct their energies, their scarce resources, to where they might do the most good. They become strategic. But everything must be on the table—this is the point of using the holistic, constructivist paradigm, and what differentiates this paradigm and type of supervision from a technicist model.

Supervising in More Democratic Ways

Democracy has to do with inclusion (Ryan, in press) and self-determination. As such, there are varying degrees of democracy for institutions, organizations, and forms of association. Achieving democratic supervision, indeed achieving democracy in any form, is more of a process than an ideal end state. Still, it's helpful to have an ideal against which to compare ourselves and our organization to see where we are. The task before us, then, is to strategize how we might make supervision more democratic, and how, through that process, to we might effect more democratic schools (Goodman, Baron, & Myers, 2001).

Beginning simply, and keeping in mind a primary criterion of democratic organizations (i.e., they permit self determination), democratic supervision honors the self-determination of the teacher: Who is he? What does she want to become? How can you help teachers reach their potential? True, other models of supervision (e.g., Acheson & Gall, 1992) honor the teacher's voice, at least rhetorically. But too often this is a supervisory ploy to get the teacher to buy in to the process of being observed, even controlled or manipulated. It can be authentic, but it is too often just empty rhetoric. The democratic supervisor needs to do the difficult work of checking his/her ego (this is part of the psychological aspect of democratic supervision alluded to earlier). It is patently undemocratic for supervisors to impose their beliefs or standards on teachers. Herein lies the crux of the paradox of an outside "expert" like me developing standards for democratic supervision. Such standards should be developed by those who are to implement them, based on their beliefs about democracy and schooling and rooted in and responsive to their local situation. Garfinkel (2002, p. 199) reminds us that "norms, directives, regulations, laws, commands, order, rules, *standards*, [italics added] plans, budgets, maps, manuals" are all of a family of instructions or instructed action that are only glosses for action. They connote nothing of the particular lived experiences of those for whom they are intended. They say little about how they are enacted in everyday practice. Such standards and rules thus violate the primary criterion of democracy, democratic organizations, and associations: that they permit self-determination.

Rather, democratic supervision is an educative process for both the teacher and the supervisor. The details have to be hammered out by those involved, just as they have to be monitored and adjusted by those concerned (see chapter 6). This is one response to the unstated question of what to do with the teacher who is practicing wholly undemocratic pedagogy. Patience, love, and understanding are the democratic supervisor's first response (Waite, 2000). The long-term strategy for moving teachers farther along the democratic developmental path is education that is grounded in love and respect. Interventions generally work better when done collectively, the collective benefits and, hopefully, the individual does too.

Other models (Glickman et al., 2004, for example) acknowledge the interplay of values and desires between the individual and the organization. However, generally, these models privilege the organization and its goals over the individual. In contrast, I side with the individual. More often than not, the individual is subsumed and consumed by the organization. There are some organizations that exist to support the individual with their development, but their number is few (Belbin, 1998). Public education is characterized by hierarchical bureaucratic organizations (Belbin, 1998; Ingersoll, 2003). Even administrators—superintendents and principals—cite bureaucratic demands as one of the major barriers they face in their work (Public Agenda, 2003). This is despite the fact that principals, for example, enjoy more power and freedom than do teachers (Ingersoll, 2003), and those at higher levels of a bureaucratic hierarchy experience more freedom and less accountability than those lower in the hierarchy (Belbin, 1998). These principals and superintendents most likely do not problematize or reflect on their own role in perpetuating and sustaining the bureaucratic and hierarchical aspects of educational organizations. [1] Pity the poor teacher, with neither power nor authority, suffering under heavy-handed systems of accountability in the form of high-stakes testing and the punitive systems of expectations, demands, and sanctions that come with them (Hargreaves, 2004). No wonder so many teachers, especially the brightest and most creative, are leaving the profession. So, yes, if it comes down to the individual teacher or the organization, I favor the teacher.

Work on and within the school community is fundamental to the creation of a more democratic and just organization. Organizational structures and norms must change if the organizational culture is to develop more democratically (Belbin, 1998). There are models of associative living other than hierarchical bureaucratic organizations available for emulation. Other forms of association can be pursued. For example, the work on learning communities is promising.

Democratic organizations promote the inclusion of the disparate voices of members (Ryan, in press). More democratic organizations are essential to fostering more democratic supervision and schooling. An example from cyberspace serves as a model of democratic processes, especially those involving communication: Wikipedia. Wikipedia (http://en.wikipedia.org/wiki/Main_Page) is a free, online encyclopedia that is open to everyone. Anyone can add or edit an entry. The process is self-correcting, as visitors (anyone) can correct factual errors and omissions. This is but one type of organization that is neither bureaucratic nor hierarchical—structures that impede the realization of democratic schooling and supervision.

Targeting the individual teacher while ignoring the school organization is wasted effort. There are probably dysfunctional, undemocratic structures, processes, or policies operant in any community, and through a process of critical inquiry and action, these can be identified and addressed. In order not to get disheartened and discouraged, teachers and supervisors must keep in

---

1 The role of principals and other administrators in the perpetuation of unjust systems, such as onerous high-stakes testing and accountability systems with heavy-handed sanctions, is similar in kind, though not in degree, to what the German sociologist Georg Simmel (1858–1918) described as the dirty work of the Nazi sympathizers of World War II. Thanks to Norman Denzin for bringing this work to my attention.

mind that the journey is long. It's as important to identify and work on the dysfunctional or undemocratic aspects of a school as it is to say you've arrived at the idealized end goal of a fully democratic form of supervision. "We're working on it," is about as authentic a response as one might expect.

Supervisors and administrators must get their priorities straight—not an easy thing to do when beset by innumerable external demands. To encourage my graduate students in the supervision classes I teach (those in the principal's certification program) to make time for supervision and set it as a priority, I recount this parable I first heard from Robert Kegan (2000), who borrowed it from another. I think it's worth telling here:

> A noted motivational speaker was giving a presentation when, in the midst of it, he withdrew an empty pitcher from beneath his podium. He filled it with large rocks and asked the audience, "How many of you would say this pitcher is full?" Several audience members raised their hands. Then he produced a small bowl from beneath his podium and proceeded to shake small pebbles into the pitcher, topping it off. "How many now think it's full?" he asked. Fewer people raised their hands, but many did. Then he took a bowl of sand and emptied it into the pitcher, shaking it to let the sand settle between the pebbles and large rocks. "Now how many think it's full?" Few people raised their hands this time, but some still did. Then he took a glass of water and poured it into the pitcher until the water level topped the pitcher. "Now?" he asked. Almost no one raised a hand this time. "What is the lesson here?" he asked his audience. Someone responded, "You can always get more in?!" "No," he said, "it's that you can't get the big rocks in unless you put them in first!"

The point I hope my supervision students take from this is that if they value supervision, its ends, and its tasks, they have to set *that* as a priority, otherwise they won't fit it in. This is true for democratic forms of supervision as well.

I encourage my students, administrators-in-training, and potential supervisors to be resilient. I urge them to be like that child's toy, the clown punching bag that's weighted on the bottom so each time it's knocked over, it pops right back up. Striving toward democracy, democratic supervision, and more just institutions is like working to bowl a perfect 300 game or write the great American novel. Indeed it's like all those ideal goals I mentioned at the outset of this chapter; they all take continual attention, work and patience, but the struggle is worthwhile and the effort is never wasted.

Professional Development Activity

The standards for democratic supervision listed in this chapter are meant to be suggestive and not exhaustive. Certain standards that you or others might feel are important to consider may not be included. Because most innovations are adaptations, adoptions, or inventions, you and your colleagues will have the opportunity, through this professional development activity, to come up with and implement your own standard(s) for democratic supervision where you live and work.

First, identify those colleagues who would agree to work to make your classrooms and school more democratic. It really doesn't matter whether or not you consider your school or classroom to be democratic already, the path to democratic supervision (and, by extension, classrooms and schools) is a journey and not an end. There is always room for growth.

Next, secure the support of your administrators. For teachers, this might be the vice principal and/or principal; for principals, this might be your district curriculum director or superintendent. (Note: There are those who prefer to operate under the radar and those who believe it is better to ask forgiveness than to ask permission. They will initiate changes before alerting those higher up in the organization. This is a tactical decision you must make based on your knowledge of your situation. Be advised, though, to make changes systemic, eventually everyone will need to be on board.) If your district or state has a required teacher evaluation/assessment protocol or instrument, see if you can get a waiver by substituting the form of democratic supervision you come up with. If not, your democratic supervision will need to be a parallel system, at least initially.

Next, assemble your colleagues. (Treats are always nice, because as everyone knows, the first rule of staff development is that if you don't feed the teachers, they'll eat the children!) Begin discussion. You might want to use some of these questions to spark a dialogue: What do we hope to accomplish? How do we know what democratic supervision would look like? Who is to be involved? How?

Then, begin a discussion about parameters: Do we want and need formal roles for our meetings (i.e., convener, recorder, time-keeper, etc.)? Just how formal do we want to be? How will we organize ourselves?

You will probably want to begin with a joint reading and group discussion of this chapter, and perhaps some of the others. You may, however, decide that you still don't know enough about democracy, democratic supervision, and how to implement it. In that case, further book study is a possibility. Discuss the standards presented here: Do they make sense? Are any standards missing that you feel are important? Can you combine one or more? Select one from the list or through your discussions to concentrate on for a given period of time, say a week or two or a month. Consult Pajak's (2000) book of supervision models, select an appropriate model, and integrate the democratic supervision standard you've chosen with the model. (You might want to use the standard you've chosen to frame your supervision conferences.) Meet periodically to discuss how the implementation is going and to problem solve.

Then you have to decide on next steps: Will you select another supervision model to try, or perhaps another democratic supervision standard? Will you involve more people in the project? Will you expand beyond supervision to make other aspects of your school and/or district more democratic?

Assessment

In your discussions, you'll want to assess the project. Use the standards listed and judge how you've done against them, individually and collectively. Use them in both a formative and a summative fashion; that is, how can we get better and should we completely stop what we're doing and concentrate on something else? Take the second standard as an example. The standard encourages more self-directed individuals and collectivities through democratic supervision. Ask yourself, either formally or informally, did this occur as a result of your democratic supervision efforts? If so, how? What evidence do you have that this occurred? If not, what can be done to improve the outcome?

First, each member should answer these questions for themselves. Next, the group members should come together to share their individual answers to the questions and discuss the group response or assessment of the activities. Then it's time to cycle back: Are your aims still valid (that is, are you still committed to fostering democratic supervision)? If so, should you continue or alter some aspect of the project, as mentioned above? Allow for divergence and allow time for these efforts to take root. Most of all, celebrate your successes, both large and small.

References

Acheson, K., & Gall, M. D. (1992). *Techniques in the clinical supervision of teachers: Preservice and inservice applications* (3rd ed). New York: Longman.

Alfonso, R. (1986, April). *The unseen supervisor: Organization and culture as determinants of teacher behavior.* Paper presented to the annual meeting of the American Educational Research Association, San Francisco.

Belbin, R. M. (1998). *The coming shape of organization.* Oxford: Butterworth-Heinemann.

Deal, T. E., & Patterson, K. D. (1999). *Shaping school culture: The heart of leadership.* San Francisco: Jossey-Bass.

Deming, W. E. (1986). *Out of the crisis.* Cambridge, MA: Massachusetts Institute of Technology, Center for Advanced Engineering Study.

Dewey, J. (1916/1944). *Democracy and education: An introduction to the philosophy of education.* New York: Free Press.

Eisner, E. (1999, April). *Curriculum studies on the threshold of the 21st Century: Challenges and opportunities.* Invited presentation given to the annual meeting of the American Educational Research Association, Montreal, Quebec, Canada.

Garfinkel, H. (2002). *Ethnomethodology's program: Working out Durkheim's aphorism.* Lanhan: Rowman & Littlefield.

Glickman, C. D., Gordon, S. P., & Ross-Gordon, J. M. (2004). *SuperVision and instructional leadership: A developmental approach (6th ed.).* Boston: Pearson Education.

Goodman, J., Baron, D., & Myers, C. (2001). Bringing democracy to the occupational life of educators in the United States: Constructing a foundation for school-based reform. *International Journal of Leadership in Education, 4,* 57–86.

Gramston, R. J., Lipton, L. E., & Kaiser, K. (1998). The psychology of supervision. In G. R. Firth & E. F. Pajak (Eds.), *The handbook of research on school supervision* (pp. 242–286). New York: Macmillan.

Grimmett, P. P., & Housego, I. E. (1983). Interpersonal relationships in the clinical supervision conference. *The Canadian Administrator, 22,* 1–6.

Hargreaves, A. (2004). Distinction and disgust: The emotional politics of school failure. *International Journal of Leadership in Education, 7,* 27–41.

Hunter, M. (1973). Appraising teacher performance: One approach. *The National Elementary Principal, 52,* 62–63.

Ingersoll, R. G. (2003). *Who controls teachers' work: Power and accountability in America's schools.* Cambridge, MA: Harvard University Press.

Kegan, R. (2000, April). *Inward bound: Transformational learning for professional development.* Workshop given to the annual meeting of the American Educational Research Association, New Orleans, LA. April 27, 2000.

Lucio, W. H., & McNeil, J. D. (1969). *Supervision: A synthesis of thought and action* (2nd ed.). New York: McGraw-Hill.

Pajak, E. (2003). *Honoring diverse teaching styles: A guide for supervisors.* Alexandria, VA: Association for Supervision and Curriculum Development.

Pajak, E. (2000). *Approaches to clinical supervision.* Norwood, MA: Christopher-Gordon.

Public Agenda. (2003). Where we are now: Twelve things you need to know about public opinion and public schools. Retrieved November 16, 2004 from http://www.publicagenda.org/research/PDFs/ where_we_are_now_combined.pdf

Rothberg, D. (1999). Transpersonal issues at the millennium. *The Journal of Transpersonal Psychology, 31*(1), 41–67.

Ryan, J. (in press). *Inclusive leadership.* San Francisco: Jossey-Bass.

Sarason, S. B. (1996). *Revisiting the culture of school and the problem of change.* New York: Teachers College Press.

Sarason, S. B. (2004). *And what do YOU mean by learning?* Portsmouth, NH: Heinemann.

Schommer, M. (1994). Synthesizing epistemological belief research: Tentative understandings and provocative confusions. *Educational Psychology Review,6*(4),
293–319.

Sergiovanni, T. J. (1992). Why we should seek substitutes for leadership. *Educational
Leadership, 49*(5), 41–45.

Varenne, H., & McDermott, R. (1999). *Successful failure: The school America builds.* Boulder, CO: Westview Press.

Waite, D. (1992). Instructional supervision from a situational perspective. *Teaching
and Teacher Education, 8,* 319–332.

Waite, D. (1995). *Rethinking instructional supervision: Notes on its language and culture.*
London: Falmer Press.

Waite, D. (1998). Anthropology, sociology and supervision. In G. R. Firth & E. F. Pajak
(Eds.), *The handbook of research on school supervision* (pp. 287–309). New York:
MacMillan.

Waite, D. (2000). Identity, authority, and the heart of supervision. *International Journal
of Educational Reform, 9*(4), 282–291.

Waite, D. (2002a). Critical new directions in educational leadership. *Education and Society, 20*(1), 29–42.

Waite, D. (2002b). Is the role of the principal in creating school improvement
over-rated? *Journal of Educational Change, 3*(2), 161–165.

Waite, D. & Allen, D. (2003). Corruption and abuse of power in educational administration. *The Urban Review, 35,* 281–296.

Waite, D., Boone, M., & McGhee, M. (2001). A critical sociocultural view of accountability. *Journal of School Leadership, 11,* 182–203.

Waite, D., & Nelson, S. W. (in press). Educational leadership reconsidered. *La Revista
Espanola de de Pedagogia.*

4

Standards of Ethical Learning and Teaching

Robert J. Starratt

Meet the Author

Robert J. Starratt

Robert J. Starratt, known to his friends as "Jerry", is a professor of educational administration at the Lynch School of Education at Boston College. His publications include Ethical Leadership (Jossey Bass), Centering Educational Administration (Lawrence Erlbaum), Building an Ethical School, (Falmer Press), Leaders With Vision (Corwin Press), The Drama of Leadership (Falmer). The Drama of Schooling/ The Schooling of Drama (Falmer, and eight editions of Supervision: A Redefinition (McGraw Hill), coauthored with Tom Sergiovanni. He and his wife live in Newton, Massachusetts with their dog, Salli, and their bird, Lovey, and several inquisitive squirrels and family of cantankerous cows.

Successful supervision:

♦ Establishes good working relationships with teachers and support staff based on respecting and trusting their professional and moral competence, and based on genuinely caring for them in their intrinsic goodness

♦ Encourages teachers to establish good working relationships with each student, based on understanding the student's cultural and immediate social environment and respecting all students' present talents and interests and their huge potential

♦ Identifies and articulates personal and civic values and meanings in the curriculum being taught by teachers with whom supervisors work

♦ Encourages teachers as they plan their curriculum to articulate the personal and civic value of the material under study

♦ Encourages teachers to translate various units of the curriculum they are teaching into personally and publicly meaningful learnings that foster student's sense of identity, membership, and participation in the natural, cultural, and social worlds

♦ Encourages teachers and learners to develop a sense of responsible participation in the world, reflected in the material under study in the classroom

♦ Encourages teachers to develop rubrics with learners for personally authentic learning

This chapter will propose some initial standards to guide supervisors who are promoting ethical pupil learning and a practice of teaching that would support such ethical pupil learning. I say initial standards for two reasons. First, the literature dealing with the preparation and professional development of supervisors is, by and large, bereft of a treatment of pupil learning as a moral activity, although we may find such treatments of the moral character of learning in the more general literature on education (e.g., Dunne, 1995; Hogan, 1995; Starratt, 2004). Second, this initial effort is seen as a starting conversation among educators who teach courses in supervision, those who engage in supervision in the field, and the teachers they supervise. That conversation will fill out, refine, and improve this initial set of standards as well as generate further examples of supervisory and teacher practices that cultivate and enhance the moral character of the pupil's learning.

At the outset, we need to clarify the focus of these particular supervisory standards. These standards are not intended to be limited to moral issues within the relationship of supervisor and teacher, such as sexual harassment, the authoritarian bullying of teachers, racial stereotyping, psychological manipulation, arbitrary and unfounded criticisms of teachers, etc. These initial standards imply a prohibition against such behaviors. Nor are these supervisory standards meant to be limited to the supervision of explicitly moral instruction. For example, what might be embedded in processes of classroom management; articulations of rules against and reason for prohibiting cheating, bullying, stereotyping and scapegoating in the classroom; explicit curriculum units devoted to character education or sex education; curriculum units dealing with the moral implications of religious teaching such as the Ten Commandments or the Beatitudes, although these standards might implicitly guide supervisory engagement with such instruction.

Rather, these standards are intended to support the cultivation and enhancement of the moral character of *all* forms of learning. These standards are based on the assumption that the learning of the formal academic curriculum is a moral activity as well as an intellectual activity. To solidify our understanding of the moral character of school learning, the following section attempts a brief exposition of what that moral character might be. Without such an exposition, the relatively bold proposal of standards for supervising ethical learning might appear incomprehensible.

The Moral Character of School Learning

Let us start by asking why we study what we study in school. Policy makers today tend to answer, "So we can get a good job, and can compete in an increasingly demanding and sophisticated work environment." Although preparation for participation in the workforce is one important goal in education, it is by no means is the only goal. In a society that declares a dedication to life, liberty, and the pursuit of happiness, schools are meant to help young people grow toward a fuller humanity, to develop what Melanie Walker refers to as "human capabilities" (Walker, 2004). This question could be rephrased as: What difference does attention to these subjects make in our efforts to understand who we are, how we might live our lives, and what we should value?. Conversely, we can ask what these studies tell us about the mistakes, pitfalls, habits, perspectives, attitudes, and self images that are self-destructive, harmful, childish, or repugnant. In other words, contrary to what it means to be a reasonably mature and socially responsible human being. The answer to these questions about the rationale behind the school curriculum is that these studies have much to do with basic human concerns (Carr & Steutel, 1999; Dunne, 1995; Hogan, 1995;). These studies can (though not necessarily will) help us understand who we are as the natural beings (situated in the world of nature as described by the natural sciences); as sociocultural beings (situated in the world of culture and society as described by the arts and humanities and the social and human sciences); and as historical beings (belonging to communities whose traditions and journeys have a past, a present, and a future, and whose members have built that past and are expected to build its future). As human beings, we are both circumscribed and privileged by these worlds, bound to and in partnership with these worlds. These studies bring to light the intelligibility of these worlds and our own intelligibility as members of these worlds. They illuminate our relationships to these worlds so that we may participate in them with responsibility, integrity, and purpose. Participation in these worlds obviously means that the learning process involves not only an intellectual appreciation of the architecture and grammar of these worlds (in the role of spectator, participant observer, or aesthetic critic), but also the exercise of various practical skills to negotiate and engage these worlds (as autonomous and intentional agents, as fully functioning members of these worlds). These aspects of the learning process constitute the "good," the intrinsic value of learning.

These studies can (again, not automatically will) gradually and cumulatively engage us in a conversation, both personal and public, with these worlds in which we can ask: How do you work? How do you help me (us) understand how I (we) work? How is my (our) immediate life-world like your world? What do you teach me (us) about my (our) possibilities, my (our) limitations, my (our) responsibilities? How are you inside me and I inside you? With capable teachers, these studies can develop into ongoing conversations with the worlds expressed and interpreted through the academic subjects that comprise the school curriculum. In these conversations learners listen to the voices of those worlds talk back to them. Learners can become more fully present to those worlds and thus to the various relationships of the learners to those worlds. These relationships gradually reveal increasing complexity and responsibilities, in response to which learners continue to shape their self-understanding both individually and communally.

Such a justification for engaging the school's "subjects" at this level of learning seems to be lacking in the current articulation of the school's learning agenda. Instead, we hear other metaphors: the curriculum is "delivered" by teachers to students who, in turn, "master" the curriculum. The mastery is revealed by identifying or producing preordained "right answers" that are then tallied in numbers and percentages, revealing what the student has "achieved."

Clearly, this understanding of learning refers to a one-way appropriation of a prefixed menu of abstract, right answers (no credit for left answers) that are presumed to objectively correspond with the true and real state of affairs, uniformly and universally agreed on by the adult world, if not the world of scholars (Shepard, 2002). There appears to be no concern in the process of preparing for these tests with either the self-knowledge of one's humanity in relationship to these worlds or one's responsibilities to these worlds. Achieving right answers seems an end in itself. It is a sign of hard work and conformity to a dominant adult world that has constructed this artificial obstacle course of puzzles, riddles, problems, abstract classifications, formulas, definitions and technical vocabulary, the mastery of which is supposed to predict a successful future.

The view of learning that is driven by mastery of right answers forces learning into a uniform time frame for all learners to learn a specific skill or understanding. "Mastery" of such learning is equated with speed: how fast one can accumulate sufficient information and organize it into right answers, all within an allotted time frame. Again, the limited time frame of the test and the limits of the test questions are assumed to represent a legitimate sampling of the larger body of information delivered during the circumscribed time of instruction and study.

This arrangement of instructional/curriculum units into limited, one-size-fits-all time frames forces many, if not most, learners to hurry up, to scramble for some scrap of what it is they perceive the teacher to expect them to have learned, to parrot out a phrase or definition just in time before the class or the test runs out of time, or to guess at a right answer without having any clue as to why this constitutes a right answer. More often than not, learners are forced to make believe that they know what they do not know. Observe some students arguing with the teacher after a test that they should get partial credit for having a piece of the right answer.

As I have argued elsewhere (Starratt, 2004, in press), this test-fixated learning promotes an unethical type of learning. This type of learning is inauthentic and irresponsible; it promotes an attitude where the integrity of the worlds represented by the academic subjects is of no importance outside of its instrumentality in providing decontextualized right answers to someone else's questions. This form of learning is posed learning. It is phony, fake, and superficial learning. Indeed, this learning is morally harmful, because it tends to program students to approach their world in a thoroughly self-referential and exploitative learning process that treats knowledge as personal private property, as a commodity to be consumed or traded in the free market of school achievement. The learning process is then corrupted. Students are turned from an authentic encounter with the physical, the cultural, and the historical worlds to a pillaging of texts in search for answers to the teacher's or the test maker's questions.

Learning as Virtuous Activity

We can better understand the morality implied in learning when we see learning engage in three virtues: the virtue of presence, the virtue of authenticity, and the virtue of responsibility (Starratt, 2004). Virtues are ways of responding to the moral demands and opportunities proffered within the varying circumstances and settings of associated living (Flanagan & Jupp, 2001). Gouinlock (1993) suggested that virtues are responses organically related to actual problematic situations. Thus, there would be specific, virtuous responses to problematic situations in the practice of architecture, engineering, or teaching. The virtuous response would not only seek to avoid or prevent harm in those practices, but also seek to promote the good organically embedded within practice. In other words, the integrity of the practice of architecture, engineering, or teaching would imply certain virtuous ways of practicing those professions and certain ways that would violate the integrity of the practice. The practice of learning has its own integrity and calls for certain virtues.

I propose above that learning involves the virtues of presence, authenticity, and responsibility. One has to be present, as fully present as possible, to the material or topic under study. Presence implies a dialogical relationship between the learner and the material under study. With two persons, their mutual presence to each other makes a relationship possible; it is a relationship bonded by telling and listening. Each person listens to the other's words, taking them in, and with the words, taking the other person inside as one interprets what the other means. The listener then responds to the other, presenting in the response both the listener's interpretation of what the other has said, and also how the listener responds from his or her perspective or feelings to what the other has said. Thus the dialogue goes back and forth with each person disclosing more of themselves and taking in richer and fuller understandings of the other. If one of the parties to the dialogue becomes distracted and fails to be fully attentive to the other person, then the mutuality or presence is diminished, if not broken, and the integrity of the dialogue and the developing relationship is put in jeopardy. Frequently humans have ways of signaling the withdrawal of presence. They look at their watches, throw up their hands, and declare that they must rush off for an appointment, but say they hope the dialogue can be resumed tomorrow or on some other occasion. Most of us, however, have experienced talking to another person who was barely half-present to us, who was obviously preoccupied with something other than our fascinating story. We feel somewhat offended by others' feigned responses of interest when it is obvious their mind is elsewhere.

The practice of the virtue of presence in the process of learning is something that itself is learned. Some teachers will explicitly teach it under the guise of study skills or by creating a readiness set at the beginning of class. There are ways of getting the learner's attention and motivating them to focus and concentrate in anticipation of learning something of personal value to them. As the lesson progresses, teachers increase the learner's attention by posing new questions: "If x is thus and so, what does that imply for y?" And: "What does this situation suggest for its resolution?" The point behind the questions is to encourage the learner to listen to the intelligibility embedded in the subject matter talking back to the learner. The teacher is suggesting ways for the learner to be present to that intelligibility.

Although there are many nuances to being present, three seem particularly apropos in the activity of learning: affirming presence, enabling presence, and critical presence. Affirming presence accepts the person or the event as it is, in its ambiguity, its incompleteness, it particularity, and its multidimensionality. Enabling presence is open to the possibilities of the person or event to contain or reveal something special, something of deep value and significance. Critical presence expects to find both negative and positive features in persons and events. People, events, and circumstances reveal unequal relationships of power and reciprocity. Critical presence brings to light what is tacit, assumed, or presumed in situations that reflect human constructions and beliefs, rather than something prefixed as natural or essential. All of these ways of being present to what is being studied enable the dialogue between learners and one or more of the worlds under consideration in that unit of the curriculum. This kind of presence on the learners' part allows those worlds to be similarly present as affirming who the learners are, enabling learners to become more fully themselves, and critiquing the appropriate assumptions and presumptions about their mutual relationships.

The second virtue that honors the integrity of learning is authenticity. The virtue of authenticity involves human beings in their most basic moral challenge, namely the challenge to be true to themselves, to be real. The opposite of that virtue is inauthenticity: playing false, making believe one is someone other than who one is. As with presence, the virtue of authenticity is a dialogical virtue. One cannot be authentic if one is alone, locked up in a closet. One is authentic in relationship to another. Authenticity is revealed in our acting out the various social and cultural roles we play. Most basically one is authentic as a human being in response to our humanity and the humanity of the other. One is also authentic as a son or daughter, as a friend or lover, or as a father or mother. In all of these roles, one strives to be real, not a fake or cardboard character. But the expression of our authenticity has to take into account the similar effort of others to also be true to themselves. Authenticity supposes a kind of social contract, namely, that if I expect a certain latitude to be myself, to own my life and my choices, so too must I afford to others the latitude to chart the courses of their own lives (Taylor, 1992).

The practice of learning asks the learner to allow the world to be what it is and to recognize that the learner's integrity is connected to the learner's relationship to the various physical, social cultural, historical, religious worlds he or she is studying. Those worlds invite the learner into membership. Membership, however, imposes a recognition of the benefits, privileges, and responsibilities of membership. In other words, one's authenticity as a member of these worlds requires a respect for the authenticity of the ways these worlds work. Authenticity, the way of being real, is a moral good. The learner pursues this way of being real, this way of expressing goodness, always in relationship to the authentic realities of the worlds he or she inhabits, which are revealed through the activity of learning.

The practice of the virtues of presence and authenticity imply the third virtue that seeks the good of the learning process—the virtue of responsibility. This virtue is exercised by learners (and by implication, on the part of teachers) by respecting the good things about learning—namely, the good of understanding and participation in the worlds of nature, society, culture, and history.

This virtue is enacted in two ways. First, in the learning process itself, the learner adopts an attitude of respect toward what the learner is studying. The material under study, whether it be the genetic code, the physics of magnets, a poem of Wordsworth, an historical account of the battle of Richmond, the industrial revolution, a novel by William Faulkner or Katharine Ann Porter, the geography of Egypt or of Brooklyn, all have an integrity of their own. That is to say, they reveal how humans have represented the intelligibility of the natural, the social, the cultural, and the historical worlds. The learner has a responsibility in the learning process to understand those worlds in their intelligible manifestations—as they are in themselves, not as the learner would like them to be. These worlds are there not for the learners to posses as their private property, but as the habitat of their own humanity, so to speak, as the physical, social, cultural, and historical home for them. It is a home that supports their lives in all its dimensions, a home where learners can come to know who they are, and a home conferring on them the important marker of membership in a community shaping both the learners' identities and supporting their necessary quest for an agency that is distinctive and authentic.

Learners therefore do not enter into the learning process as detached tourists, cavalierly and arbitrarily deciding whether to pay attention to what's in front of them. Rather, learners choose to be responsive, to respect the value and significance of that world, and to listen to the lessons that world has to teach them. Thus, in the process of learning, the learners make the effort to listen and respond, entering into dialogue with the worlds under study.

The virtue of responsibility is enacted in a second way, which flows immediately from the learner's effort to enter into dialogue with the world under study. It is to listen to and reflect on what lessons the experience of the worlds have to teach them about living their lives, about defining themselves, about the obligations of membership in those worlds, about the unfinished agendas of those worlds, and about the possibilities of agency within those worlds. Responsibility is about responding to the many significant potential lessons offered in these focused learning experiences of the physical, social, cultural, and historical worlds. If learning does not imply a response to these worlds, then why should we even bother to study them in the first place? What purpose is served by accumulating an encyclopedic knowledge of the world if that knowledge provides no sense of who one is, no sense of how to live one's life, no sense of membership in the larger communities making up these worlds, and no sense of moral purpose? Indeed, the present insistence on accumulating this kind of encyclopedic knowledge in both a local and international competition for high test scores seems to ignore these important questions, and thereby eviscerates the moral character of learning (Carr & Steutel, 1999).

The Realpolitic of Accountability

Obviously, the politicians who set policies in education and the state and federal authorities who implement them are not about to change the test-driven approach to school learning after reading this chapter. The present policy climate defining accountability measures in schools has generated such a momentum both in the United States and throughout the world that it will take time to play itself out before the inevitable cultural and political pendulum swing eventually brings a greater balance between national uniformity and local autonomy in education (Shepard, 2002). Given the present policy climate, these virtuous approaches to authentic learning and teaching cannot be thoroughly enacted. Rather, I suggest that supervisors work with teachers to shape *some* curriculum units to illuminate and activate the moral character of learning within those units. Along the way, teachers can show students how both to prepare for tests and discover at a deeper level how these curriculum units can speak to student issues of identity, belonging, social responsibility, and self-fulfilling participation in the adult world. By experiencing some curriculum units explicitly through the exercise of the learning virtues of presence, authenticity and responsibility, say three or four a year over the course of 8 to 12 years, learners would come to appreciate the activity of learning as serving both extrinsic technical usefulness and intrinsic personal and civic moral purposes. I believe most teachers would readily embrace such a modest effort to transform the experience of learning from tedious and exclusive emphasis on extrinsic and technical knowledge into learning that can serve both extrinsic and intrinsic values in learning.

A Model of Supervision That Attends to the Moral Character of Learning

Figure 4.1 presents a model of teaching and learning towards which supervisors and teachers might strive. In this model, the three ingredients of the moral character of teaching are highlighted. In one dimension of the triangle, the teacher establishes a working relationship with the learner based on caring and respect. The teacher accepts the learner as who they are, with all the advantages, talents, and interests the learner brings to the work of learning. In the second dimension of the triangle, the teacher reencounters the curriculum unit as revealing a world of significance and value to the teacher, a world that illuminates and makes possible the teacher's identity, sense of agency and participation in that world. In the third dimension, the teacher brings the learner and the curriculum unit into mutual dialogue through the teacher's careful construction and scaffolding of a variety of learning experiences. These are shaped by the teacher's knowledge of the learner and the teacher's relationship to the world under study in that particular curriculum unit. Through these learning activities, the student encounters the world revealed in that curriculum unit and is encouraged to appreciate how this part of that world speaks to him or her about who he or she is, about the possibilities for agency in that world, about the privileges and obligations of membership in that world, and about the unfinished agenda of that world. In the process of learning these lessons, the learner will, under the guidance of the teacher, also learn to apply the intelligibility of the subject matter to responses to expected types of questions on the state exam. Under the guidance of the teacher, the learners will also be encouraged to reflect on why these questions are deemed to be important for public life.

Figure 4.1. The Moral Character of Teaching and Learning

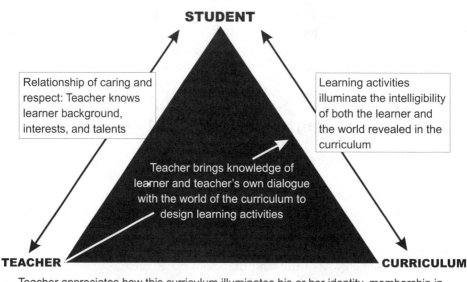

STUDENT

Relationship of caring and respect: Teacher knows learner background, interests, and talents

Learning activities illuminate the intelligibility of both the learner and the world revealed in the curriculum

Teacher brings knowledge of learner and teacher's own dialogue with the world of the curriculum to design learning activities

TEACHER

CURRICULUM

Teacher appreciates how this curriculum illuminates his or her identity, membership in that world, and the possibilities for agency and participation in it.

Professional Development Activities

Using the above model of the moral character of teaching and learning, supervisors can work with groups of teachers (either at the same grade level or focused on a particular academic discipline, such as developing good writing skills and habits). The teachers might be asked to focus on one or more students who are having difficulty with a particular subject area and its attendant curriculum standard. They might then be asked to list the various background variables of that student (e.g., ethnicity, first language, class, parental education level and occupations, family composition, neighborhood where the student lives; student's friends, interests and talents of the student, etc.). The exercise may reveal that some teachers in the group do not adequately understand the learner's backgrounds, talents, and interests. Their assignment would be to find out such information. Next, the teachers and supervisors can brainstorm, finding a variety of ways to scaffold the learning activities with this knowledge in mind. Included in these discussions would be the various ways the teachers can build a more caring and trusting relationship with those students, a relationship that communicates expectations of untapped potential in those students. Then, the supervisor and teachers can design learning activities that will create a dialogical learning relationship with the curriculum material, in which the student will listen to the material talk back to him or her. Lastly, supervisors and teachers can develop potential learning outcomes, along with rubrics that reflect a personal appropriation of the material under study, as well as a public application of that material within the context of the learner's context (e.g., working with a parent on how that curriculum material might be used in the parent's job, or how it might be useful in dealing with a family or neighborhood issue).

Another possible professional development activity would involve the supervisor with a group of teachers in discussing how a particular curriculum unit with its attendant standards speaks to them of particular personal and civic values, values that are important and useful to them, to their expression of themselves and their participation in public life. As teachers share what values they find embedded in the curriculum unit, they can build a base for bringing these values to the fore as they introduce this particular curriculum unit to their own students. In this exercise, teachers should be challenged to find something personally valuable in the material. Otherwise, why should they be teaching something that does not appear to have any particular value for them? The exercise may reveal that some of the teachers have not engaged the curriculum at this deeper level of moral dialogue and the mutual relationships to the world revealed through this curriculum. The supervisor and the group of teachers can collaboratively explore how those worlds engage their human identity and sense of agency, and communicate the privileges and obligations of members in those worlds. These discussions could then lead to additional strategies for designing learning activities that bring the learner into a similar level of dialogue with the curriculum unit. This process of designing learning activities can lead to the design of appropriate rubrics for self-assessment by the learner and assessment by the teacher.

By discussing the various dynamics of this model of the moral character of teaching and learning with groups of teachers, supervisors can cooperatively develop an ongoing agenda of reflective practice and professional development with the teachers.

All of the preceding learning and teaching analysis, as both an intellectual and moral activity, led me to propose the standards listed at the beginning of this chapter for supervisors at various levels of the school system. These standards would guide the activities of different administrative leaders in different ways, depending on the scope and focus of their responsibilities. But if embraced systemwide, they could go a long way to reestablishing the moral integrity of supervision.

References

Carr, D., & Steutel, J. (Eds.). (1999). *Virtue ethics and moral education.* London: Routledge.

Dunne, J. (1995). What's the good of education? In P. Hogan (Ed.), *Partnership and the benefits of learning* (pp. 60–82). Maynooth College, County of Kildare: Educational Studies Association of Ireland.

Flanagan, K., & Jupp, P. C. (Eds.). (2001). *Virtue ethics and sociology.* Basingstoke, Hampshire, UK: Palgrave.

Gouinlock, J. (1993). *Rediscovering the moral life: Philosophy and human practice.* Buffalo, NY: Prometheus Books.

Hogan, P. (1995). *The custody and courtship of experience: Western education in philosophical perspective.* Dublin, Ireland: Columba Press.

Shepard, L. A. (2002, January). *The contest between large-scale accountability and assessment in the service of learning: 1970–2001.* Paper prepared for the Spencer Foundation's 30th Anniversary Conference, Chicago.

Starratt, R.J. (2004). *Ethical leadership.* San Francisco: Jossey-Bass.

Starratt, R.J. (in press). Moral issues in the test-driven accountability agenda: Implications for learner centered education leadership programs. In A. Danzig, K. & W. F. Wright (Eds.), *Professional Development for Learner Centered Leadership: Policy, Research, and Practice.* Mahwah, NJ: Lawrence Erlbaum.

Taylor, C. (1992). *The ethics of authenticity.* Cambridge, MA: Harvard University Press.

Walker, M. (2004). *Human capabilities, education and "doing the public good": Towards a capability-based theory of social justice in education.* Paper presented at the annual conference of the Australian Association of Research in Education, Melbourne, Australia.

5

Standards of Collegiality and Collaboration

Sally J. Zepeda

Meet the Author

Sally J. Zepeda

Sally J. Zepeda is an associate professor and Graduate Coordinator in the Department of Lifelong Education, Administration, and Policy at the University of Georgia. Her research interest is instructional supervision focusing on differentiated and developmental approaches. Sally has written several books, book chapters, and articles chronicling the improvement of instruction. She is a member of the Council of Professors of Instructional Supervision (COPIS). In 2004, she guest edited a themed issue of NASSP *Bulletin* on instructional supervision for the National Association of Secondary School Principals. Sally teaches Supervision of Instruction, Trends and Issues in Supervision, and Supervision Theory.

Successful supervision:

♦ Creates and sustains a learning community that supports teachers as both learners and leaders

♦ Reduces isolation by encouraging teachers and other school personnel to collaborate by engaging in critical discussions about instructional practices that transcend individual classrooms

♦ Promotes a culture of cooperative work and risk taking among teachers

♦ Promotes a can-do attitude and a safety net as teachers face uncertainties associated with high stakes learning and work environments

♦ Pays attention to affective domains, including developing professional relationships, promoting openness to individual and collective improvement, and caring for teachers by nurturing relational trust, respect, personal regard, and integrity

♦ Provides momentum for the development of differentiated forms of supervision (e.g., action research, portfolio development, peer coaching) where teachers are the major actors setting the course for expanded learning opportunities

Isolation is an embedded pattern in schools with teachers working mostly alone, encountering the issues of practice without the benefit of gaining insight and constructing individual and collective knowledge by working with colleagues. The absence of collaboration points create differences between schools that develop as learning communities and schools that form as insular (Lortie, 1975), compartmentalized "egg crates" (Troen & Boles, 1994), where teachers experience the "ceiling effect" in their learning, growth, and development (Fullan, 1993, p. 17).

Instructional supervision can be a way to enhance the work of teachers individually and collectively, and in theory embraces the purposes and intents needed to support collaboration, collegiality, risk taking, and the development of a learning community. Supervision that supports collegiality and collaboration promotes:

- ◆ Face-to-face interaction and relationship building (Acheson & Gall, 2003)
- ◆ Ongoing learning (Sullivan & Glanz, 2004; Zepeda, 2003)
- ◆ Increased capacity-building for the individual and the organization (Pajak, 2000);
- ◆ Trust in the processes, each other, and the environment (Costa & Garmston, 2002);
- ◆ Change that supports teacher and student learning (Sergiovanni & Starratt, 2002)

Individual and group development processes in supervision date to the work of Cogan (1973), who envisioned practices that would position teachers as active learners "analytical of their own performance, open to help from others, and self-directing" (p. 12). Supervision can be a powerful tool in fostering collaborative learning communities (Zepeda, 2000, 2004). This chapter offers six standards to promote collegiality and collaboration to forward the overall intents and purposes of instructional supervision.

Standard 1: Successful Supervision Creates and Sustains a Learning Community

Successful supervision creates and sustains a learning community that supports teachers as both learners and leaders.

A learning community consists of "school staff members taking collective responsibility for a shared educational purpose, and collaborating with one another to achieve that purpose" (Newman, 1994, p. 1). Supervision as a community-based effort promotes growth where learning is the norm, and where all members, regardless of formalized role, are encouraged to learn together. "No profession can survive, let alone flourish, when its members are cut off from others and from the rich knowledge base on which success and excellence depend" (Barth, 1989, p. 289). Supervision that builds a learning community is nestled in an environment supporting:

1. *Interaction and participation.* People have many opportunities and reasons to come together in deliberation, association, and action.
2. *Interdependence.* These associations and actions both promote and depend on mutual needs and commitments.
3. *Shared interests and beliefs.* People share perspectives, values, understandings, and commitment to common purposes.

4. *Concern for individual and minority views.* Individual differences are embraced through critical reflection and mechanisms for dissent, and lead to growth through the new perspectives they foster.

5. *Meaningful relationships.* Interactions reflect a commitment to caring, sustaining relationships. (Westheimer, 1998, p. 17)

Standard 2: Successful Supervision Reduces Isolation

Successful supervision reduces isolation by encouraging teachers and other school personnel to collaborate by engaging in critical discussions about instructional practices that transcend individual classrooms.

Teaching is a complex process, and "learning is a messy, mumbled, non-linear, recursive, and sometimes unpredictable process" (Avery, 1990, p. 43). In other words, to refine instructional practices, teachers need time and opportunity to collaborate and form collegial relationships. Empowering supervision gives teachers opportunities to engage in ongoing conversations about practice, with classroom observations serving as the point of departure for these conversations. By providing time and opportunity for teachers to "talk about the walk" of classroom instruction, a more collaborative culture emerges where the "traditional norms of isolation and autonomy" are supplanted with "opportunities for interaction" (Dorsch, 1998, p. 2).

Collaboration is a complex, multidimensional construct that supports interdependence (Little, 1990), reciprocal relationships (Rosenholtz, 1989), and authentic interactions and collegiality (Hargreaves, 1994, 1997). Hargreaves (1994, pp. 245-247) argued, in part, that collaboration:

- strengthens resolve, permits vulnerabilities to be shared, and carries people through the failures and frustrations accompanying change
- improves the quality of student learning by improving the quality of teaching
- permits sharing of the burdens and pressures coming from intensified work demands and accelerated change
- increases teachers' opportunities to learn from each other
- encourages teachers to see change not as a task to be completed, but as an unending process of continuous improvement

Dialogue is a critical component of supervision regardless of its form (e.g., clinical, peer coaching, cognitive coaching, and action research). However, dialogue is more than mere talk. Dialogue supports inquiry and reflection as teachers engage in building new meanings about their practices over time. Therefore, the power of the word needs to be respected and encouraged. In collaborative cultures, values are shared when "values find expression and a common lexicon is developed…values find action…values and efforts are affirmed" (Simonelli, 1996, pp. 23–24). Learning occurs when beliefs, theories, and perceptions are challenged through conversation and experience.

Supervisors support and sustain collaboration by providing opportunities for teachers to talk about teaching and learning, encouraging teachers to observe each other teaching, and modeling critical behaviors such as listening and respecting dissenting perspectives, cooperating with others, and deferring to expertise.

Standard 3: Successful Supervision Promotes Cooperation and Risk Taking

Successful supervision promotes a culture of cooperative work and risk taking among teachers.

In a school culture built on collaboration and promoting collegial relationships, teachers can discuss without the fear of retribution the issues that matter most to them, regardless of the subject or dissention of ideas among teachers and administrators. This is because

♦ Diversity of expertise among its members, who are valued for their contributions and are given support to develop

♦ A shared objective of continually advancing the collective knowledge and skills is nurtured

♦ An emphasis on learning how to learn is provided

♦ Mechanisms for sharing what is learned are provided (Bielaczyc & Collins, 1999, p. 4)

A school that promotes these behaviors and values also supports taking risks, and according to Hargreaves (1997), "cultures of collaboration among teachers seem to produce greater willingness to take risks, to learn from mistakes, and share successful strategies" (p. 68). Risk-taking is central to the work of teachers whose decisions might have consequences spanning beyond the confines of the single classroom. Confronting the unknown is "risky business" and involves loss, gains, and uncertainty. However, in environments supporting risk-taking, "faculties had the capacity to learn from losses" (Louis, Kruse, & Marks, 1996, p. 193).

Teachers who are engaged in examining their practices in public places put their professional lives in full view of their colleagues, which is why creating a risk-taking environment requires trust. When teachers work together, they expose vulnerabilities and in the process of making improvements, they take dynamic risks by challenging the status quo, versus static risks that preserve the status quo (Kehrer, 1989). Risk-taking is often avoided because the possible consequences of taking risks are losing respect, face, credibility, reputation, and possible embarrassment (Kindler, 1998; Ryan & Oestreich, 1991). Teachers may be more willing to take risks if anxiety and potential threats can be reduced (Ponticell, 2003).

Risk-taking is tied to learning and requires overcoming fears and facing new challenges. Vygotsky (1978) described the Zone of Proximal Development (ZPD) where the learner has knowledge, familiarity, and security. When confronted with new information or experiences, learners must go outside their comfort zones. With experience, comfort levels increase and fear decreases, so learning curves expand more readily (Vygotsky, 1978). While working with one another in a fault-free workplace, teachers will more openly take "risks in an environment that encourages efforts without facing retribution for less than satisfactory progress at hitting the target" (Zepeda, 1999, p. 65).

Standard 4: Successful Supervision Promotes "Can Do" and Safety Net

Successful supervision promotes a "can do" attitude and a safety net as teachers face uncertainties associated with high-stakes learning and work environments.

The discussion of high stakes and accountability abounds in the literature. Suffice it to say, teachers are now held more responsible for the success of student performance on such measures as end-of-course exams, standardized tests, and other measures. With this pressure and stress for students to "do better," teachers feel the trickle effect from principals, school boards, parents, and community members that they too must "do better." Teachers need a "safety net" where their ideas and problems of practice can be examined. These interactions will be at best perfunctory in a school that does not embrace collegiality. With collaboration, collegiality is not guaranteed, as authentic collegiality rests on mutual respect, embracement of similarities and differences, acknowledgement of expertise—all in the spirit of making collective judgment and taking action about practice while embracing a common purpose (Hargreaves, 1994; Newman, 1994).

For collegiality to prevail, community members must be able to value their purposes and intents while working toward a shared purpose. But there can be a dark side to collegiality, and according to Hargreaves (1997), "Contrived collegiality does not so much deceive teachers as delay, distract, and demean them" (p. 73). Supervisors who promote the development of collegial behaviors encourage all to model learning as a way to assist teachers in actively constructing knowledge. Successful supervision provides multiple forms of supervision (e.g., action research, peer coaching, portfolio development), so teachers can work in different ways with other teachers who face similar classroom dilemmas. These collaborative efforts promote a natural safety net for teachers as they tackle working in schools where performance is based on what students learn in the classroom.

Standard 5: Successful Supervision Pays Attention to Affective Domains

> Successful supervision pays attention to affective domains, including developing professional relationships, promoting openness to individual and collective improvement, and caring for teachers by nurturing relational trust, respect, personal regard, and integrity.

When supervisors build bridges with teachers, authentic relationships develop through supporting an inclusive sense of belonging, nurturing the growth of people, and embracing differences. Trust is a prerequisite for building positive relationships and the norms of collaboration and collegiality. Without trust, efforts will be diminished and relationships will flounder. Trust and respect build a strong foundation for the work and efforts of teachers. Relational trust rests on a foundation of respect, personal regard, and integrity.

According to Beck (1992), a "caring ethic" includes two primary goals: "promoting human development and responding to needs" (pp. 456-457). Care is promoted when people value one another and the purposes of working together. Supervisors who promote a positive and caring culture act in ways that signal to teachers they are able to seek assistance, overcome obstacles, view failure as a learning experience, and develop individual and collective strengths.

Standard 6: Successful Supervision Stimulates Development of Differentiated Forms of Supervision

> Successful supervision provides momentum for the development of differentiated forms of supervision (e.g., action research, portfolio development, peer coaching) in which teachers are the major actors setting the course for expanded learning opportunities.

Successful supervision is built on the foundation of collaboration and collegiality, and this foundation is fortified through differentiated practices that more holistically meet the career needs of teachers. Differentiated supervisory practices often incorporate the basic phases of the clinical supervision model (e.g., pre-observation conference, classroom observation, and post-observation conference), action research (Glanz, 1998, 1999), and peer coaching (Joyce & Showers, 1982) with innovations like the portfolio (St. Maurice & Shaw, 2004; Zepeda, 2002, 2003) and whole-school study groups (Murphy & Lick, 2005).

Through differentiated supervisory opportunities, teachers are empowered to make decisions about what activities and practices will meet their learning needs, what resources are needed to meet learning needs, with whom to partner, and what markers identify completion of short- and long-term learning goals (Glatthorn, 1997; Zepeda, 2003). Because differentiated supervisory options promote collaboration, teachers can be actively nurtured to become involved in discovery and refinement of practice through ongoing dialogue, reflection, and inquiry.

Professional Development Activity

This activity relates to standards of collegiality and collaboration. These standards support the proposition that successful supervision creates and sustains a learning community, reduces isolation, promotes cooperative work and risk taking, promotes a "can do" attitude, considers the affective domains in developing relationships, and supports differentiated supervisory practices to promote collegiality and collaboration. The following activities will take the reader into the field to collect and analyze data and then to develop an action plan to enhance the development of collegial and collaborative efforts and activities in the school.

Part 1: At the school site, identify what factors contribute to the development of a learning community that supports collegiality and collaboration. Starting with:

♦ The leadership team (principal, assistant principal(s), department chairs, instructional coordinators, grade level leaders)

♦ Teachers, professional staff (nurse, social worker, paraprofessionals, staff secretaries, and custodians)

For each group, identify communication patterns, opportunities for collaborative work, and learning opportunities provided for each. Spend time talking with a sample from each group. Identify what you discover as overall themes about communication patterns (how people talk, and interact with one another). For each theme, develop a strategy to enhance communication and interaction. Present your findings to the administrative team.

Part 2: At the school site, identify the programs in place that support teacher development vis-à-vis collaboration and collegiality (e.g., peer coaching, mentoring, study groups, action research). Collect documents describing these programs and choose one or two programs on which to focus time and energy. For the programs you choose to examine, identify the goals and objectives of the programs and assess how these programs support norms of collaboration and collegiality.

Part 3: At the school site, identify what differentiated opportunities exist for teachers (beginning teachers, mid-career teachers, veteran teacher). Determine:

- ♦ What structured programs involve beginning teachers and veteran teachers?

- ♦ What formal and informal opportunities exist for these teachers to focus on teaching and learning? (e.g., informal and formal classroom observations, opportunities to engage in action research with teachers within and across grade levels).

- ♦ As a leader, what would you need to do to support these programs and help them grow and develop further? What resources from within the site and the central office could be allocated to these programs?

Part 4: Develop a survey to administer at the next faculty meeting to determine the scope of collaboration (time for teachers during the day, structured and unstructured opportunities to collaborate, the extent to which teachers are involved in leadership, desired activities to promote collaboration—study groups, peer coaching, mentoring, etc.). Next,,

- ♦ Tally and share results with faculty and administration

- ♦ Form a committee to examine results, make recommendations, and develop a prioritized plan that aligns with the mission of the school and priorities in the school improvement plan.

- ♦ Based on data, forecast how the prioritized plans will enhance collaboration and collegiality.

- ♦ Develop a self-reflection on what leadership is needed to move the plan forward and the role you will play in it.

To these ends, as a supervisor, you will be involved in a cycle of defining needs and goals, developing solutions, implementing a plan, providing ongoing support, and evaluating results. These activities are circular in that one activity will inform actions and resources needed to support the plans that are developed.

Assessment Criteria

There are four criteria used in the assessment:

1. The data gathered are robust enough to identify patterns of communication that enhance and patterns that impede collaboration.

2. Based on data, the participant can identify programs for targeted school personnel (e.g., mentoring and peer coaching for beginning to career status teachers), identify areas in need of resources to support these programs, and identify what leadership is needed to enhance the ongoing development of programs.

3. The participant is able to identify key structural needs to promote collaboration (time for teachers during the day), delineate between structured and unstructured opportunities to collaborate, evaluate the extent to which teachers are involved in leadership, and knows which activities promote collaboration.

4. The participant is able to work with school personnel in defining needs and goals, developing solutions, implementing a plan, providing ongoing support, and evaluating results.

The participant's reflection of self and the leadership needed to promote a learning community and norms of collaboration and collegiality is realistic relative to the context of the school.

References

Acheson, K. A., & Gall, M. D. (2003). *Techniques in the clinical supervision of teachers* (5th ed.). New York: Wiley.

Avery, C. S. (1990). Learning to research/researching to learn. In M. W. Olson (Ed.), *Opening the door to classroom research* (pp. 32–44). Newark, NJ: International Reading Association.

Barth, R. (1989). The principal and the profession of teaching. In T. J. Sergiovanni & J. Moore (Eds.), *Schooling for tomorrow: Directing reforms to issues that count* (pp. 227–250). Boston: Allyn and Bacon.

Beck, L. G. (1992). Meeting the challenge of the future: The place of a caring ethic in educational administration. *American Journal of Education, 100*(4), 454–496.

Bielaczyc, K., & Collins, A. (1999). Learning communities: Knowledge for a lifetime. *NASSP Bulletin, 83*(604), 4–10.

Cogan, M. (1973). *Clinical supervision.* Boston: Houghton-Mifflin.

Costa, A. L., & Garmston, R. J. (2002). *Cognitive coaching: A foundation for Renaissance schools* (2nd ed.). Norwood, MA: Christopher-Gordon.

Dorsch, N.G. (1998). *Community, collaboration, and collegiality in school reform: An odyssey toward connections.* Albany: State University of New York Press.

Fullan, M. G. (1993). *Change forces: Probing the depths of educational reform.* London: Falmer Press.

Glanz, J. (1998). *Action research: An educational leader's guide to school improvement.* Norwood, MA: Christopher-Gordon.

Glanz, J. (1999). Action research. *Journal of Staff Development, 20*(3), 22–25.

Glatthorn, A. A. (1997). *Differentiated supervision.* (2nd ed). Alexandria, VA: Association for Supervision and Curriculum Development.

Hargreaves, A. (1997). Cultures of teaching and educational change. In M. Fullan (Ed.), *The Challenge of School Change* (pp. 57–84). Arlington Heights IL: Skylight.

Hargreaves, A. (1994). *Changing teachers, changing times: Teachers' work and culture in the postmodern age.* London: Cassell.

Joyce, B., & Showers, B. (1982). The coaching of teaching. *Educational Leadership, 40*(2), 4–10.

Kehrer, D. (1989). *Doing business boldly: The masters of taking intelligent risks.* New York: Times Books.

Kindler, H. (1998). The art of prudent risk taking. *Training and Development, 52*(4), 32–36.

Little, J. W. (1990). The persistence of privacy: Autonomy and initiative in teachers' professional relations. *Teachers College Record, 91*(4), 509–536.

Lortie, D. C. (1975) *School teacher: A sociological perspective.* Chicago: University of Chicago Press.

Louis, K. S., Kruse, S. D., & Marks, H. M. (1996). School-wide professional community. In F. M. Newman (Ed.), *Authentic achievement: Restructuring schools for intellectual quality* (pp. 179-203). San Francisco: Jossey-Bass.

Murphy, C. U., & Lick, D. W. (2005). *Whole-faculty study groups: A powerful way to change schools and enhance learning* (2nd ed.). Thousand Oaks, CA: Corwin Press.

Newmann, F. M. (1994). School-wide professional community. In L. Lynn (Ed.). *Issues in Restructuring Schools,* No. 6, (pp. 1–2). Madison, WI: Center on Organization and Restructuring of Schools

Pajak, E. (2000). *Approaches to clinical supervision: Alternatives for improving instruction* (2nd ed.). Norwood, MA: Christopher-Gordon.

Ponticell, J. A. (2003). Enhancers and inhibitors of teacher risk taking: A case study.*Peabody Journal of Education, 78*(3), 5–24.

Rosenholtz, S. J. (1989). Workplace conditions that affect teacher quality and commitment: Implications for teacher induction programs. *The Elementary School Journal, 89*(4), 421–439.

Ryan, D., & Oestreich, D. K. (1991). *Driving fear out of the workplace.* San Francisco: Jossey-Bass.

Sergiovanni, T. J., & Starratt, R. J. (2002). *Supervision: A redefinition* (7th ed.). Boston: McGraw-Hill.

Simonelli, R. (1996). The basic school: Recreating community for educational development. *Winds of Change, 11*(1), 22–25.

St. Maurice, H., & Shaw, P. (2004). Teacher portfolios come of age: A preliminary study. *NASSP Bulletin, 88*(639), 15–25.

Sullivan, S., & Glanz, J. (2004). *Supervision that improves teaching: Strategies and techniques* (2nd ed.). Thousand Oaks, CA: Corwin Press.

Troen, V., & Boles, K. (1994). Two teachers examine the power of teacher leadership. In D. R. Walling (Ed.), *Teachers as leaders: Perspectives on the professional development of teachers* (pp. 275–286). Bloomington, IN: Phi Delta Kappa.

Vygotsky, L. (1978). *Mind in society: The development of higher psychological processes.* Boston: Harvard University Press.

Westheimer, J. (1998). *Among school teachers: Community autonomy and ideology in teachers' work.* New York: Teachers College Press.

Zepeda, S. J. (1999). *Staff development: Practices that promote leadership in learning communities.* Larchmont, NY: Eye On Education.

Zepeda, S. J. (2000). Supervisory practices: Building a constructivist learning community for adults. In J. Glanz & L. Behar-Horenstein (Eds.), *Paradigm debates in curriculum and supervision: Modern and postmodern perspectives* (pp. 93–107). Westport, CT: Bergin & Garvey.

Zepeda, S. J. (2002). Linking portfolio development to clinical supervision: A case study. *The Journal of Curriculum and Supervision, 18*(1), 83–102.

Zepeda, S. J. (2003). *Instructional supervision: Applying tools and concepts.* Larchmont, NY: Eye On Education.

Zepeda, S. J. (2004). Leadership to build learning communities. *The Educational Forum, 62*(2), 144–151.

6

Standards of Reflective Practice

Daisy Arredondo Rucinski

To learn from experience is to make a backward and forward connection between what we do to things and what we enjoy or suffer from things in consequence. Under such conditions, doing becomes a trying; an experiment with the world to find out what it is like; the undergoing becomes instruction—discovery of the connection of things (John Dewey, 1916, p. 1).

Meet the Author

Daisy Arredondo Rucinski

Daisy Arredondo Rucinski, is associate professor in educational leadership at Seattle University. She earned a Ph.D. degree from the University of Washington. Arredondo Rucinski teachers doctoral seminars on reflective, ethical and moral leadership development, conducts research on teacher evaluation and instructional supervision, and is currently involved in research in Santiago, Chile on improving teaching through assessment and development of reflection using dialogue, cognitive coaching, and mentoring. She has an article on assessment of reflection in a 2004 Boletin de Investigaction Educacional, 19(2).

Successful supervision:

♦ Reviews actions and accepts feedback about actions and perceptions of those actions in conversations with others

♦ Plans actions, describes plans, and checks plans with others

♦ Interprets and constructs meaning in conversations, and inquires about interpretations of others

♦ Invites feedback and asks questions about assumptions, perspectives, and beliefs about self and others

♦ Openly accepts criticisms for actions and decisions and does not become defensive when questioned by others

♦ Accepts responsibility for decisions or actions taken; does not rationalize behaviors or blame policy, others, or practices for actions or decisions

♦ Asks questions about the effects of actions or decisions on others (e.g., colleagues, employees, clients, students, on policy and/or future practice)

♦ Asks questions about the extent to which the actions or decisions are moral or ethical

♦ Asks questions about the results of actions or decisions on disenfranchised, underrepresented, and/or marginalized populations

Background

Within the past 15 years, much has been written about reflective practice. For anyone who works within a school, reflective practice is a way of learning from what we do, experience, and understand about any knowledge or teaching method we are using. It is a way of rigorously examining our actions and decisions and improving the overall quality of our work. Reflective practice is also a powerful way to develop new skills, knowledge, and professional practices to help our students learn more effectively. In addition, because engaging in reflective conversations with colleagues is essential to the development of collaborative learning communities, it is an important part of any school's instructional supervision and professional development program.

This chapter presents background information about reflective practice and a rationale for its use; it describes and explains the standards identified above, presents a professional development activity for enhancing fluency in the use of reflective practice, and explains how the standards can be assessed. The standards for reflective practice presented in this chapter were developed with ongoing research about levels of reflection as indicators of cognitive developmental changes among personnel involved in school reform efforts. This chapter has been written primarily for an audience of school-based practitioners—teachers, principals, and others in leadership positions—who want to use reflective practice within their school communities. In addition, I hope the information presented will be useful to graduate students, university professors, and administrators interested in reflective practice.

Why Is Reflective Practice Important?

In recent years, a number of educational researchers and writers have argued that despite decades of school reform efforts and innovations, schools have basically remained the same (see, for example, Elmore, 1995, 1996; Osterman & Kottkamp, 2004; Tyack & Cuban, 1995). These educators argued that to bring about real school reform, both individuals in schools and whole school cultures must change. They argued that real reform does not occur unless the core technology, defined as the teaching and learning process, is changed. They suggested that individual behavioral change is controlled by cognitive beliefs, assumptions, and action theories, and is essential to change the core technology of schools. Such cognitive changes cannot occur with a simple "fix-it" mentality toward school reform efforts. For example, if professional development is focused on presentations of new strategies or ideas and has this simple perspective toward change, then it is unlikely to result in real reform (Fullan, 2000; King & Newmann, 2000; Osterman & Kottkamp, 2004;). We know from other research on school reform that professional development activities have had minimal effects on teaching practices (Little, 1993), and that innovations, even when implemented well, do not remain in place over long time periods (Fullan, 2000; Fullan & Hargreaves, 1996; Hargreaves, Earl, & Ryan, 1996). Although some reviewers of comprehensive school reforms have reported positive overall student achievement gains under certain conditions (Desimone, 2002; Murphy & Datnow, 2003), critics have argued that these reported effects are more likely caused by flaws in evaluation designs, large numbers of the evaluations being completed by nonindependent evaluators, and an over-reliance in judgments based on first-year changes in achievement (Pogrow, 2005). Elmore (1996) explained these results in terms of reforms that were not focused on the core work of schools—that is, on the basic teaching and learning process and how teachers think about knowledge and learning. Tyack and Cuban (1995), on the other hand, attributed the underlying stability of schools in the face of decades of change efforts to a sensible response from teachers, when in their assessment, local conditions and support for real change do not exist.

We also know from the reflective practice literature that when small, piece-meal innovations are implemented, even those based on sound research, an individual's habitual behavior, controlled and guided by implicit beliefs and assumptions and often shared across the organizational culture, remains the norm and eventually resurfaces in behaviors and actions that result in the innovation being weakened or completely destroyed (Argyris, 1992; Argyris & Schön, 1978; and Schön, 1987). Such regression in schools is even more likely to happen when the innovation is implemented in isolated classrooms, which is often the case. To explain why this happens, Argyris and Schön (1978) used two constructs: "espoused theories" and "theories-in-use".

Espoused theories are ideas or theories we often use to explain what we believe. In other words, they are our practical theories about how to operate in the world. They exist at a conscious level and are changed with relative ease. To illustrate, I might emerge from a professional development activity or a graduate class with a newly learned idea or theory about how children learn abstract words. According to this theory, learners are more likely to remember abstract words—what they mean and how to spell them—if they create an image or mental picture of what the word means with the letters of the word superimposed (or written) on top of the image. This theory is consistent with what I know about memory, so it makes sense to me and it becomes my espoused theory. Following this learning experience, if someone asks me what I believe about how children learn to spell abstract words, I readily describe this new idea or theory, and if I am like most folks, I believe that such espoused theories guide my actions. According to psychologists, however, this is usually not the case. Instead, our behaviors are driven by theories-in-use.

Carrying our simple example still further, perhaps on the following day, I notice three abstract words among those that I want my third-grade students to remember and learn to spell. Instead of asking them to create a "picture in their minds" of what the word means, and then to "see themselves" writing the word over the picture, I instruct them to look up the words in their text and to spell out the words as they say them aloud so they will remember them for a spelling test after lunch. This action with my third graders would be a failure to use the recently learned idea or theory (i.e., my new espoused theory) about how children learn to spell, in my own classroom. Instead, my teaching action would be guided or controlled by a very different theory-in-use.

Theories-in-use are more powerful than espoused theories in guiding our behaviors and actions because they exist at the tacit (Polanyi, 1967) or subconscious level and are not easily articulated. They are deeply engrained in our subconscious and are part of us, because we have constructed them from our past experiences. They are constructed from critical incidents in work or life situations, in schools, from experiences with our parents, role models, teachers, and mentors. These theories-in-use are difficult to change because they are connected to habitual behaviors that have developed over time. They are part of what makes us unique individuals. In addition, many of our theories-in-use are shared across communities and as such are reinforced within our cultural contexts. This is why cultures remain stable over long periods of time.

One of the reasons that theories-in-use are difficult to change is that we have not rigorously examined them. They tend to remain part of what Polanyi called the "tacit dimension" and part of our tacit knowledge until they are made explicit and we become conscious of them. Theories-in-use show up and can be observed in our behavior, especially by individuals who know us well enough to know some of our espoused theories. If, in our work situations, we often say we believe a certain theory to be true and then do not follow that theory into practice, it is glaringly obvious to those around us. This is what is happening when someone says, "She doesn't walk her talk" or "He is not practicing what he preaches". In the fourth reflective practice standard listed above, we examine our actions and decisions to identify the underlying tacit assumptions and beliefs, so that we may look for discrepancies between what we say we believe and what we do. Until then, we are usually not aware that some of our behaviors are different from our espoused theories.

Discrepancies between espoused theories and theories-in-use may exist for long periods of time. Reflective practice provides a rigorous and structured way of examining and identifying these discrepancies. Once identified, discrepancies are believed to create cognitive dissonance (Festinger, 1957), which then may become an impetus for changing behaviors, especially in a supportive environment (Vygotsky, 1962). Behaviors reflecting our theories-in-use are more likely to shift in the direction of espoused beliefs because our espoused beliefs are connected to self-esteem and may be more acceptable. If we have made a verbal commitment to a particular belief, for example, some self-esteem is involved. That tension between our self-esteem and the cognitive dissonance created by our knowledge of the discrepancy may tend to push our behaviors into congruence with our stated beliefs. For example, recent research on educator beliefs has shown that reflective practice has the potential to bring about cognitive changes in our beliefs and assumptions, which may result in the implementation of school reform efforts more consistent with those stated beliefs (Arredondo & Rucinski, 1998; Beas, Gomez, Thomsen, & Carranza, 2004; Kaufman, 2004).

Some Background

Reflective practice is based on John Dewey's explanation of experiential learning (1916). Dewey's description of the experiential learning cycle includes five stages. The first two are usually collapsed by modern writers, resulting in the four commonly described: (1) experience, (2) observation and reflection, (3) abstract reconceptualization, and (4) experimentation (Osterman & Kottkamp, 1993). In the learning process, the first phase of the learning cycle begins with what Dewey described as inquiry into a problematic situation. (See Figure 6.1.) This might be a troublesome event or experience, or an unsettling situation that cannot be resolved using standard procedures. A sense of uncertainty causes the reflective practitioner to stop and examine the experience. According to Osterman and Kottkamp (1993), the person may ask, "What was the nature of the problem here? What happened? What did I do? What were my intentions?" (p. 21.). In the process of observing and reflecting on the experience, problems are clarified. A problem may be "a discrepancy between the real and the ideal, between intention and action, or between action and effects" (p. 21). Problems stimulate inquiry as part of an active search for new information, better answers, and more effective strategies in this second phase of the cycle.

Figure 6.1. Experimental Learning Cycle

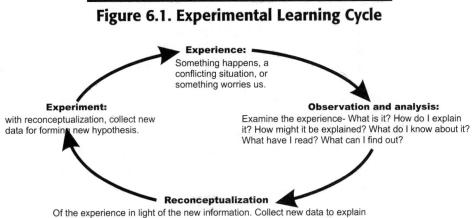

Experience: Something happens, a conflicting situation, or something worries us.

Observation and analysis: Examine the experience- What is it? How do I explain it? How might it be explained? What do I know about it? What have I read? What can I find out?

Reconceptualization Of the experience in light of the new information. Collect new data to explain the new thinking about the problem in practice; form new hypothesis.

Experiment: with reconceptualization, collect new data for forming new hypothesis.

During the third and fourth phases of the cycle, reconceptualization and experimentation occur. After observation and reflection on the experience, the learner moves into the realm of theory. Here the person uses new information to develop alternate theories or explanations that are useful in understanding what happened, or the relationship between actions and outcomes, and thus begins the search for strategies more consistent with espoused theories and likely to be more effective in achieving intended outcomes. These alternate theories become a stimulus for experimentation as we test new ideas and hunches. In short, reflective thinking and raising questions about reflective practice begins a learning process, which often leads to significant behavioral change based on underlying cognitive change. Because individuals change behaviors only after they notice and reflect on discrepancies, reflective educators argue that the use of a structured process for reflection helps them become continuous learning professionals.

Reflective Practice
Standards and Applications

The standards for reflective practice represent at least four levels of cognitive development: (1) emergent use of reflective practice, (2) competent use of reflective practice, (3) expert use of reflective practice, and (4) ethical and socially just use of reflective practice. Level one includes the first two standards, *reviews actions and accepts feedback about actions and perceptions of those actions in conversations with others*; and *plans actions, describes plans, and checks plans with others*. Level two includes the third and fourth standards, *interprets and constructs meaning in conversations and inquires about interpretations of others*; and *invites feedback and asks questions about assumptions, perspectives, and beliefs about self and others*. Level three includes the fifth and sixth standards, *openly accepts criticisms for actions and decisions and does not become defensive when questioned by others*; and *accepts responsibility for decisions or actions taken*; and *does not rationalize behaviors, blame policy, others, or practices for actions or decisions*. Level four includes the final three standards: *asks questions about the effects of actions or decisions on others (e.g., colleagues, employees, clients, students, on policy and/or future practice), asks questions about the extent to which actions or decisions are moral or ethical*; and *asks questions about the results of actions or decisions on disenfranchised, underrepresented or marginalized populations*.

The reader will notice that emergent, competent, and expert levels of reflective practice represent what King and Kitchener (1994) referred to as the first three phases in development of reflective judgment. The fourth level, "ethical and socially just use of reflective practice," represents reflective thinking about ethical and moral problems. As King and Kitchener argued, reflective thinking is a necessary but not sufficient precursor of ethical and moral judgment.

Reflective practitioners habitually have mental conversations with themselves. When groups agree to reflect together in learning communities, they participate in reflective conversations with their colleagues. In these conversations they engage in the components of reflective practice identified in the standards. They review both routine and nonroutine actions; reflect and inquire about their own and others' assumptions, beliefs, and theories; construct meaning; and ask how they might reframe the problem or situation, thus considering others' perspectives. Each of the identified standards, then, represents actions or behaviors that reflective practitioners habitually use. In collaborative group reflections, it is especially important for practitioners to consider feedback about their performances. Feedback is an important piece of acquiring new knowledge, so if they have not received feedback, reflective practitioners invite it. With this invitation for feedback, they attempt to discuss what was previously undiscussable, with the overall goal being to examine behavior so that continuous growth and development occur. Such habits of reflection allow professionals to improve their practices by making better decisions about future actions based on continuous learning. Because reflective practice gets at the deep changes needed for real individual growth, many educators believe it presents a hopeful message about our ability to bring about whole school reform and create effective learning environments for all students.

Similarly, reflective practice is useful for examining ethical and moral effects and implications of actions and decisions. This application of reflection is based on the work of scholars who have contrasted the normative duties and actions of ethical leaders with technical–rational leadership practices. The stereotype of practicing administrators often portrays them as focused on pragmatic and operational matters, and exhibiting a tendency to make decisions based on a culture of policy and procedures developed by bureaucratic school organizations. Increasingly, however, the theoretical and empirical literature in educational leadership addresses the need for educators to regard their professional responsibilities as based on moral and ethical imperatives (See, for example, Fullan, 1993; Sergiovanni, 1992; Starratt, 1991; Strike & Ternasky, 1993).

Central to the development of educational leaders who view their responsibilities as having moral and ethical implications is a conceptual framework for thinking about dilemmas in educational practice. Starratt (1991) articulated three fundamental themes of ethical conduct: critique, justice, and caring. For Starratt, these themes describe the day-to-day duties of an ethical leader. He argued that in this age of school reform, administrators have a duty to establish a school environment where the educative function can occur ethically. Hence the structure, system, and context of the school become the arena in which administrators make ethical decisions.

Following Starratt, Shapiro and Stefkovich (2001) described a model in which ethics of justice, critique, and care might be viewed within the context of the ethical codes of the profession. Codes and standards developed by educational associations place a high value on what is "in the best interest of the student" as a focus for ethical perspectives. Using the reflective process to think about the likely results of actions and decisions, asking about who will be advantaged or disadvantaged by the results, is a powerful way to examine leadership behaviors and decisions from these ethical and moral perspectives.

Reflective practice is also a powerful way of developing an understanding of new and often abstract theories and ideas. In this use of the reflective process, the learner or reflective practitioner begins with the new theory or idea in phase two of Dewey's experiential learning cycle. Learners first describe this new idea or theory in their own words. Then, moving to phase one, reflective practitioners recall or invent situations in which this new idea or theory might be applicable. During this phase, they fully describe the "experience" or "created experience" and connect it in detail to the new theory or idea. As alternative explanations and new information develop from insights in this phase, an enhanced perspective of the new ideas or theories for experimentation results. Following this, reflective practitioners experiment with the new idea or theory, test it in practice, collect new data, and begin the cycle anew. Obviously, new skills or procedural knowledge can also be developed by reflecting on them in this manner and by mentally "practicing" them.

Several researchers have described different levels of reflection in attempts to assess the overall quality or type of reflective practices being used. (See, for example, Ross, 1989; Zeichner & Liston, 1985.) The standards for reflective practice presented in this chapter are currently being used to assess changes in teacher-mentor dialogue in schools in the Seattle area and in Santiago, Chile. I have argued that these nine standards represent all four cumulative levels of reflection: emergent, competent, expert, and ethical and socially just use of reflective practices. These standards can be used to teach the components of reflective practice as a self-assessment to improve practices, as well as for assessments of group use of reflective practices in collaborative conversations.

The standards were synthesized from a review of the literature on reflective practice. They were originally developed for a 34-item survey used as part of an alumni assessment of reflective, ethical, and moral leadership practices. This was two out of five integrated curricular strands within a doctoral program in educational leadership. The self-assessment survey was administered to program graduates and an observer form of the survey was administered to selected workplace colleagues of the program graduates. Survey ratings collected from the alumni and their workplace colleagues on the reflective practice standards were then compared to determine discrepancies between espoused theories and theories in use (Arredondo-Rucinski & Bauch, 2005).

Developing and Assessing the Reflective Practice Standards

Using the standards for reflective practice within schools requires each individual within the learning community to become familiar with the components of reflection. As an example, to illustrate the type of activity used to develop fluency with these components, the following professional activity and assessment criteria are presented for the fourth standard: *Invites feedback and asks questions about assumptions, perspectives and beliefs about self and others.*

Professional Development Activity

To develop fluency with the fourth standard, an individual *invites feedback and asks questions about assumptions, perspectives, and beliefs* (about self and others), to locate and better understand discrepancies between beliefs and actions. Depending on the level of knowledge and skill with reflective practices, an examination of beliefs activity is helpful. During this activity, individuals first write a strong belief that they hold—one that they think affects their teaching or leadership behaviors. An example might be, personal characteristics of students should not be called to attention in the classroom, even in teacher attempts at humor. They might write this belief in the center of a circle.

Then the participants are asked to recall several experiences with this belief, and to write each on a spoke drawn from the circle. In doing so, individuals often remember critical incidents with the selected belief. For example, in one workshop on reflection a teacher remembered an incident in her freshman college speech class when she had been ridiculed for her "Ozark hill country accent." She was asked to talk about her background, as soon as she began to talk, the professor said, "Oh my God, you will be my quarter project!" Then this teacher was asked to repeat—Pygmalion style—almost everything she said aloud in class thereafter. She subsequently suppressed the memory of this critical incident and for years afterwards remained largely silent during group discussions. Many years later, in the reflective practice workshop, she recalled this incident as a basis for her strong belief that no child should ever be ridiculed in class.

Once participants have listed memories about their beliefs, they might share them in small groups and then generate examples of how their beliefs might look in practice. They should ask what teacher or leadership behaviors would be occurring in situations where behaviors are consistent with the identified beliefs. As time permits, individuals examine other beliefs in this fashion and journal about their experiences. At other times they bring these journals to meetings to share with colleagues. The identification of discrepancies and examinations of practices can be a very powerful way of changing the professional dialogue within a school.

This initial examination of beliefs activity is followed with readings, discussions, and observations about defensive behaviors (see, for example, Argyris, 1992). Ask why such behaviors surface and how they can be changed. Change can occur in work with faculty dialogue; communication and relationship skills, including conflict resolution; or in practice with framing reflective questions and sharing information that fosters the development of higher levels of collaborative reflective dialogue within the school. One elementary school in the Seattle area, for example, used a part of faculty meetings throughout a whole year to develop and then use reflective practice skills. Faculty in this school attributed the higher achievement scores on the state assessment to this habit of using reflective dialogue on a regular basis.

Criterion for Assessment

The major criterion for assessment of the fourth reflective practice standard is evidence of its use in conversations, shared journals, and individual professional development plans prepared by faculty and staff throughout the school. This evidence might include collected oral or written examples posted in faculty rooms; journals containing example of the standards, shared at faculty meetings; or comments made about the standard in conversations or written goals. Formal self-assessments and tallies of observational data can also be made and shared across the learning community.

Conclusion

This chapter presented nine standards for reflective practice. I have argued that these standards represent four cumulative levels of reflective thought, ranging from emergent use of the standards, to competent use, to expert use, and last, to ethical and socially just use of the standards. A rationale for the use of reflective practice is that it has the potential to move individuals and therefore whole school communities toward real school reform through changes in the underlying beliefs and assumptions about knowledge and learning. Components of reflective practice can be learned through professional development activities and used within regularly scheduled school meetings to foster the collaborative conversations about teaching and learning believed to be essential for developing a school learning community.

References

Argyris, C. (1992). *On organizational learning.* Cambridge, MA: Blackwell.

Argyris, C., & Schön, D. (1978). *Organizational learning.* Reading, MA: Addison-Wesley.

Arredondo, D. E., & Rucinski, T. T. (1998). Using structured interactions in conferences and journals to promote cognitive development among mentors and mentees. *Journal of Curriculum and Supervision, 13*(4), 300–327.

Arredondo Rucinski, D. E., & Bauch, P. A. (2005). *Assessing ethical, reflective, and social justice constructs in educational leadership programs.* Manuscript submitted for publication.

Beas, J., Gomez, V., Thomsen, P., & Carranza, G. (2004). Practica reflexiva y cambio cognitivo del professor (reflective practice and teachers' cognitive change). *XIV Congreso Mundial del las Ciencias de la Educacion: Educadores para una Nueva Cultura.* Santiago, Chile: Andros Impresores.

Desimone, L. (2002). How can comprehensive school reform models be successfully implemented? *Review of Educational Research, 72*(3), 433–479.

Dewey, J. (1916). Experience and thinking. *Democracy and education* (chap. 11). Retrieved January 15, 2005 from Institute of Learning Technologies: http://www.ilt.columbia.edu/publications/Projects/digitexts/dewey/e_e/chapter11.html

Elmore, R. F. (1995). Teaching, learning, and school organization: Principles of practice and the regularities of schooling. *Educational Administration Quarterly, 31*(3), 355–374.

Elmore, R. F. (1996). Getting to scale with good educational practice. Harvard *Educational Review, 66*(1), 1–26.

Festinger, L. (1957). *A theory of cognitive dissonance.* Stanford, CA: Stanford University Press.

Fullan, M. (2000). The three stories of education reform. *Phi Delta Kappan, 81*(8), 581–584.

Fullan, M. (1993). *Change forces: Probing the depths of educational reform.* New York: Falmer Press.

Fullan, M., & Hargreaves, A. (1996). *What's worth fighting for in your school.* New York: Teachers College Press.

Hargreaves, A., Earl, L., & Ryan, J. (1996). *Schooling for change: Reinventing education for early adolescents.* London: Falmer Press.

Kaufman, D. (2004). *Structured dialogue: Influencing teacher reflection, judgment, and responses to diverse students.* Unpublished doctoral dissertation, Seattle University, Seattle, WA.

King, M. B., & Newmann, F. M. (2000). Will teacher learning advance school goals? *Phi Delta Kappan, 81*(8), 576–580.

King, P. M., & Kitchener, K. S. (1994). *Developing reflective judgment: Understanding and promoting intellectual growth and critical thinking skills in adolescents and adults.* San Francisco: Jossey-Bass.

Little, J. W. (1993, Summer). Teachers' professional development in a climate of educational reform. *Educational Evaluation and Policy Analysis, 15*(2), 129–151.

Murphy, J., & Datnow, A. (Eds.). (2003). *Leadership lessons from comprehensive school reform.* Thousand Oaks, CA: Corwin Press.

Osterman, K. F., & Kottkamp, R. B. (1993). *Reflective practice for educators: Improving schooling through professional development.* Newbury Park, CA: Corwin Press.

Osterman, K. F., & Kottkamp, R. B. (2004). *Reflective practice for educators: Improving schooling through professional development.* (2nd ed.). Thousand Oaks, CA: Corwin Press.

Pogrow, S. (2005). *Are comprehensive school reform models really effective? Implications for meta-analysis on program effectiveness and policy.* Manuscript submitted for publication.

Polanyi, M. (1967). *The tacit dimension.* New York: Anchor Books.

Ross, D. D. (1989). First steps in developing a reflective approach. *Journal of Teacher Education, 40*(2), 22–30.

Sergiovanni, T. J. (1992). *Moral leadership: Getting to the heart of school improvement.* San Francisco: Jossey-Bass.

Shapiro, J. P., & Stefkovich, J. A. (2001). *Ethical leadership and decision making: Applying theoretical theoretical perspectives to complex dilemmas.* Mahwah, NJ: Erlbaum.

Schön, D. S. (1987). *Educating the reflective practitioner.* San Francisco: Jossey-Bass.

Starratt, R. J. (1991). Building an ethical school: A theory for practice in educational leadership. *Educational Administration Quarterly, 27*(2), 185–202.

Strike, K. A., & Ternasky, P. L. (1993). *Ethics for professionals in education: Perspectives for preparation and practice.* New York: Teachers College Press.

Tyack, D., & Cuban, L. (1995). *Tinkering toward utopia: A century of public school reform.* Cambridge: Harvard University Press.

Vygotsky, L.S., (1962). *Thought and language.* Cambridge: MIT Press.

Zeichner, K. M., & Liston, D. P. (1985). *Teaching and teacher education.* New York: Pergamon Press.

7

Standards
of Critical Inquiry

John Smyth

Meet the Author

John Smyth

John Smyth is Emeritus Professor, Flinders University of South Australia and currently holds the Roy F. & Joann Cole Mitte Endowed Chair in School Improvement, Texas State University-San Marcos. He also holds positions as: Professorial Fellow, School of Education, University of Ballarat; Professor, Wilf Malcolm Institute of Educational Research, University of Waikato, New Zealand; and Adjunct Professor, School of Education, Charles Darwin University. He is author/ editor of 15 books. His latest works are *Teachers in the Middle; Reclaiming the Wasteland of the Middle Years of Schooling* (with McInereny 2006) and *'Dropping Out' Drifting Off, Being Excluded: Becoming Somebody Without School* (with Hattam and others, 2004), both published with Peter Lang, New York.

Successful supervision:

- Asks whose interests are being served through teaching and schooling
- Facilitates effective teaching for the least advantaged in the school and its community
- Provides the opportunity for students to have ownership and voice in their learning
- Assists educators to develop, enhance, and promote school–community relations in teaching
- Pursues questions about why teaching is enacted the way it is, what sustains particular practices, and how to pursue alternatives
- Examines learning in terms other than "deficit" and focuses instead on the wider forces that interfere with teaching and learning
- Has a paramount concern with ensuring the advancement of a socially just curriculum

Rationale

It is important that I say something about where the press for a set of standards for critical inquiry in instructional supervision comes from. I need to explain what I mean by this because the notion of standards for critical inquiry is an idea that rests very uneasily with me and that on the surface appears to be highly contradictory (see Smyth, 1991, 2001).

We live in difficult and confusing times, so we need different perspectives to make sense of and to act on the world to change it. The reason we need a different lens, language, and discourse with which to speak about supervisory practices in schooling is that existing approaches are inadequate to the task. To continue to think about schools in terms of the long shadow of the now largely discredited and outmoded mass-production education is to live a fantasy, the effects of which are extremely damaging to those most affected. Willms (2003) put it succinctly:

> Most schools still operate along the same lines as the old mass-production facilities. Bells ring, students move through a fragmented curriculum, and the hours fly by. The quality of student learning is measured by narrow tests, and, increasingly, teachers' salaries and school resources are being tied to test scores. Teachers have little time or incentive to work together as professionals in the service of children's learning. Most teachers cope by simply walling themselves off inside their own classrooms and teaching the best that they know how. How can the schools be restructured to produce a high-quality education? (p. 608).

We could add to this the reality that the forms of language largely dominating the way we talk about what goes on inside schools are still in the vice-like grip of this mass-production mentality, and this situation appears to be getting worse by the day. Take, for example, words like the following, which are deeply embedded in how schools are spoken about, at least officially:

- Accountability
- Curriculum audits
- School charters
- Mission statements
- Strategic reviews
- Profiles
- Instructional delivery systems
- Stakeholders
- Targeted groups
- Operational procedures
- Competency standards
- Benchmarks
- Line management
- Leaner organizations
- Quality assurance
- Advanced skills assessment
- Student learning outcomes
- Total quality management
- Corporate managerialism
- Performance management
- Performance indicators
- Performance appraisal
- World's best practice

We need a process that allows us to move beyond such an emaciated and intellectually impoverished view of schooling and the dispirited narratives accompanying it, and to think and talk about what a new pedagogical imagination might look like, one that acknowledges the reality that "adults and children are able to read their world more accurately and, as a result, to act within it more critically" (Ernst & Statzner, 1994, p. 201). But at the heart of

this are some significant and protracted problems, which require a preparedness to confront and supplant, at the most fundamental levels, some of the
most cherished and deep-seated aspects of American education. Possibly the
most central of these are the abundant evidence that "too many people leave
school scarred" (Varenne & McDermott, 1999, p. xi) and the exclusive
construction of schooling in terms of failure or success.

The starting point in this reclamation is to begin thinking and talking
about "how limiting these categories are…build[ing] the case for a new way
of thinking about education and schooling" (Varenne & McDermott, 1999, p.
x)—one that is against the divisive vocabulary of individuals succeeding and
failing. As Varenne & McDermott (1999) put it:

> Somehow the people of the United States have organized a terrible
> problem for themselves: They have made individual learning and
> school performance the institutional site where members of each
> new generation are measured and then assigned a place in the so-
> cial structure based on this measurement. Learning has become an
> instrument for so much else than education that the vocabulary
> commonsensically talk about learning and education cannot be
> trusted (p. xi).

A crucial ingredient in this reclamation project is the language and practice of critical inquiry in instructional supervision. We need to begin to shake
loose the current language used to describe and analyze what goes on inside
schools, classrooms, teaching, and learning. Unless we do this, what is re-
garded as valuable and legitimate will continue to reflect a distorted,
one-sided, and corroded view. In other words, we need ways of speaking
about what goes on inside schools that reflect the authenticity, integrity, and
indigenous nature of teaching and learning. Otherwise, the work of schools
will continue to be invaded and colonized by alien and interloper discourses,
which portray them antagonistically and in entirely synthetic terms.

To begin to put some definition to what I am talking about here, the pre-
vailing discourses and ideologies of schools are overwhelmingly highly
reductionist and they are simply not up to the task. They are largely derivative of the military and a set of business and corporate views long deemed
bankrupt. Even at the most fundamental level, they are far too linguistically
inept and diminished to be taken as serious contenders for ways of representing either the complexity or the diversity of what goes on in the average
school. For example, they are insufficiently sophisticated and nuanced to be
able to capture the richness, tentativeness, provisionality, or improvised nature of what transpires in much modern teaching and learning. The mechanistic input–output metaphor of the Newtownian machine is struggling to
pass the laugh test in most complex schools and classrooms as a form of real-

istic representation. For instance, it fails because it continues to be solidly wedded to notions of authoritarianism, racism, gender blindness, deficit views, victim-blaming, bullying, and other technologies of power that sort and construct false antieducative hierarchies.

There is little awareness within this view of schooling that teaching and learning might just be a multivoiced, meaning-making process with a high degree of contestation and negotiation at the essence. What goes on and what gets to be perpetrated instead of this more robust view is a silencing of marginalized lives and a further privileging and advantaging of the lives and perspectives of the already advantaged.

Standards for Critical Inquiry in Instructional Supervision

Successful supervision, from this perspective:

1. Asks whose interests are being served through teaching and schooling.

    In many respects, this is a pivotal standard in any attempt to re-configure and redefine instructional supervision. Central to this standard is asking who benefits, both at the classroom and general school level. Continuing to confuse or fudge this is the single factor most likely to lead to the kind of unexamined drift in which what occurs is naturalized or made to appear as if it is natural or commonsense. In these situations, as educators we often go along with ideas, policies, and practices even when they are not in the interests of students or the advancement of learning. What I am referring to in particular are policies and practices that are orchestrated at a distance from schools and classrooms, and are imposed for what seem on the surface to be compelling reasons— accountability; to inform parents; to ensure quality; to enable benchmarks or statewide comparisons; to foster national or international competitiveness. These might be fine ideals but they are often presented in ways and for reasons that appear incontrovertible or unquestioned. In other words, as articles of faith! We have to ask how a policy or practice is authentically advancing student learning. Obtaining a negative answer to this, or even ones that are not affirming, ought to raise further questions and lead us to ask why this is being done. If there is a serious intent to place students at the center of what schools are doing, then we are entering a zone in which there is a need for serious debate and discussions about direction and priorities, and the need for a realignment.

2. Facilitates effective teaching for the least advantaged in the school and its community.

    The starting point for this standard is that what occurs in class-rooms and schools ought to benefit all students, not just those from advantaged backgrounds. Bringing this about is a compli-cated issue, and it has much to do with how the teacher encour-ages and facilitates engagement by all students, not just a few. It goes beyond the individual teacher as well, to the kind of school culture that permits, encourages, and indeed requires this to be an issue and agenda for all teachers. One of the most significant reports to canvass this issue in the United States in recent years entitled *Engaging Schools* (National Research Council, 2004) put it these terms:

    > When students from advantaged backgrounds become disengaged, they may learn less than they could, but they usually get by or they get second chances; most eventually graduate and move on to other opportuni-ties. In contrast, when students from disadvantaged backgrounds in high-poverty, urban high schools be-come disengaged, they are less likely to graduate and consequently face severely limited opportunities (p. 1).

    While acknowledging the complexity of what is involved here, the report also highlights the kinds of areas around which educa-tors need to be asking themselves questions:

    > Engaging adolescents, including those who have be-come disengaged and alienated from school, is not an easy task (pp. 1–2)....Engaging schools promote a sense of belonging by personalizing instruction, show-ing an interest in students' lives, and creating a sup-portive, caring social environment. (p. 3)

    The focus here, therefore, is on asking questions about how teaching is continually trying to advance forms of learning that are aiming to actively include those who might be considered least welcome in schools—those of color, in poverty, homeless, transient, minority groups, those for whom English is a second language, recent immigrants, those otherwise placed at disad-vantage, and those for whom the middle-class institution of schooling is alien or antagonistic. In a sense, then, the question is how the school—both widely and at the level of individual class-rooms—is operating for students who least fit and how their lives, cultures, experiences, and aspirations are not only ac-knowledged but actively incorporated into curriculum, teaching, and learning.

3. Provides the opportunity for students to have ownership and voice in their learning.

It is becoming increasingly clear in research literatures as diverse as school reform, adolescent and youth health, motivation and learning theory, youth culture, and children-at-risk that one of the key elements on whether students learn or not is the extent to which they are given a meaningful measure of control over what and how they learn. It sounds like such an obvious point (and there is mounting and compelling evidence) that whether or not young people learn has a lot to do with how much they are given a say over the content and substance of their learning. If we teach in ways that deny this, then we are running a real danger of having large numbers of students who switch off, disengage, or out-right refuse to learn the things that we as adults say are good for them. Working in these ways is not the same as saying that all learning should be student-driven, because that is clearly unten-able. Rather, we know that good teaching involves finding ways of negotiating learning with students within boundaries. What students want to do, how they want to learn, and the interests they bring with them to classrooms can be negotiated within a broader framework or set of essential learnings. It takes skill to do this, but it can be done and is being done in many classrooms.

The essence of this standard is the view that students should be treated as coeducators or coconstructors of their learning with teachers and other students (Smyth, 2005). When we do this and make it a candidate for examination in instructional supervision, Cook-Sather (2002) said we are seriously questioning

> that we know more than the young people of today about how they learn or what they need to learn in preparation for the decades ahead. It is time that we count students among those with the authority to par-ticipate both in the critique and in the reform of educa-tion. (p. 3)

What is fundamentally at issue here, then, is the rather profound but not always widely practiced pedagogical point that success-ful learning, especially for categories of students regarded as having been placed at risk, does not occur when they are re-garded as ignorant or empty vessels to filled up with knowledge. Rather, successful learning in young people indicates it to be more of a process akin to "authorizing students' perspectives" (Cook-Sather, 2002, p. 3). To put it another way, this is a call

> to count students among those who have knowledge and the position to shape what counts as education, to reconfigure power dynamics and discourse practices within existing realms of conversations, and to create new forums within which students can em-brace...[learning]. (p. 3)

In practice this means a preparedness to jettison the view that in schools where students are under-performing, the answer lies in some kind of "scripted approaches [that] attempt to teacher-proof the curriculum by rigidly specifying teacher ac-tions, and essentially removing all creativity and professional judgement from the classroom" (Sawyer, 2004, p. 12). The alter-native being argued for here, and which ought to be a candidate for scrutiny as a standard in instructional supervision with a crit-ical inquiry agenda, is the notion of creative teaching, which dis-plays a high degree of improvisation and a very different agenda whereby "teachers are [regarded as being] knowledgeable and expert professionals, and are granted creative autonomy in their classrooms" (Sawyer, 2004, p. 12). The basic insight behind this standard of instructional supervision, construed from a critical inquiry perspective, is that learning is "a creative improvisa-tional process" (Sawyer, 2004, p. 14) and teaching is more like a coconstruction than following some preformulated script.

4. Assists educators to develop, enhance, and promote school–community relations in teaching.

Teaching ought to be an activity embedded in some set of wider contexts and structures, and the most obvious starting place is the immediate community of the school. Put another way, things work better when there is an authentic dialogue between schools and their communities. Teaching is not an activity that works well when it is hermetically sealed or walled off from the context in which it occurs. There needs to be an active and ongoing dis-cussion among the school, the parents, and the community. This might happen in a variety of ways. For example, having students undertake investigations in the community or engage in com-munity work projects that allow them to draw learning skills is a crucial way of providing understandings about the school's agenda in the community and how the community might have relevance and meaning to the school. One way this might be given expression is through the way the interests and expertise of the community are valued and brought into teaching and learning in the school. In such instances, school–community relations become a crucial way of both heading off difficulties born by ignorance or misunderstanding and of sustaining both the school and community in difficult times when complex issues have to be sorted out.

The overall intent here is to promote ways in which students and schools feel valued and understood in their communities, and communities in turn feel they have something of value to offer their local schools. Such forms of interchange are crucial for a student to see that what they bring to schools, although sometimes different from mainstream school values, is nevertheless understood and valued. Spoken about in these terms, schools are responsive to communities and what transpires in such relationships are schools and communities that are empowered. Learning in these contexts provides a way for students to see that what is occurring beyond the classroom walls is valuable, relevant, legitimate, and has a vibrant place within school. Also, important forms of knowledge are left behind by students in contexts, situations, and agencies of which they temporarily become a part. What is being broken down here is the malaise of ignorance and isolation as schools create a venue within which issues can both be systematically and analytically identified and pursued, but also collectively and jointly owned beyond the school.

The kind of critical curriculum questions that such approaches permit include discussions across the school–community boundary about why things are the way they are, how they got that way, and what set of conditions/relationships support the status quo.

5. Pursues questions about why and how teaching is constructed and enacted the way it is, what sustains particular practices, and how to pursue alternatives.

    When teaching practices are not punctured, interrogated, or illuminated by questions, it is likely the result will be ritualized and unproblematic teaching. Under these circumstances, teaching becomes characterized by the deadening hand of habit, and the burnout of teachers and alienation of students is an assured outcome. As mentioned earlier, when teachers wittingly or unwittingly go along with other people's schemes, they become script-followers. What gets lost in the process is the opportunity for teachers to creatively reinvent their teaching in ways that fire the imagination of students, and part of firing the imagination involves being innovative, experimental and risk-taking in terms of teaching and learning. Taking risks can, of course, only occur in circumstances where teachers are not punished for making mistakes, and this means having educational leaders who foster and encourage a climate of courageous innovation.

Questions that might be permitted, indeed fostered here, include:

- Where does this way of doing things come from?
- Is this the best way to learn?
- For whom?
- What do students say about this?
- Are there other better alternatives?
- How might these alternatives work better for us?
- How do I foster multiple ways of learning?
- What happens when I do this?
- Who helps who to learn in my classroom?
- What does this say about the way power works here?
- How can we keep the option of continually revising the way we do things around here open?

6. Examines learning in terms other than deficit terms and focuses instead on the wider forces that interferee with teaching and learning.

When children, their families, cultures, and backgrounds are blamed for not learning, this is a clear indication of a deep-seated mismatch between the values, beliefs, and assumptions of the school and the factors allegedly at work when learning does not occur.

Looking for the interferences to learning is a qualitatively different entity than suggesting that blame be lodged within the student (Smyth & Hattam, 2004). The starting point in any such reexamination is the appropriateness of the pedagogical activities and the suitability of the sensitivity and support being provided by the teacher and the school more generally. Although it may be easier to locate the reasons for not learning within the student, in the end this is unhelpful. A more satisfying strategy is to try and locate what it is about the way the school, or the dominant culture of which the school is a part, has become implicated in producing impediments to the student's learning. In this conceptualization, the focus is shifted off the student, the lack of motivation, or the alleged cultural deficiencies of the student or their family as the sources of failure to learn. The spotlight is put instead on how particular forms of pedagogy or the wider culture of the school, or even society, are structured in such as way as to "fail" students or impute that they are engaging in failing behavior. This is a perspective that involves a whole lot more than repositioning blame—it seeks to find alternative explanations and to use those as a basis upon which to construct success-oriented forms of learning.

7. Has a paramount concern with ensuring the advancement of a socially just curriculum.

    This is a recursive standard in an important sense because it forces participants in the supervisory process to focus on and ask, yet again, how what they are doing in the educative sense is inclusive. In other words, how is what is going on in the teaching, curriculum, pedagogy, classroom, school, and community relationships illustrative of respecting and valuing the lives, experiences, cultures, and aspirations of all who are a part of that learning community. The imperative is to provide evidence that this is occurring through the supervisory process, rather than claiming its existence by assertion.

Professional Development Activity

Imagine you were the supervisor who had to engage with the teacher and the parents in the real situation described in the extract from the newspaper article below. Drawing on the information presented in this chapter, describe what you would do and how you would act in this situation. Specifically, what practical actions would you adopt as a consequence?

> The instructions were easy enough for a seven-year-old to understand: Choose a word from the box on the right to complete the sequence on the left. I watched as my second-grade daughter, Maya, read "bear, wolf" then carefully checked her options in the box before writing "fox" on the line. She charged down the page, pausing only at number 5: "work, office." The answer the worksheet

was going for was "job." Maya chose "fun." I let it slide. She'd already demonstrated that she understood the assignment. And secretly, I was pleased by her choice. My husband and I like our jobs, and our office environments reflect that. His has beanbag chairs and employees who have known Maya since preschool. Mine has stacks of magazines, a stereo, and a hallway of people to visit.

Offices are fun to this kid.

But whoever marked Maya's paper didn't realize that. The homework came back with an "X" on number 5. Even worse, she'd had to erase "fun" and replace it with "job"—a bad workplace metaphor if I've ever seen one.

I don't know where to direct my frustration with this. Not at the teacher, whom I respect a great deal, and who wrote me a friendly and apologetic note when I brought up the issue, even agreeing with my point of view. And not at the classroom aide, who's just earning her hourly wage. So should it be directed at a school that depends on parent volunteers to mark student homework? At a school district grappling with a multimillion-dollar deficit, where worksheets are used to reinforce concepts teachers might otherwise review with students themselves? Or at the worksheet publishers, whose products are so inferior that students themselves notice typos and mistakes? No, I suspect my frustration is with something much larger: with whatever—myself included—has already trained my daughter to shrug her shoulders and erase her answer without question, complacently accepting someone else's standard of right and wrong. (Edelman 2004)

As an instructional supervisor with a commitment to the notions of critical inquiry advanced here, how would you judge your own performance in responding to the teacher, the parent, and the child in the instance just described? Here are some possibilities worth thinking about: they are indicative more than prescriptive, and they are meant as a basis for individual or collective self-reflection and discussion on whether the standards are being achieved.

  ♦ Whose interests are being served in this instance by having students respond to worksheets with reductionist answers? Where did the idea come from that this is an educative way to operate with children? Is it educationally defensible? What sustains and maintains this idea?

- ♦ Where is the space for teacher–student engagement about what might be an appropriate answer to the worksheet question, and why?

- ♦ When answers are struck out as being wrong with no attempt at explanation or opportunity to pursue reasoning processes, what message is this conveying to students and is this acceptable?

- ♦ What alternatives to this activity were considered and why was this option selected as being most appropriate?

- ♦ How inclusive is this teaching activity to the life experiences and family background of this student? How was that decision made?

- ♦ What about other students from backgrounds where work is not an option, or where work is not of a professional or middle-class kind? How socially just is this as a learning activity?

- ♦ What processes exist within the school for informed dialogue among teachers about why they teach in these ways or why they do what they do? Is an unreflective school something we should be endorsing or encouraging? Why are such opportunities denied teachers?

- ♦ How does the school engage with parents and care-givers as partners in the education of children? How helpful is it to handle situations like the one described here by sending "apologetic notes" to parental complaints? Isn't this too reactive? Shouldn't the school be more proactive in providing a venue for parents to understand what the school is doing and why?

Note

The ideas contained in this chapter come generally from published papers that have emerged from project grants received by the author from the Australian Research Council from 1992–2004. I also wish to express my appreciation as the holder of the Roy F. and Joann Cole Mitte Endowed Chair in School Improvement in the College of Education at Texas State University–San Marcos, for the generous support from the Mitte Foundation during the writing of this chapter.

References

Cook-Sather, A. (2002). Authorizing students' perspectives: toward trust, dialogue, and change in education. *Educational Researcher, 31*(4), 3–14.

Edelman, H. (2004, November 20). My daughter's subtle lesson: reading, writing and rigidity. *Austin–American Statesman,* A17.

Ernst, G., & Statzner, E. (1994). Alternative visions of schooling: an introduction. *Anthropology and Education Quarterly, 25*(3), 200–207.

National Research Council. (2004). *Engaging Schools: Fostering High School Students' Motivation to Learn.* Washington, DC: National Academies Press.

Sawyer, K. (2004). Creative teaching: collaborative discussion as disciplined improvisation. *Educational Researcher, 33*(2), 12–20.

Smyth, J. (1991). *Teachers as collaborative learners: challenging dominant forms of supervision.* London: Open University Press.

Smyth, J. (2001). *Critical politics of teachers' work: An Australian perspective.* New York: Peter Lang.

Smyth, J. (2005). When students have power over their own learning: "student voice" as a response to "dropping out." In A. Cook-Sather, & D. Thiessen (Eds.), *International handbook of student experience in elementary and secondary schools.* Dordrecht, Netherlands: Kluwer.

Smyth, J., & Hattam, R. (with Cannon, J., Edwards, J., Wilson, N., & Wurst, S.). (2004). *"Dropping out," drifting off, being excluded: Becoming somebody without school.* New York: Peter Lang.

Varenne, H., & McDermott, R. (1999). *Successful failure: The school America builds.* Boulder, CO: Westview Press.

Willms, J. (2003). *Student engagement at school: A sense of belonging and participation. Results from PISA 2000.* Paris: Organisation for Economic Cooperation and Development.

8

Standards of Diversity

Geneva Gay

Meet the Author

Geneva Gay

Geneva Gay is Professor of Education at the University of Washington, Seattle where she teaches graduate studies and teacher education courses in Multicultrual Education and Curriculum Theory. Her areas of interest and specialization are intersections among race, ethnicity, and culture in educating under-achieving African, Asian, Latino, and Native American students. Her writings address these issues as they relate to teacher education, curriculum development, and classroom instruction in PreK-12 schools. She also is a nationally and internationally known consultant who works with local and sate educational agencies, community service groups, colleges and universities, and professional organizations on understanding cultural and racial differences in teaching and learning, and improving the school achievement of students of color.

Successful supervision:

♦ Provides a variety of opportunities for teachers and students to develop and disseminate desirable public and private visions, values, knowledge, and skills about diversity in U.S. history, life, culture, and education

♦ Provides systematic assessment and constructive feedback to teachers and students about building their emerging competencies in ethnic and cultural diversity

♦ Makes necessary resources available and facilitates their use, ensuring that ethnic and cultural diversity are woven into all aspects of the educational enterprise in ways that are appropriate to task, domain, context, and audience

♦ Determines if multiple ethnic, cultural, social, and experiential perspectives are used in analyzing challenges and providing opportunities for learning about and responding to diversity

♦ Monitors teaching and learning activities for and about cultural diversity to ensure that they are always multiethnic, multiracial, multidisciplinary, and multidimensional

♦ Helps classroom teachers and other educators develop a deep knowledge and critical consciousness of how cultural diversity influences the educational opportunities, programs, practices, and outcomes for students from different ethnic groups, and develop skills to make these processes more multicultural

♦ Ensures that comprehensive approaches are used to teach and learn about ethnic, racial, cultural, and social diversity on a regular basis throughout the educational process

♦ Helps teachers and students determine and continually improve the quality of their teaching and learning about ethnic and cultural diversity with respect to relevance, accuracy, and significance

♦ Assists teachers to systematize their decision making, problem solving, implementation actions, and progress monitoring for making all aspects of the educational enterprise more inclusive of and responsive to ethnic, racial, cultural, social, and linguistic diversity

Nine Standards For and About Diversity

Nine standards of education for and about diversity are proposed in this chapter. They are illustrative, not conclusive, of the many possibilities that can be discerned from the scholarship in multicultural education. Because they are intended to be applied at different levels and dimensions of the educational enterprise, the proposed standards are, of necessity, rather general and broad. They should be applied to teachers working with students; supervisors and staff developers working with teachers and each other; and policy makers and administrators working with personnel recruitment and retention and with educators involved in multicultural program design, implementation, and evaluation. Related benchmarks, or action indicators, of different performance proficiency levels for these standards vary by dimension of the educational enterprise; they are the conveyers of context, task, content, and audience specificity. For further refinement and elaboration on the standards of education for and about diversity discussed here, as well as to expand the list of possibilities, three documents are recommended: They are: "Curriculum Guidelines for Multicultural Education" (1992), *Diversity Within Unity* (2000), "Teacher Reflection and Race in Cultural Context" from *Theory Into Practice* (2003).

The suggested education standards for and about diversity have many of the general features of standards. First, they reflect the major goals, principles, content, and priorities of their disciplinary foundations (which is the field of multicultural education), although not the entire body of knowledge. Second, they symbolize some values and ideological emphases. Among these are accepting the legitimacy of cultural diversity in schools and society at large; developing better understandings of and respect for cultural, ethnic, and racial differences; and promoting social justice, equality of educational opportunities, and improved academic performance for students from diverse groups. Third, all standards of education for diversity need extensive descriptions and operational details about how they function in action to make their implementation in school practice more effective. Limited space does not permit this level of explanation here. However, a professional development activity for one of the standards is included. It illustrates the process of explicating specific practice components related to general ideas about building school staff member capacity (and by extension, the school itself) for an education that includes diversity.

Rationale for Standards on Education for Diversity

The increase of ethnic, racial, cultural, and linguistic diversity in U.S. society and schools is indisputable. But, how to most effectively deal with the challenges it poses in the educational enterprise is not nearly as uncontested. Although scholars of multicultural education agree on some fundamental principles, purposes, and components of teaching and learning about diversity, the level of consensus among school practitioners is not nearly as high. This difference in accepting the validity and significance of diversity in education is partly because of variances in where, what, and how scholars, researchers, theorists, and practitioners engage in the educational enterprise. There tends to be a higher degree of consistency among scholars in a field of study than among practitioners who teach applied knowledge about related disciplines and subjects in Pre-K–12 schools, colleges, and universities. Scholars are a much smaller professional community than their public school practitioner peers and tend to engage in greater depth of analysis in a given area of study. Their relatively small size and narrow specializations give them an advantage over Pre-K–12 school practitioners, who are much larger in number, routinely have to do more varied things in performing their jobs, and work with a wider range of students who have less of a knowledge base about the subjects they teach. Consequently, the work of school practitioners invites broader scope (rather than depth) in the treatment of the many concepts, knowledge, and skills taught.

When these general differences of place, function, and person are applied to issues of educating about diversity, there often are conceptual, ideological, and knowledge gaps between scholars and practitioners. Most school teachers and administrators have good intentions about implementing the ideas and proposals suggested in the scholarship on multicultural education. Unfortunately, many do not have the knowledge base and pedagogical skills needed. Others are still struggling with how to resolve what they see as inherent tensions between the national ideals of the United States embedded in the motto *E Pluribus Unum* and recognizing, accepting, and promoting diversity in schools and society. Confusion is still rampant over calls for diversity, equity, and excellence in education. Too many educators continue to believe that to treat students differently based on their cultural heritages, ethnic identities, and background experiences is synonymous to discrimination, and to promote diversity is to compromise high-quality performance and standards of excellence. This confusion drives some educators to question the merits of education for diversity, to judge it divisive and counterproductive, and to re-define it in ways that reaffirm their comfort levels and serve their own pro-poses. These reactions have different consequences on efforts to implement multicultural education, but in general they produce distortions, inaccuracies, and misconceptions that are not consistent with the thinking, research, and writing of multicultural education scholars.

Whatever the motivation of many school practitioners, big gaps often exist between theoretical conceptualizations of multicultural education (used here as analogous to education for and about ethnic, racial, cultural, and so-cial diversity), and how (or if) it is implemented in practice in Pre-K–12 schools and classrooms. One way to bridge this gap is to use more carefully crafted and articulated guidelines for translating theoretical principles into actual practice. This might be accomplished by ordering multicultural educa-tion school reform around performance standards that are applicable to mul-tiple levels of participation in the educational enterprise and by providing professional development experiences to help educators acquire the knowl-edge and skills these standards require. Once this is accomplished, they are in a better position to do likewise for students and sharpen the entire institution's value commitments to and practices of diversity on multiple fronts.

When filtered through the lens of supervision, these suggestions pose a practical design and management question. That is, can the major goals and content of education about diversity be configured into a set of manageable performance standards that can be facilitated and monitored by a host of dif-ferent "supervisors" to better accomplish higher levels of multicultural knowledge, attitudes, and skills for their respective constituencies? The pro-posals made above suggest that this can and must be done, given the kind of inclusive, systemic, and systematic efforts such a project requires. In these proposals, supervisors are conceived broadly to mean anyone in the educa-tional enterprise who routinely provides instructional assistance to other people within the educational enterprise. Thus, classroom teachers are in-cluded in this conceptualization (along with school principals, teacher lead-ers, central office administrators, programs managers, and teacher educators) because they supervise students.

This broad concept of supervisors is consistent with two important argu-ments related to diversity. First, advocates contend that multicultural educa-tion is everybody's business. Although marginalized groups of color play a central role, educating for diversity is really about everyone for everyone, and its implementation requires the participation of students and educators throughout the entire educational system in all school settings. In making these points, Gay (1997) argued that the benefactors of multicultural educa-tion are "both the privileged and the oppressed; the European–American majority as well as the many minority groups of color; the valiant and the vanquished; men and women" (p. 5). Barber (1991) added compelling support for this position in his analyses of the kind of education that is needed for democracy, freedom, and civic living. He suggested further that positioning diversity in the center of this agenda is not something new; it is as old (if not older) as the nation itself. Therefore, education for and about diversity is imperative to the realization of the democratic dream (Banks, 1990, 1991/92; Parker, 1997; Sigel & Hoskin, 1991). These statements do not preempt variance in how different components of multicultural education are practiced in different educational environments.

Other scholars, such as the contributors to the *Handbook of Research on Multicultural Education* (Banks & Banks, 2004; Gay, 1988; and Bennett, 2003) connected diversity to educational equity and excellence, suggesting that one cannot be achieved without dealing simultaneously with the other. Why is this so? Because cultural heritages, experiences, and perspectives are important filters through which school knowledge and skills become meaningful to ethnically diverse students. Incorporating them into the educational process is a viable way to improve the quality of learning opportunities and achievement for African, Asian, Latino, and African–American students (for further discussion see Gay, 2000; Lipka, Mohatt, & the Ciulistet Group, 1998; McCarthy, 2002; Nieto, 2002; Pai & Adler, 2001; Tharp & Gallimore, 1988; Villegas & Lucas, 2002).

These kinds of explanations for improving the quality of educational opportunities and outcomes are growing in magnitude and significance as educators grapple with the persistent achievement gaps among students from different ethnic, racial, social, cultural, and linguistic groups. They demand a thorough understanding of the conceptual relationships between diversity and education and learning how to translate them into school programs and practices. Twiss (1997) and Gay (2000) reminded us that good intentions about dealing with diversity in education are insufficient; they must be accompanied by appropriate knowledge, skills, and actions. As Twiss said, "good intentions in cross-cultural instructional situations may fail because of the mechanisms underlying attributional differences or the assumptions or inferences we make about the causes of behavior" (1997, p. 53). Acquiring specific cultural knowledge about different ethnic groups can minimize these mistakes and failures. Therefore, knowing about the culture of different ethnic groups, valuing diversity, and skills in culturally responsive pedagogy are fundamental components of multicultural professional development experiences for educators. In other words, educators must genuinely care about diversity, and act deliberately and constructively in doing something about it throughout the educational process.

Another argument that connects education for diversity to a broad-based conception of supervision is the idea that multicultural education is a comprehensive undertaking. Its effective implementation requires changes in curriculum, instruction, administration, classroom and institutional climates, counseling and guidance, performance appraisals, and policy making, as well as school–community, parent–teacher, teacher–student, and student–student relationships. Facilitating and overseeing these reforms far exceeds the skills and responsibilities of any one dimension of the educational enterprise or a single class of supervisors. Administrators can't do it alone and neither can teachers or policy makers. Instead, they need to pool their differentiated abilities and efforts to accomplish the best systemic results. Otherwise, imbalanced actions and effects are likely to occur, with some segments taking more than their fair share of responsibilities and others assuming less. In addition to inviting fragmentation, such approaches call into question the integrity of the school's overall commitment to diversity. Conversely, the active involvement of all segments of the institution in educating for and about diversity signals institutional investment and ownership. The sheer energy and time involved in managing and monitoring such an undertaking require supervision at multiple levels. Indeed, education for and about diversity is everyone's business and benefit!

When all else is said and done, education for and about diversity is a collective endeavor that requires multiple-levels of engagement for all members of a school staff. They must simultaneously learn and teach, design and do, lead and follow, and operate individually and collectively. It is imperative, then, that standards, benchmarks, and related programs that govern the supervision of the preparation for and practice of diversity in the educational enterprise include these attributes. To the extent that they do, supervisors will be better multicultural education facilitators, teachers will be better multicultural instructors, students will be better multicultural learners, and schools will be better multicultural places for everyone to live, work, and connect.

Sample Professional Development Activity

Teacher educators, classroom teachers, school principals, curriculum developers, guidance counselors, and others who must be actively involved in implementing education for and about diversity do not automatically have the knowledge and skills needed. These competencies have to be developed in a variety of preservice and ongoing staff development activities. The nature of the standards (and related benchmarks) determine the major substantive parameters of these learning experiences, not how they are taught. All staff members may participate in professional development on the same standards, but how they engage with them should vary according to who they are and their roles and functions in the educational enterprise. Therefore, specific, competency-centered professional development on diversity is more effective than whole-staff and generalized learning experiences.

The sample professional development activity described next focuses on standard 6 above, which states "successful supervision helps teachers and other educators develop a deep knowledge and critical consciousness of how cultural diversity influences the educational opportunities, programs, practices, and outcomes for students from different ethnic groups, and develop skills for making these processes more multicultural." It deals specifically with analyzing the current status of ethnic and cultural diversity in local or particular educational programs and practices, and how it can be improved. Four major assumptions underlie this activity: (1) current diversity efforts in education are inadequate, (2) recognition and understanding of inadequacies are prerequisites to high quality action reform, (3) personal self-awareness, institutional analyses, and programmatic assessments are essential components of developing critical awareness for implementing diversity, and (4) educational change strategies must be informed by knowledge about diversity that is different from what has been traditionally used. Furthermore, "critical cultural consciousness" is not merely criticism. Rather, it focuses on analyzing and critiquing how diversity is typically dealt with in education, from the perspectives of individual and institutional ideologies, policies, programs, and practices, and then envisioning new possibilities for change that are more constructive and productive (Gay & Kirkland, 2003).

This professional development activity has four phases that will move participants through processes of knowing, thinking, feeling, doing, and reflecting. Its ultimate goal is to empower both the individual members and the collective members of a school's professional staff to personify and promote cultural diversity in everything they do, *all of the time.*

In the first phase, the participants will examine their personal beliefs and ideologies about ethnic and cultural diversity in general, and its role in the educational process specifically. Different prompts should be used to elicit these ideas, such as doing free-writes on the role of diversity in schools and society; responding to a real or contrived scenario declaring the merits of color-blindness and racelessness in educating diverse students; and creating acrostics and acronyms that capture the ideological positions of the participants on ethnic and cultural diversity. After these documents are completed individually, they should be shared in groups and compared for similarities and differences. Then, regroup the participants according to similar beliefs and engage in conversations about the reasoning behind their ideologies and creations. This phase of the activity can be concluded by having the participants read a critique of "color-blindness" written by a scholar, such as *The*

Colorblind Perspective in School: Causes and Consequences by Janet Schofield (2001). Another quick reference that can help the participants to further crystallize their thinking about the place of diversity in education is *Acceptance and Caring are at the Heart of Engaging Classroom Diversity* by Lindy Twiss (1997).

In the second phase of this activity, the participants will collect data on how diversity is currently addressed in their respective areas of the educational enterprise. For example, school administrators might compile information on the demographic distribution of the school's student population by ethnic groups across grade levels, enrollment in various curricular options (i. e., advanced placement subjects, gifted and talented, special education, English language learning), frequency and types of disciplinary referrals, extracurricular activities, and participation in student leadership functions (such as student government and honor society). Counselors might collect statistics on the kinds of self-initiated contacts made to their offices for services and supports by members of different ethnic groups, and how these vary by age and gender within and across ethnic groups, and identifying the most and least problematic school adjustment issues encountered by members of different ethnic groups.

Classroom teachers might collect similar data about student participation in classroom interactions, when and what kinds of learning experiences about diversity they typically provide, how students from different ethnic groups react to these experiences, and how ethnic and cultural diversity is represented in textbooks and other instructional materials. The analyses of instructional materials should be multiethnic, thorough and comprehensive, including quantitative and qualitative data about the full range of information presented in varied formats (such as the narrative text, visual illustrations, learning activities and projects, highlights and special features, questions and prompts, additional resources, background information on authors, events, etc.). Educators across school functions (i. e., teachers, instructional aides, clerical and janitorial staff, counselors, administrators, etc.) can work together to describe and document their perceptions of and interactions with students from different ethnic groups, the conditions under which these occur, and how diversity is conveyed through schoolwide activities such as hall and classroom decorations, relationships among students from different ethnic groups, award presentations, assembly programs, and interactions with different community-based, ethnically different groups, individuals, and events. Once these data are collected and summarized they could then be analyzed for patterns or trends within and across different areas (teaching, counseling, extracurricular activities, administration, etc.) of school functioning.

The third phase of this professional development activity focuses on actions for change. The results from the comparison of the participation trends of ethnically diverse students and issues in school programs and practices can be used to identify areas that need to be changed to achieve a more comprehensive and inclusive representation of diversity across school life. The school staff members then work collectively to prioritize these needs, decide on broad timelines for change, and determine the resources required to accomplish the reform goals. Next, members of school staff work in job-alike groups to determine area-specific actions needed to achieve the school-based diversity improvement plan. For example, teachers may be grouped according to subjects, grades, subjects within grades, or topics across subjects and grades. All members of the job-alike teams should agree to participate in the implementation of the action plans and have specific tasks to perform. It also would be helpful if opportunities and invitations are provided for members of the school staff to make individual contributions to the change process. For instance, some teachers might work on changing how they interact with diverse students in the classroom, some may focus on establishing better informal relationships with students outside the classroom, and still others could choose to modify content about diversity in specified units of instruction. Interested members from different segments of the schoolwide staff may decide to redesign how diversity is portrayed in the visual representations and symbolic images of the school to make them more inclusive and explicit about the institutional acceptance and commitment to ethnic and cultural diversity.

In the fourth phase, conclude the professional development activity with a communal sharing of action plans from the small groups. Plan future sessions to coordinate, monitor, and assess the progress of the reform efforts and reflect on the current learning experiences. These reflections should include both personal and professional elements, such as what the individuals learned about their personal needs and capabilities, their individual areas of work and the school as a whole as related to diversity, and how they feel about their ability to make worthy contributions to creating more desirable learning spaces and opportunities for diversity to flourish among themselves, their students, and their institution. Have the participants revisit their initial ideas about the viability of a "color blind" approach to diversity in view of the revelations and learnings that occurred throughout this professional growth experience.

Assessment Criteria

As is the case with teaching and learning experiences with students, professional development activities for the school staff should be assessed to determine the progress the participants made toward achieving the goals, and how well the design of the learning activities matched the components of high quality education for and about diversity as described in multicultural scholarship. Some criteria that can be used to make these assessments about the activity described above are:

♦ Participants are open to critically analyzing their beliefs about and behaviors toward diversity, and reexamining them in view of countervailing evidence.

♦ School staff members accept individual and collective ownership of and responsibility for making personal and institutional changes to improve the quality of education for diversity.

♦ Data collected about diversity in schools (or the lack thereof) are comprehensive and have substantive depth in that they include all aspects of the school and different types of participation and performance specific to various ethnic groups.

♦ Data about cultural diversity in the local school are disaggregated by variables *within* ethnic groups, such as age, gender, grade, and subject, as well as *by* ethnic groups. Plans for reform also reflect this variability.

♦ The professional fund of knowledge on education for and about diversity is evoked in making sense of particular or localized school achievements, challenges, needs, and plans for reform, as well as the progress made in achieving new goals.

♦ Participants become more conscious about the presence and influence of cultural diversity in schooling and deliberate about making it more constructive, visible, inclusive, habitual, and facilitative in all aspects of school life.

♦ Increased knowledge and consciousness about ethnic, racial, and cultural diversity are reflected in the behaviors of school staff members as they fulfill their respective job responsibilities; there are high levels of congruency between their diversity reform plans and their actual behaviors.

References

Banks, J. A. (1990). Citizenship education for a pluralistic democratic society. *The Social Studies, 81*(5), 210–214.

Banks, J. A. (1991/92). Multicultural education for freedom's sake. *Educational Leadership, 49,* 32–36.

Banks, J. A., & Banks, C. A. M. (Eds.). (2004). *Handbook of research on multicultural education* (2nd ed.). San Francisco: Jossey-Bass.

Banks, J. A., Cookson, P., gay G., Hawley, W. D., Jordan Irvine, J., Nieto, S., Stephan, W. G. (2000). *Diversity within unity: Essential principles for teaching and learning in a multicultural society.* Seattle, WA: Center for Multicultural Education, University of Washington.

Barber, B. R. (1992). *An Aristocracy for everyone: The politics of education and the future of America.* New York: Oxford University Press.

Bennett, C. I. (2003). *Comprehensive multicultural education: Theory and practice* (5th ed.). Boston: Allyn & Bacon.

Curriculum guidelines for multiethnic education (1992). *Social Education, 56*(5), 274–294.

Diversity within unity: Essential principles for teaching and learning in a multicultural society (2001). Seattle, WA: Center for Multicultural Education, University of Washington.

Gay, G. (1988). Designing relevant curricula for diverse learners. *Education and Urban Society, 2*(4), 327–340.

Gay, G. (1997). The relationship between muticultural and democratic education. *Social Studies,* 88(1), pp. 5–11.

Gay, G. (2000). *Culturally responsive teaching: Theory, research, & practice.* New York: Teachers College Press.

Gay, G. (2002). Preparing for culturally responsive teaching. *Journal of Teacher Education, 53*(2), 106–116.

Gay, G., & Kirkland, K. (2003). Developing cultural critical consciousness and self-reflection in preservice teacher education. *Theory Into Practice, 42*(3), 187–187.

Lipka, J., Mohatt, G. V., & the Ciulistet Group. (1998). *Transforming the culture of schools: Yup'ik Eskimo examples.* Mahwah, NJ: Erlbaum.

McCarthy, T. (2002). *A place to be Navajo: Rough Rock and the struggle for self-determination in indigenous schooling.* Mahwah, NJ: Erlbaum.

Nieto, S. (2002). *Language, culture and teaching: Critical perspectives for a new century.* Mahwah, NJ: Erlbaum.

Pai, Y., & Adler, S. A. (2001). *Cultural foundations of education* (3rd ed.). Upper Saddle River, NJ: Merrill.

Parker, W. C. (1997). Navigating the unity/diversity tension in education for democracy. *Social Studies,* 88(1), pp. 12–17.

Schofield, J. W. (2001). The colorblind perspective in school: Causes and consequences. In J. A. Banks & C. A. M. Banks (Eds.), *Multicultural education: Issues & perspectives* (4th ed., pp. 247–267). New York: Wiley.

Sigel, R. A., & Hoskin, M. (Eds.). (1991). *Education for democratic citizenship: A challenge for multi-ethnic societies.* Hillsdale, NJ: Erlbaum.

Teacher reflection and race in cultural context. *Theory Into Practice, 42*(3).

Tharp, R. G., & Gallimore, R. (1988). *Rousing minds to life: Teaching, learning, and schooling in social context.* Cambridge, England: Cambridge University Press.

Twiss, L. L. (1997). Acceptance and caring are at the heart of engaging classroom diversity. *The Reading Teacher, 50,* 602–604.

Villegas, A. M., & Lucas, T. (2002). *Educating culturally responsive teachers: A coherent approach.* Albany: State University of New York Press.

Part 3

Process Standards

9

Standards for Clinical Supervision

Elaine Stotko, Edward Pajak, and Lee Goldsberry

The teacher's self is the primary instrument with which the teacher must work, and the choices made about how to use that self effectively assists or hinders students in the process of learning.

(Combs, 1982, pp. 82–83)

Meet the Authors

Elaine M. Stotko

Elaine M. Stotko is Chair of the Department of Teacher Preparation at John Hopkins University. She has a master's degree in Teaching English as a Second Language from the University of Illinois at Urbana-Champaign and a Ph.D. in Linguistics for teachers, children's understanding of derviational morphology, alternative programs for teacher certification, and collaboration among arts and sciences and education faculty to improve teacher education programs. A past president of the Project 30 Alliance, she is currently Chair of AACTE's Special Study Group on Arts and Sciences Collaboration with Teacher Education.

Edward Pajak

Edward Pajak is Professor and Chair of the Department of Teacher Development and Leadership at John Hopkins University. He has authored or co-edited a number of books, including: *Honoring Diverse Teaching Styles: A guide for Supervisors* (2003); *Approaches to Clinical Supervision* (2000); *Handbook of Research on School Supervision* (1998); and *The Central Office Supervisor of Curriculum and Instruction* (1989).

Lee Goldsberry

Lee Goldsberry, Associate Professor of Education at the University of Southern Maine, has been studying supervision of teaching for three decades. He is convinced that, done well, supervision is both a model for and a powerful encouragement for excellence in teaching ... and that it is seldom done well. Gratefully, he is also Jan's husband, Kim's and Kirk's father, Jennie's, Dan's and Kate's step-father, and Cora's and Emily's grandfather.

Successful supervision:

♦ Is grounded in a thorough understanding of the students and the context in which the teacher works

♦ Is grounded in a comprehensive understanding of pedagogy and encourages a deliberate and articulate connection between classroom activities and the instructional goals of the teacher for the students

♦ Elicits from each teacher, a meaningful discussion of student learning progress and consideration of how adaptive teaching strategies contribute to present and future learning of diverse and individual students

♦ Provides a framework in which many learning and communicative styles are possible, given the instructional needs of the students, and refrains from imposing any one style on the teacher

♦ Models that learning to teach is a developmental process, and thus modifies feedback to make it accessible to the teacher and to address the most important dimensions of teaching or areas of immediate need

♦ Helps teachers (and supervisors) articulate and document how seemingly small episodes of teaching relate to a larger vision for educating students and promotes supportive collegial relationships among educators to develop a collaborative learning community in a school

♦ Models qualities of tactful and skilled communication, goal clarity, data-based performance assessment, and guided self-evaluation

♦ Seeks to help teachers build their professional identity through thoughtful connections among clear goals for students, documentation of student accomplishment, a personal mission or platform for teaching, and careful analysis of personal teaching performance

Overview

How do we distinguish success from failure? How do we know that the houses we live in, the roads we drive on, and the buildings we work in are safely constructed? What protects us from malpractice when we consult a physician, an attorney, or an architect? Clearly, some shared sense of what distinguishes competent performance from incompetent performance is necessary for us to judge any form of complex work, whether we are considering the result of a science or an art.

Both state and national professional associations have adopted content standards to help guide curriculum and create a shared definition of success for students. Also, the Interstate New Teacher Assessment and Support Consortium and the National Board for Professional Teaching Standards, among other groups, have established performance standards to help guide assessments of beginning and accomplished teaching.

The most powerful argument used by those who advocate the use of standards in education is that high standards are necessary to ensure uniform, high-quality learning opportunities are available to every student, in every school and classroom, everywhere in the country. Proponents of standards also emphasize the idea that standards are *public* statements. The result should be that *everyone* knows the expectations for an instructional unit, a course, or a program of study: students, teachers, parents, taxpayers, and employers. A further result is supposed to be that if students are not learning, then everyone recognizes the fact and will do something about it.

What is clinical supervision? Clinical supervision is a *process* for improving instruction that combines classroom observation and feedback. Clinical supervision can be conducted by people in various roles, including teachers, mentors, peer coaches, team leaders, department chairs, principals, content specialists, or university supervisors.

Proponents of standards seek to ensure both excellence and equity in classrooms. Traditionally, clinical supervision has addressed the intended or probable influence of teacher behavior on student learning, rather than actual outcomes relating to student achievement. From its first appearance (Goldhammer, 1969) through more recent manifestations (Zeichner & Liston, 1996), however, clinical supervision has embraced equity and social justice as worthwhile goals.

It may be only a slight exaggeration to say the standards movement in American education is a direct result of the *failure of instructional supervision* to ensure excellence and equity in classrooms. The reason may be that throughout its history, clinical supervision has emphasized process almost exclusively over outcomes.

Morris Cogan formulated the idea of clinical supervision in the 1950s while on the faculty of Harvard University, where he coordinated a Master of Arts in Teaching program that prepared liberal arts graduates for careers in teaching. Despite an internship lasting an entire year, he recognized that it did not provide a satisfactory induction experience for beginning teachers. Cogan and his colleagues invented both the concept and techniques of clinical supervision—essentially, a preconference between a teacher and a supervisor, a classroom observation, and a post-observation conference—as a way to provide meaningful feedback to beginning teachers that would improve their success.

Cogan's name for this strategy, *clinical* supervision, suggested a close affinity with professions like psychiatry, social work, and nursing, and represented a deliberate departure from the imagery of industrial management (Garman, 1986). In fact, Cogan (1973) and his colleagues (Goldhammer, 1969; Mosher & Purpel, 1972) unanimously held that every lesson should be considered a hypothesis posed during the pre-observation phase and tested in the laboratory of the classroom. Data gathered during observations, according to the Harvard group, was intended solely as formative feedback (i.e., determining whether or not the "hypothesis" was supported by the evidence) and never for summative evaluation of the teacher (Pajak & Arrington, 2004).

But to blame clinical supervision alone for the ills of the schools would be naïve or disingenuous. In reality, standards have also failed to produce equitable learning opportunities in every classroom for every student. The reason, we suggest, is that standards emphasize outcomes to the exclusion of process. More and better clinical supervision in classrooms is now needed to address this failure of standards, by achieving a better balance between what we want to attain and how we attain it.

The standards we seek must not oversimplify the skilled service and decision making of either teachers or supervisors. If we sought to produce millions of identical gizmos, our methods would be quite different. Because human beings are so much more complex, we understand that "differentiated" approaches are not only desirable, but they are also absolutely necessary for success. Because supervisors assist teachers with very diverse abilities, talents, and backgrounds with acquiring specific knowledge, skills, and dispositions, our methods must adapt to these differences or fail.

Clinical supervision has not been used in a standards-rich environment for a long enough time to know whether this marriage will be successful. However, the emphasis on explicit teacher and student outcomes places important decisions about content and instruction in the hands of experts far removed from the classroom. Removing opportunities for teachers to engage in conversations about the appropriateness of curriculum relegates teachers to the status of technicians who simply deliver content to students (Wraga,

1999). In such an environment, supervision is likely to emphasize monitoring and inspection, along with a focus on enforcing teacher fidelity to externally determined content.

Experienced educators understand that teaching well requires more than simply communicating accurate information to students through correct application of technique. Teaching well demands a high level of self-investment and personal identification with one's work. Successful teachers are those who are able to connect with their students as people and actually influence how their students choose to live their lives.

Similarly, clinical supervisors should be responsive to every teacher's individual style and personal sources of satisfaction and meaning (Pajak, 2003). If the internal coherence and integrity of the teaching act are violated or the professional identity of the teacher is marginalized, then the worth of technical competence, which performance standards reinforce, is severely diminished. In other words, a major limitation of traditional standards is that their very objectivity (what exists externally) can be entirely unconnected with who teachers and students are as human beings.

Standards for Clinical Supervision

What is clinical supervision? Why does this form of supervision deserve its own standards? As the editor of this volume suggests, supervision is often equated with instructional leadership in the practical world of schools. Hence, when an educational leader engages in staff-development planning, curriculum work, or interprets assessments of student learning, they may be said to be "doing supervision." As all good teachers know, there are various activities that contribute to the supervision of learning. Providing knowledgeable and tactful feedback to learners regarding their performance is an indispensable and invaluable part of supervising learning. So, too, are there various activities that contribute to the supervision of teaching. Likewise, providing knowledgeable and tactful feedback to teachers regarding their performance is an indispensable and invaluable part of supervising teaching. Thus, clinical supervision is the subset of supervision in schools that is sharply focused on providing meaningful feedback on teaching performance with the specific intent of helping teachers reflect upon and improve their own practice.

Ask experienced teachers about their experiences with supervision and the answer to why this particular part of supervision deserves its own standards will likely become apparent. Many teachers (and some educational leaders) equate supervision of teaching with formal teacher evaluation—which they usually consider to be both unhelpful and inaccurate. In short, performance feedback in the form of clinical supervision is either absent in many schools or simply poorly done. Why is this? Perhaps one contributing factor is that school leaders and school boards simply have not considered standards for such important work.

In this spirit we offer this discussion. The standards suggested here are drawn from three qualities that we believe distinguish clinical supervision from less specific forms of educational leadership: providing regular and meaningful feedback to individual teachers based on observed teaching; addressing the pedagogy and learning climate of the teacher's setting, that is, it is context-specific (i.e., classroom-specific); and modeling good teaching in keeping with the stakeholders' views of good teaching, but at the same time demanding reflective assessment of those practices.

Three crucial implications logically arise from these qualities:

1. Clinical supervision is supervision of *teaching*, not teachers.

2. Clinical supervision requires skills and knowledge about teaching that not all education leaders possess (or need to possess). Therefore, one need not have the title *supervisor* to deliver good clinical supervision, but whoever does clinical supervision needs specialized knowledge and skills related to teaching.

3. Clinical supervision requires face-to-face discussion with a teacher in which the teacher actively considers how specific aspects of the teaching currently serve (and could possibly better serve) the intended learning for the students with whom they work. These discussions, when done well, also actively contribute to the growth of the teacher as a professional through a reflective examination of the teacher's beliefs about teaching and learning.

We believe that the standards listed in this chapter reflect this concept of clinical supervision.

Standard 1: Clinical Supervision Is Grounded in Understanding of Students and Context

Clinical supervision is grounded in a thorough understanding of the students with whom and the context in which the teacher works.

This standard subsumes a few issues relevant to clinical supervision. First, the supervisor should have a firm grasp of the specific developmental levels of the students, the curricular aims for the lesson and overall subject being taught, and implications of these considerations for the selection of pedagogical methods. Second, the supervisor should know the context of the school and be familiar with the students who attend it. Third, the supervisor should know the level of control granted to the teacher by the administrative structures in place at the school and/or district. For example, what decisions can the teacher make regarding instruction, curriculum materials, scheduling, discipline and so on? The level of teacher decision making may be a function of experience, as in the case of interns or student teachers, or a function of administrative decisions, such as when a particular reading method or curriculum is required by a district.

Pajak and Arrington (2004) described what they call "opportunity to teach" standards, which delineate the conditions that make successful teaching possible. These conditions include a reasonable workload, adequate resources and support, and a level of control and decision-making power in keeping with the responsibility and accountability that the teacher is being asked to accept. Supervision in contexts where such an opportunity to teach standards is not met is likely to be focused on how to best help the teacher survive the teaching assignment or on how the teacher might provide students with the most effective, if not optimal, instruction possible under the circumstances. But it seems unlikely that supervision in such contexts could also focus effectively on the professional identity of the teacher. In other words, for supervision to be focused on student and teacher development, contextual conditions for successful teaching must be met.

Standard 2: Clinical Supervision Grounded in Understanding of Pedagogy

Clinical supervision is grounded in a comprehensive understanding of pedagogy and encourages a deliberate and articulate connection between classroom activities and the instructional goals of the teacher for the students.

It is unlikely that unannounced classroom visits, though useful for some evaluation purposes, will result in effective clinical supervision experiences. Through pre-observation and post-observation discussions, both the supervisor and teacher can reflect on both the potential and actual success of classroom activities with respect to curriculum and classroom management goals and student achievement. If the focus of supervision is to be truly upon the best interests of the students in a particular classroom and the professional identity and development of a particular teacher, goals must be discussed and negotiated and not reduced to a list of standards or competencies imposed by an external agency. Even as the supervisor works to ensure that the teacher is able to meet the goals of the various stakeholders with regard to student learning—the school improvement team, the district, or a teacher education program in the case of student teachers—they must also demand reflection on the part of the teacher as to the validity of such goals.

Standard 3: Clinical Supervision Elicits
Salient Educational Consideration from Teachers

Clinical supervision elicits from each teacher meaningful discussion of student learning progress and consideration of how adaptive teaching strategies contribute to present and future learning of diverse and individual students.

Supervisors need thoughtful preparation if they are to lead the sort of inquiry suggested by the standards presented here and in the other chapters included in this volume. Clearly there is a great need for skilled supervisors who can facilitate the kind of face-to-face communication focusing on both the goals and the delivery of high-quality learning experiences. However, in many cases, neither the supervisor's own personal experience with supervision nor the required preparation for certification as a supervisor of teaching provides them with the vision or skills needed to engage in intense and focused interaction with the teachers they observe. What passes for supervisory communication in too many cases is a vapid written narrative that neither reinforces specific highlights of teaching performance nor identifies any meaningful area for improvement (Guthrie & Willower, 1973). Supervisors need preparation in thoughtful and collaborative modes of communication.

The professional development activity suggested in this chapter provides one avenue to such preparation by requiring the supervisor to use the skill of active listening (Goldsberry & Nolan, 1983; Nolan & Hoover, 2004) to focus on the teacher's *espoused platform* (Goldsberry, 1997; Nolan & Hoover, 2004; Sergiovanni & Starratt, 2002) or preferred *teaching style* (Pajak, 2003) so that supervision connects to an articulated and understood relationship between the teacher's ideals and his or her actual practices in the classroom. Active listening allows the supervisor to help make the connections between the teacher's intentions and real classroom context, students, and practice visible. It also paves the way for meaningful dialogue on the improvement of instruction.

Standard 4: Clinical Supervision Provides for Diverse Styles

Clinical supervision provides a framework in which many learning and communicative styles are possible, given the instructional needs of the students, and refrains from imposing any one style on the teacher.

The supervisor should support each teacher in finding a unique voice and teaching style by not insisting on any one "best" method of instruction. This does not mean that teachers are free to ignore the overall goals of instruction as determined by the school or other stakeholders or to limit themselves to only one preferred method. However, supervisors should recognize their ways of perceiving and processing information may vary from those of the teachers. Therefore, it is important for supervisors and teachers to clarify the language of supervision to avoid misunderstandings (Pajak 2003). Just as teachers are expected to adjust their teaching to the preferred learning styles of their students, supervisors should adapt their words and behaviors to communicate successfully with teachers. Where differences of opinion or style truly interfere with the clinical supervision process, the supervisor should be prepared to bow out, if possible, in favor of another supervisor who may be able to work more effectively with the teacher. The supervisor should be open to learning new methods and content as well.

Standard 5: Clinical Supervision Models
That Learning to Teach Is a Developmental Process

Clinical supervision models that learning to teach is a developmental process and, thus, modifies feedback to make it accessible to the teacher and to address the most important dimensions of teaching or areas of immediate need.

The supervisor will view some problems as evidence of development or as opportunities for teacher learning and growth, rather than as mistakes to be eradicated. The supervisor should refrain from trying to fix each and every problem and, as much as possible, allow the teacher the developmental time needed to improve. However, because the ultimate goal of clinical supervision is improved student learning, the supervisor must also be ready to recognize instructional practices that are likely to cause harm to children and intervene as necessary. Directive, nondirective, and collaborative approaches should be employed appropriately to facilitate professional growth. Care should be taken, however, that the directive approach actually contributes to the teacher's developmental needs and not the supervisor's need to control.

Standard 6: Clinical Supervision Helps Teachers (and Supervisors) Articulate and Document

Clinical supervision helps teachers (and supervisors) articulate and document how seemingly small episodes of teaching relate to a larger vision for educating students and promotes supportive collegial relationships among educators to develop a collaborative learning community in a school.

Clinical supervision can certainly serve as a resource for teachers to become knowledgeable about ways to link state and national standards, the local curriculum, and federal, state, and local mandates and regulations to actual practice. However, the supervisor should avoid reducing observations and feedback to a mere laundry list of standards, so as not to subvert creative and reflective practice. Indeed, discussions about standards should include reflection on their appropriateness for the particular students within a context of learning, equity, and social justice.

While encouraging the individual voice and talents of a particular teacher, supervisors should also draw on their own knowledge and experience to help ensure appropriate consistency across the same content taught to different learners. That is, key concepts and understandings of the subject matter field should be maintained for all learners and effective supervision can help to provide such consistency.

Standard 7: Clinical Supervision Models Special Qualities

Clinical supervision models qualities of tactful and skilled communication, goal clarity, data-based performance assessment, and guided self-evaluation.

Effective clinical supervision, though always collegial, provides the teacher with a large repertoire of instructional strategies through the demonstration of action research applied to teaching and learning. As appropriate and when invited, the supervisor can step into the teacher's role to model ways of solving instructional and classroom management problems. But more effectively, the teacher can see the strategies of goal setting, hypothesis testing, data-based feedback, and self-assessment being implemented during the course of the clinical supervision cycle. The supervisor also knows that there is no one-size-fits-all observation instrument that works for every teacher, every subject, every grade level, or every circumstance. In other words, clinical supervision should be practiced according to accepted principles of what constitutes effective instruction.

Standard 8: Clinical Supervision Helps Teachers Build Their Professional Identity

*Clinical supervision seeks to help teachers build their professional iden-
tity through thoughtful connections among clear goals for students, documentation of student accomplishment, a personal mission or platform
for teaching, and careful analysis of personal teaching performance.*

Supervisors understand and are able to help teachers use effective methods of collecting and interpreting data from students to improve classroom
practice. Although many teachers are able to design interesting and enter-
taining classroom activities, supervisors should push teachers to constantly
question the value of their instructional choices with regard to student learning. Teachers' choices should be guided at all times by what is objectively and
demonstrably best for students, rather than by good intentions, local culture,
expediency, personal preference, or mere habit. This necessarily implies significant self-knowledge acquired through examination of one's own motives,
beliefs, and behaviors, as well as a consciously deliberate mastery of multiple
techniques to teach all students.

Professional Development Activity

The Espoused Platform

What should the students be learning? What kinds of feedback should
students get on their work, and why? How should a teacher alter the feedback in consideration of the individual student's history or preferences?
When teachers respond to questions like these, they are revealing their espoused platform, their individual ideals for what teaching should try to accomplish connected to their own strategies for achieving these good ends.
Hence, a platform-based approach to supervision connects to an articulated
and understood relationship between the teacher's ideals and actual practices in the classroom. By basing supervisory work on each individual
teacher's convictions and strategies, one both engages the idealism and commitment that draws most teachers to their good work and helps dissipate the
commonly voiced attitude that supervision is a top-down imposition of the
supervisor's preferred style of teaching (Pajak, 2003).

Active Listening

In general, active listening seeks to understand how another person per-
ceives the world or more specific elements of life. When adapted for supervisory conferences, the skill is focused on supervisors discovering teachers'

perceptions relating to the teachers' own preferred teaching styles. Goldsberry and Nolan (1983) identify seven specific movements characterizing different elements that may contribute to effective active listening. Participants should observe the moves the leader uses and how they contribute to the quality of the conversation.

Active Listening Moves

Structuring moves set the topic or boundaries for the discussion. For example:

- ♦ What are your goals for this unit?
- ♦ Tell me about the students you teach.
- ♦ Why is studying DNA important?

Probing moves seek more information about what has been said. For example:

- ♦ Can you tell me more about the critical thinking that you want?
- ♦ What do you mean when you say "higher level questions"?
- ♦ Why do you believe getting the students to raise questions is important?

Linking moves connect the topic under discussion to a related topic. For example:

- ♦ You mentioned several cognitive goals; do you have affective goals, as well?
- ♦ That plan seems solid. What might you see or hear that would cause you to adapt it during the class?
- ♦ You said developing a "spirit of inquiry" in one of your foremost goals. How do you assess a student's "spirit of inquiry"?

Feeling checks ask for the teacher's emotional responses. For example:

- ♦ You really seem excited to develop this new unit. Are you?
- ♦ Do you find the students' attitudes toward math frustrating?.
- ♦ How did that interaction make you feel?

Summarizing moves simply review or tentatively interpret what has been said. For example:

- ♦ You want every student to understand the composition and importance of DNA, and you hope that several students will find it engaging enough to focus their self-selected project on it.

Monitoring nonverbal cues: look for gestures or intonations that have meaning.

Sending nonverbal cues: attend to how your own gestures and intonations are perceived (from Goldsberry & Nolan, 1983).

The Activity

In the following professional development activity, the leader of the activity first explains the espoused platform concept and the active listening process. He or she then demonstrates an episode of active listening with a volunteer from the group. The active listening is focused on the volunteer's espoused platform and generally begins with factual questions as to the nature of the job. As most often the volunteer is a classroom teacher, these questions would address subject(s) taught, the nature and number of students taught, years of experience, and description of the school context. Next,[1] Good leaders focus on teachers' sense as to how they influence students—their goals for their learning. Often one goal that seems important to a teacher is then pursued by asking what the teacher does to accomplish the goal. The leader tries to accurately summarize the teacher's strategies, connecting them to the goals they are intended to serve. Depending on the context, the leader may shift focus to a district goal (possibly improved assessment of learning) to a concern of the teacher (if such a concern can be elicited), or to a discussion of specific students (if differentiation of instruction is of interest).

One of the keys to a successful demonstration is developing an explicit connection between the teacher's ideals for teaching and their regular strategies for teaching. Thus, the crucial bridge between one's personal goals for teaching and the practices one uses is articulated, illuminating part of the espoused platform. Of course, another key to the demonstration is to build upon what the teacher says—as opposed to what the leader may *want the teacher to say*. When the goal is to capture the teacher's perceptions and beliefs, questions or moves that lead the teacher to the leader's point of view are counterproductive.

During the demonstration, other participants are asked to record observations about the leader's moves. They are explicitly directed to separate what they actually see and hear (the *descriptive documentation*) from their interpretations or judgments of those actions. Following the demonstration,

---

1 The sequence of these topics varies considerably depending on the teacher's demeanor and preferences. The aim here is not to provide a protocol to follow; rather, it is to offer one potential course of discussion. Responding to and illuminating the teacher's sense of connection and flow takes priority over following an agenda set by the supervisor.

observers are asked to share their observations—first, through simple descriptions without interpretation and then by connecting judgments or interpretations to the observed behavior. After identifying moves that seemed most helpful and any that may have been counterproductive to active listening, participants divide into groups of three to replicate the exercise in active listening. One person serves as the leader who is practicing active listening; one person serves as the educator discussing his or her own platform; and the third person serves as a process observer, again collecting descriptive information regarding the leader's performance.

After giving each triad time to complete the demonstration and to give constructive feedback to the leader, the entire group reassembles to discuss the uses of active listening and the value of discussing espoused platforms for supervision. Often participants note the disparity between the level of discussion elicited by this brief exercise and the level of discussion experienced as a part of supervision in schools. Experienced teachers often report that such focused discussions seldom occur as part of supervision and that when they do, they are generally "supervisor dominated." Even when those engaged in the exercise are themselves supervisors, seldom does anyone report that such fruitful interactions are already a part of the supervisory routine. Another common observation is that active listening is not the *only* way a supervisor should interact with a teacher. Of course, there are times when active listening is really dysfunctional. Still, the ability to use the skill *when it is indeed helpful* is needed to serve the standards suggested.

Although any of these standards might be a topic explored using platform-based, active listening to capture a teacher's perspective on the standard, standards 3, 5, 6, 7, and 8 in particular, listed at the start of this chapter, seem to require such skilled communication.

A Final Thought About Standards

Standards can be helpful to our aims of attaining a sound and just educational experience for each child or they can become part of the ethereal conversation that never touches a single classroom. In our view, clinical supervision offers a vehicle for reaching into classrooms in a meaningful way. The supervision we envision for our schools calls for educational leaders (be they called supervisor, teacher, coach, or principal), for teachers, and for learners of all ages to be engaged in inquiry into how we learn and into how we can succeed with each learner when our ambitious aims may, at times, seem unrealistic. Through the clinical supervision we advocate, such rich conversations about how to translate our educational hopes for each learner into reality should be commonplace in our schools. When such focused and collegial conversation becomes routine in a school, we have no doubt that the students will profit. When supervision regularly contributes to that standard of collaborative inquiry in each school and classroom, we will have a standard of excellence.

References

Cogan, M. L., (1973). *Clinical supervision.* Boston: Houghton-Mifflin.

Combs, A., (1982). *A personal approach to teaching: Beliefs that make a difference.* Boston: Allyn & Bacon.

Garman, N., (1986). Clinical supervision: Quackery or remedy for professional development? *Journal of Curriculum and Supervision, 1*(2), 148–157.

Goldsberry, L. (1997). *Platforms and Portfolios.* Paper presented at Portfolios in Teacher Education: A working conference on using portfolios in teaching and teacher education, Cambridge, MA.

Goldsberry, L., & Nolan, J. F. (1983). *Active listening skills for reflective conferences.* Unpublished manuscript. Pennsylvania State University, University Park.

Goldhammer, R., (1969). *Clinical supervision: Special methods for the supervision of teachers.* New York: Holt, Rinehart & Winston.

Guthrie, H. D., & Willower, D. J. (1973). The ceremonial congratulation: An analysis of principals' observation reports of classroom teaching. The High School Journal, 6, 84–290.

Mosher, R. L. & Purpel, D. E., (1972). *Supervision: The reluctant profession.* New York: Houghton-Mifflin.

Nolan, J., & Hoover, L. A. (2004). *Teacher supervision and evaluation: Theory into practice.* Hoboken, NJ: Wiley/Jossey-Bass

Pajak, E. (2003). *Honoring diverse teaching styles: A guide for supervisors.* Alexandria, VA: Association for Supervision and Curriculum Development.

Pajak, E., & Arrington, A. R., (2004). Empowering a profession: Rethinking supervision, evaluation, and teacher accountability. In M. A. Smylie & D. Miretzky (Eds.), *Developing the teacher workforce.* National Society for the Study of Education Yearbook, 103(1), 228–252.

Sergiovanni, T. J., & Starratt, R. J. (2002). Supervision: A redefinition. New York: McGraw-Hill.

Wraga, W. G., (1999). The educational and political implications of curriculum alignment and standards-based reform. *Journal of Curriculum and Supervision, 15*(1) 4–25.

Zeichner, K. M., & Liston, D. P., (1996). *Reflective teaching: An introduction.* Mahwah, NJ: Erlbaum.

10

Standards for Teacher Evaluation

Patricia E. Holland

Meet the Author

Patricia E. Holland

Pat Holland is Associate Professor of Educational Leadership and Culture Studies at the University of Houston. Her research and publications are in the areas of instructional supervision and teachers' professional development. She is currently studying teachers' development in a context of urban high school reform. Recent publications include articles in the *NASSP Bulletin, Journal of Technology in Education, Journal of Curriculum and Supervision,* and a chapter in *Current Issues in School Leadership* (Prentice Hall, 2004), and an edited book, *Beyond Measure: Neglected Elements of Schooling in an Age of Accountability* (Eye on Education, 2004). Her Ph.D. was awarded by the University of Pittsburgh.

Successful supervision:

♦ Employs differentiated procedures for teacher evaluation. These procedures are appropriate to respective levels of teachers' professional development.

♦ Requires teachers and administrators to work as collaborative partners to identify teachers' professional development goals, appropriately assess those goals, analyze data collected as evidence of effort toward and accomplishment of the goals, and interpret the implications of such evidence for the improvement of teaching and learning

♦ Evaluates teachers using data derived from multiple sources and points in time. Ideally, data are also provided by multiple evaluators.

♦ Recognizes that evaluation of teaching is both formative and summative; however, the majority of evaluation resources are used for formative evaluation processes

♦ Ties evaluation of teaching both to individual teachers' professional development goals and to school and/or program improvement goals

♦ Ensures that evaluation policies and the goals and outcomes that are the basis for evaluation of teaching are well defined, plainly articulated, and clearly communicated. Administrators and teachers are well informed about these policies and goals.

Neither teachers nor school administrators have a very high opinion of the teacher evaluations that are required bureaucratic rituals in schools. For teachers, particularly experienced ones, it is at best an empty formality to have their classrooms observed each year by an administrator who may know little about the particular teacher's curriculum or content area. For administrators, the time spent completing the same paperwork year after year to document teachers' observed performance is considered irrelevant to improving teaching or learning in their schools.

Unfortunately, teachers and administrators consider this process of teacher evaluation to be "supervision." It is little wonder, therefore, that Starratt, an eminent scholar in the field, argued that supervision itself must be abolished because it has become indistinguishable from such evaluation practices. Starratt explained his position:

> I want to make clear at the outset what I mean by supervision.....I am speaking of supervision, as experienced by most teachers, as evaluation of classroom teaching. Whether that practice follows the procedures under the rubric of clinical supervision, human resource development supervision, democratic supervision, classroom effectiveness supervision, or whatever, it does not matter. No matter how sophisticated the procedure, if it involves a supervisor observing a classroom teaching episode, a post-observation conference with a teacher, and a written report that goes into a teacher's file, then that is the supervision I propose we abolish. (Starratt, 1997, p. 4)

Starratt is not the only supervision scholar to denounce conventional teacher evaluation and to attempt to separate such evaluation practices from supervision. In fact, the close association of teacher evaluation with supervision that has developed over the past couple of decades led other scholars (Garman, 1982; Gordon, 1992; Nolan, 1989; Waite, 1997) to claim that supervision is totally separate from evaluation. Waite (1997) remarked that "evaluation done under the guise of supervision is little better than a poke in the eye with a sharp stick" (p. 57). This aptly captures the sentiment behind the more nuanced arguments that evaluation and supervision are distinct functions.

Adding to the confusion of whether evaluation and supervision are, in fact, distinct functions is the question posed by Holland and Garman (2001) about the legitimacy of supervision. According to these authors, such legitimacy is founded in legal mandates that govern the practice of supervision. That practice, they argued, is defined as

> one of *evaluation* described in terms of administrators' assessment and rating of teachers' job performance for purposes of determining their employment status, including their possible dismissal. (p. 102)

It is, therefore, a matter of legislation that equates supervision with evaluation of teaching. It is through such legislation that supervisors obtain both the authority and the responsibility to enter classrooms to observe and rate the performance of teachers on criteria determined by legislators or their delegated representatives as hallmarks of good teaching.

Despite what those of us who are supervision scholars might wish to be the case, educators and legislators equate evaluation of teaching with supervision. By denying this reality and attempting to distance ourselves from evaluation, we are, in fact, abandoning the teachers and supervisors we profess to serve, leaving them to suffer the constraints and inadequacies of current evaluation practices. We would better serve our practitioner colleagues as well as the field of supervision by accepting responsibility for evaluation of teaching. A good beginning is to develop and advocate standards for evaluating teaching that make the process meaningful to educators while addressing the legitimate concerns of legislators to hold teachers accountable as public employees for their performance. The standards proposed in this chapter would not only accomplish these goals, but would also make evaluation of teaching an aspect of supervision consistent with the emphasis on teachers' professional development through reflection, collaboration, and inquiry.

Standards for Teacher Evaluation

Before considering each of the six standards proposed in this chapter for the evaluation of teachers and their performance, it is important to note that these standards are designed to counter the rigid standardization that currently characterizes these evaluations. In fact, the uniformity of a single, standardized procedure used to evaluate all teachers within a given school, district, or state makes it less likely that such evaluations will yield useful information for judging or improving teaching. To achieve these goals, evaluation of teaching should be governed by standards that inform and guide an individual teacher's practice, rather than by arbitrary behavioral indicators that prescribe it. With this distinction in mind, the following six standards for evaluating teaching in ways that integrate such evaluation with good supervisory practice are proposed.

Standard 1: Successful Supervision Employs Differentiated Procedures for Teacher Evaluation

Successful supervision employs differentiated procedures for teacher evaluation. These procedures are appropriate to respective levels of teachers' professional development.

This standard indicates a view of teaching as a professional skill that is continuously learned and developed throughout a teacher's career. As such, evaluation of a teacher's practice needs to provide assessment of those aspects of teaching that are appropriate to a teacher's particular level of experience and skill development. For example, a novice teacher may very well benefit from an evaluation based on a checklist to simply determine the presence or absence of effective classroom management elements and lesson design, whereas an experienced teacher's evaluation might focus more narrowly on the development or refinement of a particular aspect of teaching, such as questioning for higher-order thinking or ways to structure cooperative learning groups that best serve their students and content area.

Although differentiating the strategies used to evaluate teachers may at first glance seem cumbersome, it is quite likely to be less time consuming and more useful in the long run. Under current practices, the time and energy teachers and administrators spend on evaluation yields little more than bureaucratic paperwork. There is certainly little evidence that conventional evaluations offer administrators much leverage to remove incompetent teachers or provide teachers with information they can use to improve their teaching. Differential evaluation would allow administrators to hold teachers who are inexperienced or new accountable for demonstrating proof of their proficiency as determined by a required observation checklist, while affording the experienced teacher a customized contract for individual professional development and assessment.

A rationale for the differentiation of evaluation of teaching lies not only in its utility, but also in its association with similar approaches in the field of supervision. Glatthorn (1997) used the term "differentiated supervision" to describe a tiered system of supervision that provides intensive assistance to those teachers who need it and a menu of professional development options to more skilled teachers. Glickman, Gordon, and Ross-Gordon (2003) presented a developmental model of supervision that matches a style of directive, collaborative, or nondirective supervision to a teacher's level of professional maturity. These models of supervision offer guideposts for the evaluation of teaching, such as the one developed by Danielson and McGreal (2000), that are based on teachers' levels of experience and skill.

Standard 2: Successful Supervision Requires Collaboration and Partnership

> *Successful supervision requires teachers and administrators to work as collaborative partners to identify teachers' professional development goals, appropriately assess those goals, analyze data collected as evidence of effort toward and accomplishment of the goals, and interpret the implications of such evidence for the improvement of teaching and learning.*

This second standard is based on a view that a major purpose of evaluation of teaching is to improve a teacher's instructional capability. It is a view that takes as its justification what Natriello (1990) identified to be a well-documented purpose of the evaluation of teaching, namely to influence and improve teachers' performance. This standard also takes into consideration McGreal's (1988) observation that to accomplish such improvement, evaluation of teaching must "provide a process that allows and encourages supervisors and teachers to work together to improve and enhance instructional practices" (p. 2).

The essential point of this standard is its depiction of administrators who evaluate and the evaluated teachers as "collaborative partners." This characterization of the working relationship between evaluators and teachers is a marked departure from conventional evaluation practice in which administrators function as external and neutral agents in the evaluation of teaching process. Instead, this standard would have administrators act as what Garman (1982) described as "connected participants" who engage with teachers out of a sense of mutual commitment to and responsibility for teachers' professional growth. To use the language of evaluation theory, administrators become "stakeholders" in the evaluation process.

This second standard also delineates the nature of the work to be done by administrators and teachers in their collaborative partnership. It is work with familiar echoes of what has become a dominant process in the field of supervision, i.e., clinical supervision (Cogan, 1973; Goldhammer, Anderson, & Krajewski, 1980), in that it focuses administrators and teachers on examining and interpreting data that document a teacher's work. It is important to note that data, according to this standard, are construed more broadly than just the classroom observation data involved in clinical supervision and in the derivative forms of conventional, observation-based teacher evaluations that are based on clinical supervision.

Standard 3: Successful Supervision Evaluates Teachers Using Multiple Data Sources

> *Successful supervision evaluates teachers using data derived from multiple sources and points in time. Ideally, data are also provided by multiple evaluators.*

A major criticism of the typical practice of basing teacher evaluation on a single classroom observation is that it encourages teachers to perform a "dog and pony show." In other words, to present an observation lesson that is vastly different and improved in complexity and sophistication from their ordinary daily teaching. Those who voice this criticism—most often, teachers—appear to be unaware that such observation-based evaluations are only designed to produce what evaluation theorists describe as "demonstration proofs," that is, evidence that teachers are *capable* of certain teaching practices, not that they *actually* perform them. Ignoring the distinction between the possible and the actual teacher performance is a critical flaw in terms of its value for making informed decisions about teacher quality, retention, and development that such evaluations are supposed to offer.

A standard for teacher evaluation that calls for multiple forms and sources of data provides direction for what the Joint Committee on Standards for Educational Evaluation has identified as criteria of *utility* and *accuracy* that personnel evaluations must satisfy (Stufflebeam & Sanders, 1990). The first of these criteria, utility, requires "that evaluations provide information useful to individuals and to groups of educators in improving their performance" (Stufflebeam & Sanders, 1990, p. 422). The second criterion, accuracy, requires that the evaluation provide relevant information about the work of teachers throughout the school year, not just during a formal observation. Data such as teachers' lesson plans, samples of instructional materials and activities, examples of student work, student evaluations, and data on student learning are examples of the kinds of information that can lead to more useful and accurate teacher assessment.

Scriven's (1988) Judgment-Based Teacher Evaluation (J-BTE) scheme for teacher evaluation offers an example of this type of evaluation, one that relies not only on multiple sources of data to yield better evaluations, but also on the participation of multiple evaluators. The J-BTE scheme argues for the "pooled professional judgment" of at least three evaluators "because the appraisal of a teacher is so complicated, it is clearly too risky to leave decisions as important as summative appraisal to one judge" (p. 67).

Standard 4: Successful Supervision Recognizes the Nature of Teaching Evaluation

Successful supervision recognizes that evaluation of teaching is both formative and summative; however, the majority of evaluation resources are used for formative evaluation processes.

This standard is one that closely links evaluation of teaching and instructional supervision. That link is forged by the shared purposes of supervision and formative evaluation, i.e., to identify a teacher's current levels of knowledge and skill and use them as the basis for a coherent and documented plan for that teacher's continued learning and professional development. Although supervision scholars are quite willing to accept this formative aspect of evaluation as within the purview of supervision, they have been less willing to accept responsibility for the summative evaluations that determine teachers' tenure or dismissal, and, likely, salary increments. Supervision scholars reject the rationale that mandated state and district evaluation practices for summative evaluation are actually forms of supervision that can lead to improved instruction (Hazi, 1994). They also contend that it is impossible for the same person to have the hierarchical power to perform such evaluations and still be able to establish the kind of trusting relationship that is necessary for a supervisor to help a teacher improve their teaching (Nolan, 1997).

This standard is also an attempt to invert what has become the hegemony of summative evaluation in schools. By placing greater emphasis on formative evaluation, this standard encourages supervisory interactions in which teachers assume an active role in the kinds of inquiry and activities that further their development as professionals (Holland & Adams, 2002). Putting more emphasis on formative evaluation serves to reinforce the role of supervision by encouraging teachers to reflect on and critically examine their own practice, and to explore alternatives for expanding their teaching repertoire. These formative evaluation activities can then serve as the basis for summative evaluations that provide evidence of teachers' growth and development.

Standard 5: Successful Supervision Ties Teaching Evaluation to Professional Development Goals and School and/or Program Improvement Goals

> *Successful supervision ties evaluation of teaching both to individual teachers' professional development goals and to school and/or program improvement goals.*

This standard comes directly from an emphasis on formative evaluation over summative evaluation by focusing on teachers' individual goals for their professional development. As the basis for evaluation, such individual goals address an emerging interest in new forms of teacher evaluation that support what Heartel (1991) described as a "professional model of teaching." This model stands in contrast with the traditional "bureaucratic model of the educational system and the work of teaching" (Heartel, 1991, p. 3). In that bureaucratic model, evaluation of teaching is the sole province of administrators, requires the use of a uniform instrument, and is used only for summative purposes. In contrast, a professional model of teaching emphasizes formative processes that link evaluation of teaching with teachers' own interests in and commitment to their professional development. As such, evaluation of teaching within a professional model of teaching is more consistent with long-held theories and practices of instructional supervision.

As this standard indicates, teachers' individual professional development goals are a necessary basis for evaluation of their teaching skills and abilities, but are not sufficient. School and program improvement goals must also be considered. Establishing explicit relationships between the teacher's individual goals and the overall school goals furthers the professionalized view of teaching that is a component of school reform efforts (Darling-Hammond, 1990; Little, 1993; Smylie, 1996) by encouraging teachers to understand their work within the larger contexts of which it is a part. As McLaughlin (1990) also pointed out, "an evaluation system located within a broader improvement effort can foster accountability through its investment in professional norms and values" (p. 413). Such accountability for common goals helps teachers as they work together with their fellow teachers and with administrators to develop a frame of mind of collegiality that has been an important aspect of supervision over the past several decades (Cogan, 1973; Garman, 1982).

Standard 6: Successful Supervision Ensures Clarity of Evaluation Policies, Goals, and Outcomes

Successful supervision ensures that evaluation policies and the goals and outcomes that are the basis for evaluation of teaching are well defined, plainly articulated, and clearly communicated. Administrators and teachers are well informed about these policies and goals.

Although this final standard states what should be obvious requirements of any teacher evaluation system, it is important to articulate the need for all parties involved in the evaluation process to have a clear and shared understanding of both the process and its purpose (Stufflebeam & Sanders, 1990). Such clarity is more easily achieved by traditional summative evaluation in which teachers are treated uniformly as they are evaluated on the basis of a common instrument. However, such clarity is more difficult when the emphasis is on formative evaluation processes that require considerable individualization to meet teachers' particular needs and interests.

This standard calls for a formalization of those formative elements of teacher evaluation. Strategies for such formalization include the options of individual plans that teachers develop to describe the professional development activities for which they can be held accountable, teacher portfolios that document teachers' work and learning, and also may include evidence of their students' performance. These strategies allow teachers to individualize their professional development efforts within the scope of common protocols for documentation and assessment.

There are also strategies for formalizing teachers' collegial efforts toward school improvement. These strategies include study groups and task forces who meet on a regular schedule and pursue a documented agenda. Critical Friends groups (Bambino, 2002; Dunne, Nave, & Lewis, 2000) offer another collegial strategy through their use of prescribed methods for reflection and interpretation of events of teaching and learning.

All of these individual and collegial strategies reframe evaluation of teaching from a bureaucratic process that is "done to" teachers to a professional activity in which teachers determine the ways they can continue to develop their own practice and participate in joint deliberation with supervisors in judging its worth and value. This view of evaluation as a professional process is one that aligns evaluation of teaching with the practice of supervision.

Why Standards for Teacher Evaluation Are Important

Standards for teacher evaluation can help change the current negative views that teachers and supervisors have of such evaluations. Standards accomplish this objective by portraying teacher evaluation as a process committed to fundamental aspects of successful supervision; namely, *clarification, interpretation,* and *deliberation.*

Standards for teacher evaluation provide *clarification* of the process and purpose of such evaluations. For instance, the focus on differentiating evaluation procedures for teachers at differing knowledge and skill levels not only establishes the growth and improvement of teachers' performance as a primary purpose of teacher evaluation, but also aligns evaluation with supervision as a process where the benefits to teachers development as professionals are central. Also, an emphasis on formative evaluation makes it clear that teachers' learning and growth are vital concerns to be supported and informed by evaluations of their teaching. Additionally, the standards require teachers, along with their supervisors, to clarify and make explicit each teacher's individual professional development goals as well as the ways those individual goals further overall school or program improvement goals.

Standards for teacher evaluation also reflect successful supervision in the importance both give to *interpretation* of teaching performance and the thoughtful explication and analysis of evidence about how such performance reflects a teacher's values and professional development goals. The standards emphasize the importance of the *process* of interpreting teaching evidence in what can be characterized as an interactive conversation with the evidence and with supervisors who are part of the social world from which that evidence comes. The purpose of that conversation is to help teachers shape and reshape an understanding of the lived experience about their teaching practice. The emphasis on interpretation aligns with successful supervision rather than traditional evaluations that seek only to provide empirical evidence and explanations about teachers' performance, which can then be used as tools to shape and control that performance. The standards empower teachers as active agents in interpreting their own practice. Furthermore, evaluation of teaching as an interpretive process views the products of interpretation as tentative and provisional accounts of teachers' knowledge and understanding at particular points in time. Therefore, evaluation of teaching, just like successful supervision, is never finished.

Finally, the standards for teacher evaluation support the kind of *deliberation* that is central to successful supervision. The standards promote genuine dialogue between teachers and supervisors about the different perceptions that may exist about the teaching practices being evaluated. The use of data from multiple sources, for example, encourages teachers and their supervisors to consider complex and possibly conflicting evidence and articulate the often tacit interpretations of what that evidence means in light of teachers' individual professional development goals. It is a deliberative process that informs teachers' efforts to reach both personal and schoolwide improvement goals. As Schwandt (2002) noted, such deliberation differs from traditional evaluations in which the evaluator attempts to manage dialogue and deliberation within the parameters of what the evaluator determines to be the evaluation's design and purpose. These standards involve teachers as well as the supervisors who evaluate them in both the evaluation's design and its implementation. Rather than being objects of study as in traditional evaluation, the standards empower teachers to influence and make judgments that direct the course of their work and how it can best be evaluated. It is reasonable to assume if teachers have this power, they will be more likely to find evaluations of their teaching useful and meaningful, and also more willing to be held accountable for their teaching practice.

Professional Development Activity

For this activity, you need a copy of the evaluation of teaching process documents used in a school or district—your own or one to which you have ready access. These documents are to include a thorough description of the evaluation process and any forms or instruments used to evaluate teachers.

Carefully review the evaluation documents and place numbers corresponding to the six standards discussed in this chapter on the documents in all places where evidence of each standard occurs. (Using a different color for each number is a good idea.)

Then, prepare a 100 to 200 word description about how each of the six teaching evaluation standards are addressed in the process that you are examining. For each of the six evaluation of teaching standards, recommend a change that will make the evaluation process more consistent with each standard.

Next, interview a supervisor who uses the evaluation teaching process you have reviewed. Ask that supervisor to discuss the changes you have recommended in terms of how they meet the following standards as defined and identified by the Joint Committee for Personnel Evaluation Standards:

> The propriety standards require that evaluations be conducted legally, ethically, and with due regard for the welfare of evaluatees and clients.

> The utility standards are intended to guide evaluations so that they will be informative, timely, and influential.

> The feasibility standards call for evaluation systems that are as easy to implement as possible, efficient in their use of time and resources, adequately funded, and viable from a number of other standpoints.

> The accuracy standards require that the obtained information be technically accurate and that conclusions be linked logically to the data. (retrieved from http://www.eval.org/EvaluationDocuments/perseval.html))

Finally, Prepare a written report of the supervisor's comments and revise your recommended changes to the current evaluation of teaching process in light of those comments.

Assessment Criteria

- ♦ Content analysis of evaluation of teaching documents and written descriptions of evidence of the six evaluation of teaching standards are comprehensive.

- ♦ Recommended changes for each standard offer evidence that the standards are well understood.

- ♦ The written interview report provides a thorough account of the supervisor's comments on the recommended changes to the current evaluation process.

- ♦ Postinterview revisions of recommended changes to the current evaluation of teaching process indicate awareness of the Personnel Evaluation Standards.

References

Bambino, D. (2002). Critical friends. *Educational Leadership, 59*(6).

Cogan, M. (1973). *Clinical supervision.* Boston: Houghton-Mifflin.

Danielson, C., & McGreal, T. (2000). *Teacher evaluation to enhance professional practice.* Alexandria, VA: Association for Supervision and Curriculum Development.

Darling-Hammond, L. (1990). Teacher evaluation in transition: Emerging roles and evolving methods. In J. Millman and L. Darling-Hammond (Eds.), *The new handbook of teacher evaluation: Assessing elementary and secondary school teachers* (pp. 17–32). Newbury Park, CA: Sage.

Dunne, F., Nave, B., & Lewis, A. (2000). Critical friends groups: Teachers helping teachers to improve student learning. *Phi Delta Kappa Center for Evaluation, Development and Research Bulletin, 28.*

Garman, N. (1982). The clinical approach to supervision. In T. Sergiovanni (Ed.), *Supervision of teaching* (pp. 35–52). Alexandria, VA: Association for Supervision and Curriculum Development.

Glatthorn, A. (1997). *Differentiated supervision* (2nd ed.). Alexandria, VA: Association for Supervision and Curriculum Development.

Glickman, C., Gordon, S., & Ross-Gordon, J. M. (2003). *SuperVision and instructional leadership: A developmental approach.* Needham Heights, MA: Allyn & Bacon.

Goldhammer, R., Anderson, R., & Krajewski, R. (1980). *Clinical supervision* (2nd ed.). New York: Holt, Rinehart, and Winston.

Gordon, S. (1992). Paradigms, transitions, and the new supervision. *Journal of Curriculum and Supervision,8*(1), 62–76.

Hazi, H. (1994). The teacher evaluation–supervision dilemma: A case of entanglements and irreconcilable differences. *Journal of Curriculum and Supervision, 9*(2), 195–216.

Heartel, E, (1991). New forms of teacher assessment. *Review of Research in Education,17,* 2–29.

Holland, P., & Garman, N. (2001). Toward a resolution of the crisis of legitimacy in the field of supervision. *Journal of Curriculum and Supervision, 16*(2), 95–111.

Holland, P., & Adams, P. (2002). Through the horns of a dilemma between instructional supervision and the summative evaluation of teaching. *International Journal of Leadership in Education, 5*(3), 227–247.

Joint Committee for Personnel Evaluation Standards Retrieved August 30, 2005 from http://www.eval.org/EvaluationDocuments/perseval.html.

Little, J. (1993). Teachers' professional development in a climate of educational reform. *Educational Evaluation and Policy Analysis, 15*(2), 129–151.

McGreal, T. (1988). Evaluation for enhancing instruction: linking teacher evaluation and staff development. In S. Stanley and W. Popham (Eds.), *Teacher evaluation: Six prescriptions for success* (pp. 1–29). Alexandria, VA: Association for Supervision and Curriculum Development.

McLaughlin, M. (1990). Embracing contraries: Implementing and sustaining school reform. In J. Millman and L. Darling-Hammond (Eds.), *The new handbook of teacher evaluation: Assessing elementary and secondary school teachers.* (pp. 403–415). Newbury Park, CA: Sage.

Natriello, G. (1990). Intended and unintended consequences: Purposes and effects of teacher evaluation. In J. Millman and L. Darling-Hammond (Eds.), *The new handbook of teacher evaluation: Assessing elementary and secondary school teachers.* (pp. 35–45). Newbury Park, CA: Sage.

Nolan, J. (1989). Can supervisory practice embrace Schon's concept of reflective practice? *Journal of Curriculum and Supervision, 5*(1), 35–40.

Nolan, J. (1997). Can a supervisor be a coach? In J. Glanz and R. Neville (Eds.), *Educational supervision: Perspectives, issues and controversies* (pp. 100–112).Norwood, MA: Christopher-Gordon.

Schwandt, T. (2002). *Evaluation practice reconsidered.* New York: Lang.

Scriven, M. (1988). Evaluating teachers as professionals: The duties-based approach. In S. Stanley and W. Popham (Eds.), *Teacher evaluation: Six prescriptions for success.* Alexandria, VA: Association for Supervision and Curriculum Development.

Smylie, M. (1996). From bureaucratic control to building human capital: The importance of teacher learning in education reform. *Educational Researcher, 25*(9), 9–11.

Starratt, R. (1997). Should supervision be abolished? In J. Glanz and R. Neville (Eds.), *Educational supervision: Perspectives, issues and controversies* (pp. 4–12). Norwood, MA: Christopher-Gordon.

Stufflebeam, D., & Sanders, J. (1990). Using the personnel evaluation standards to improve teacher evaluation. In J. Millman and L. Darling-Hammond (Eds.), *The new handbook of teacher evaluation: Assessing elementary and secondary school teachers* (pp. 416–428). Newbury Park, CA: Sage.

Waite, D. (1997). Do teachers benefit from supervision? In J. Glanz and R. Neville (Eds.), *Educational supervision: Perspectives, issues and controversies* (pp. 56–70). Norwood, MA: Christopher-Gordon.

11

Standards for Supervision of Professional Development

Stephen P. Gordon

Meet the Author

Stephen P. Gordon

Stephen P. Gordon is a professor on the faculties of the educational administration and school improvement programs at Texas State University-San Marcos. He also is the co-director of the National Center for School Improvement, located at Texas State. He is author of the book *Professional Development for School Improvement: Empowering Learning Communities* (Allyn & Bacon) and co-author of the books *How to Help Beginning Teachers Succeed*, with Susan Maxey (ASCD) and *SuperVision and Instructional Leadership: A Developmental Approach*, with Carl D. Glickman, and Jovita M. Ross-Gordon (Allyn & Bacon). Steve also was lead consultant for the Association of Supervision and Curriculum Development's video series *Improving Instruction through Observation and Feedback*. Steve received his doctorate in Supervision from the University of Georgia.

Successful supervision:

- ◆ Involves participants in the planning, delivery, and evaluation of professional development programs
- ◆ Facilitates job-embedded professional development
- ◆ Assists teachers with gathering and analyzing data on student learning as part of professional development
- ◆ Offers opportunities for dialogue on curriculum, teaching, and learning as part of the professional development process
- ◆ Differentiates professional development activities to address differences in career phase, adult learning style, teaching assignment, teaching style, interests, and concerns
- ◆ Assists teachers as they engage in self-assessment and personal reflection as a basis for self-directed professional development

Professional development, historically considered a task of supervision (Allen, Fillion, Butters, Gordon & Bently, 2004; Gordon & Nicely, 1998), has come a long way in the last few decades. It now has a large research base, has expanded beyond traditional training to include a variety of purposes and formats (Gordon, 2004; Gordon & Nicely, 1998), has its own set of standards (National Staff Development Council, 2005), and is emerging as a separate field of practice and study (Gordon, 2004). In this chapter, I will focus on standards for supervision of school-focused professional development. Such professional development should be facilitated by supervisors from the central office, certainly must include the school principal, and usually involves assistant principals and teacher–leaders. With these factors in mind, let us take a closer look at each of the proposed standards.

Supervision Standards
for Professional Development

Standard 1: Successful Supervision Involves Participants

*Successful supervision involves participants in the planning, delivery,
and evaluation of professional development programs.*

A prerequisite for planning professional development at the school level
is a collective vision for the type of graduates the school wishes to prepare
and the type of learning environment needed to develop such graduates. If a
collective vision does not exist, the entire school community (including
teachers, staff, parents, and other members of the community that the school
serves) needs to develop one. Once the collective vision exists, the overall
goal of needs assessment is to identify gaps between the vision and the current state of affairs and then to determine how professional development can
help to close those gaps.

Historically, when asked if teachers were involved in planning professional development, schools reported that teachers were involved through
completion of needs assessment surveys. Assessing teachers' learning needs,
like assessing students' learning needs, is best accomplished by using a variety of data gathering methods. At the school level, surveys can be accompanied by small and large group discussions, classroom and campus observations, analysis of student work and achievement data, prioritizing activities
like the nominal group technique, and a variety of other methods. Comparison and synthesis of different data types will provide a more complete picture of teachers' learning needs in relation to the school's vision and improvement goals.

Needs assessment data should be gathered not only on topics for professional development, but also on preferred frameworks (training, peer coaching, study groups, etc.), preferred times for participation (summer, released
time, after school, etc.), and preferred sources of assistance (district, university, intermediate unit, critical friend, etc.). Once professional development
topics have been chosen, additional data need to be gathered about teachers'
levels of readiness and concern regarding the chosen topics so the developmental needs of various groups and individuals can be addressed.

Supervisors can best coordinate a needs assessment not by designing surveys, leading discussion groups, or reviewing student achievement data by
themselves, but rather by facilitating teams of teachers as they carry out such
tasks and compare data they have gathered. By involving as many teachers
as possible in needs assessment, supervisors not only increase the likelihood

the results will be considered valid, but also foster participants' professional growth from the earliest stages of program development.

Once professional development needs have been identified, it's time to plan learning activities intended to meet those needs. Experts on constructivist teaching and learning tell us that we should engage K–12 students in planning units of instruction. It only makes sense supervisors should engage adult learners in planning professional development activities. An essential aspect of effective teacher planning is making teachers aware of the wide variety of professional development frameworks available. This can be done through awareness sessions, study groups, and visits to other schools where promising frameworks are utilized effectively. Teachers may also need some preparation on the planning process and planning tools (e.g., flow charts, Gantt charts, planning matrices) but such preparation need not be elaborate. A key role for the supervisor is liaison between teachers and administration in the procurement of resources and scheduling of professional development activities (sometimes the role of liaison morphs into negotiator and broker).

Teacher participation in the delivery of professional development is another key element of this standard. There is nothing wrong with bringing in outside presenters and facilitators. Indeed, one characteristic of successful professional development programs is external support (Gordon, 2004). However, the school that does not utilize its own teachers as staff developers is failing to take advantage of its most powerful professional development resource. A school that uses its own teachers as staff developers can increase the types and frequency of professional development and always has its staff developers available for follow up. Teachers view other teachers from their school as more understanding of teacher needs and more credible than outsiders. Teachers are more active in professional development activities led by peers and believe their peers provide more practical ideas for classroom application (Wu, 1987). Using teachers as staff developers fosters the development of a professional school culture (Ginocchio, 1990) and enhances the personal growth of the teacher who participates in staff development (Cunningham, 2002).

The same principles that apply to other aspects of program development also apply to program evaluation. Teachers should be involved in planning for evaluation, gathering and analyzing data, drawing conclusions, and revising the program based on evaluation results. Allowing teachers to evaluate their own professional development programs provides a variety of opportunities for reflective collaboration. First, participants decide on critical questions they wish to ask about the program. Next, they decide what types of data they will gather to answer their questions and how they will gather that data. A well-done evaluation will require participants to explain why evaluation questions are relevant and how the evaluation is credible and rigorous (Fetterman, 1996). Reviewing data and drawing conclusions create opportunities for professional dialogue, and allowing teachers to participate in program revision creates commitment to continuous improvement.

Standard 2: Successful Supervision Facilitates Job-Embedded Professional Development

It makes sense that professional development connected to one's daily work is more relevant and has more impact than other types of professional development. However, we must remember that regardless of formal job descriptions, teachers' work is a personal and social construct. In successful schools, teachers do not conceptualize their professional responsibilities as limited to their classrooms; they are concerned with the learning of all students in the school as well as the community that the school serves. Classroom, school, and community, then, are viewed by successful teachers as related levels of professional responsibility.

The thread that connects the various levels of professional responsibility (classroom, school, community) is student learning, and teachers affecting student learning do so directly through curriculum development, teaching, and student assessment. It is unfortunate that in recent years policy makers have attempted—through state-mandated curricula and high-stakes achievement tests—to greatly reduce teacher decision making in the first and last of these three areas. Curriculum development, teaching, and student assessment in reality are highly interactive and interdependent aspects of the same process—part of the same "job."

Student and adult development are connected in successful schools, with adult development viewed as part of a teacher's professional responsibility. Teachers assume the responsibility of helping each other develop personally and professionally. Teachers and parents collaborate to develop the capacity for both to assist student growth and development.

The natural connections discussed above—of classroom, school, and community; of curriculum, instruction, and student assessment; and of student, teacher, and parent development—should be fostered by the school's professional development program so that these connections become increasingly clear. Making these connections will help teachers define their own professional responsibilities as well as what job-embedded professional development means to them. Making these connections can expand teachers' concept of relevant professional development to include activities like the following:

- ◆ Mapping curriculum
- ◆ Designing interdisciplinary curriculum

- Learning new instructional strategies and adapting those strategies to their students
- Observing and coaching each other
- Participating in study groups
- Developing and testing alternative forms of student assessment
- Collaborating with other teachers to connect school learning to the local community and larger society through such programs as service learning, place-based learning, and democratic learning
- Developing partnership with parents characterized by mutual respect, dialogue, and shared decision making
- Conducting classroom, team and schoolwide action research

Job-embedded professional development can include any of the above and much more, but does not include professional development that teachers do not perceive to be connected to their daily work lives. The latest instructional trend sweeping the nation, the recently purchased computer program that so impressed the principal at a state conference, the new district goals developed by a central office task force—none of these can be the stuff of job-embedded professional development unless they are connected to teachers' work lives as personally and socially constructed by teachers themselves.

One implication of the need to embed professional development in teachers' work is more site-focused professional development. This does not mean that there should be no more attendance at districtwide workshops, regional conferences, and so on, but that off-site professional development should be selected because it relates to teacher and school improvement goals, and provisions are made for assisting with the application of outside learning at the classroom and school level. Another implication is for community-based professional development that enables teachers to learn how to better collaborate with parents and other community members, and to explore avenues for integrating school and community development.

Standard 3: Successful Supervision Assists Gathering and Analyzing Data on Student Learning

Successful supervision assists educators to gather and analyze data on student learning as part of professional development.

This standard includes but goes well beyond teachers reviewing the results of standardized achievement tests. One value of many state-developed standardized tests is the reporting of disaggregated test results. These results enable teachers to analyze test results for various racial/ethnic, economic, and special needs groups, and to adjust their instruction accordingly. A clear disadvantage of the high-stakes achievement tests developed by most states, however, is the tendency to focus exclusively on test results at the expense of a variety of other ways to diagnose student needs and measure student progress. One important responsibility of supervisors is to foster a balanced approach to student assessment, with teachers gathering and analyzing a variety of student assessment data. Another key role for supervisors is to convey the concept of gathering and analyzing data on student learning as a form of professional development in its own right, not just as a basis for subsequent professional development.

We have known for a long time that in diagnosing and evaluating student learning at the classroom level, effective teachers rely less on traditional test results and more on observation of students, detailed note-taking on student performance, and correcting daily student work (Brophy & Evertson, 1976). Professional development can help teachers to use such informal techniques more effectively. Gathering and analyzing data on student learning need not be done as a solitary act. Teams of teachers who teach the same students or same content areas can collaborate in this work.

One professional development program I examined involved a team of elementary teachers using student data to improve expository writing. The project began with the teachers reading and discussing literature on expository writing. Based on their study, the teachers developed an analytical scale to assess students' writing. Teachers practiced using the scale by separately scoring the same student writing samples and comparing their scores for reliability. After scoring the writing samples and comparing results, the teachers engaged in dialogue about their students' writing and their use of the scale. Eventually, the teachers were comfortable enough with the scale to gather baseline data on their students' writing skills. Throughout the remainder of the school year, the teachers continuously analyzed student writing samples, identified specific target areas for improvement, explored new instructional strategies, developed and implemented classroom action plans, gathered and analyzed new writing samples, shared results, and modified action plans. A comparison of baseline scores with end-of-year scores on the analytical scale indicated considerable growth in the students' expository writing skills.

Schoolwide action research is another vehicle for connecting the gathering and analysis of data on student learning with professional development. Teachers can gather and analyze *preliminary data* on student learning to help select a focus for action research, then gather and analyze *target data* on the focus area that will allow educators to collaborate on a schoolwide action plan, and finally gather and analyze *evaluation data* throughout the action research process to measure progress toward improved student learning, modifying the action plan as necessary.

Standard 4: Successful Supervision Offers Opportunities for Dialogue

Successful supervision offers opportunities for dialogue on curriculum, teaching, and learning as part of the professional development process.

Based on ideas originally developed by physicist David Bohm, Senge (1990) proposed dialogue as an important aspect of learning within organizations. "Those involved in a dialogue engage in 'participatory thought,' become observers of their own thinking, and develop common meaning. For dialogue to take place, participants must suspend their assumptions and regard each other as colleagues" (Gordon, 2004, p. 194).

Heckman (1993) maintained that authentic dialogue on school practice goes beyond whether a given practice works or not and examines assumptions on which the practice is based.

> Questions are raised about the reasons for a criterion of effectiveness and the practices that are being evaluated. Why this criterion? What conceptions of effectiveness undergird this criterion? Why these conceptions? What alternative ideas of effectiveness could guide the creation of other practices, and what other criteria could be invoked? (pp. 266–267)

Teachers can apply the type of critical analysis Heckman described to a host of important topics in curriculum, teaching, and learning. A few examples follow:

- Whether teachers or external experts should develop curriculum
- The gaps between the formal curriculum and what teachers really teach
- Whether it is appropriate to "teach to the test"
- Teachers' level of comfort with a new instructional strategy they are being asked to implement in their classrooms
- The effects of high-stakes testing on student learning
- Whether the needs of diverse learners are addressed by current practices

A list of examples like these makes it clear that supervisors need to foster a supportive, trusting environment if critical dialogue is going to take place. At the heart of a supportive, trusting environment are positive personal relationships between supervisors and teachers, and among teachers. The supervisor needs to take the lead in developing positive relationships with teachers, modeling relationship-building to the school community.

Beyond the need for a supporting, trusting environment, it is important that supervisors and teachers understand the purpose of dialogue is not to debate issues, engage in traditional rationale problem solving, or resolve conflict. Rather, the aims of dialogue are exploration of ideas, critical reflection, consideration of alternative perspectives, and collective learning. There currently are several professional development frameworks that include opportunities for dialogue—including peer coaching, study groups, action research, and collaborative writing, to name a few—but these frameworks are all fairly structured and none of them has dialogue as its sole purpose. The openness and fluidity required for deep, transformative dialogue might best be fostered by the creation of small dialogue groups. Dialogue groups require expert facilitation and, at least initially, a supervisor trained to facilitate dialogue can serve in that role. In addition to regular meetings of small dialogue groups, periodic opportunities for large-group dialogue can be provided.

Standard 5: Successful Supervision Differentiates Professional Development Activities

Successful supervision differentiates professional development activities to address differences in career phase, adult learning style, teaching assignment, teaching style, interests, and concerns.

Based on what we know about adult learning and the teaching career, the traditional one-size-fits-all concept of professional development is open to criticism on a variety of fronts. First, we know that teachers have different professional development needs in different phases of their careers (Gehrke, 1991; Krupp, 1987; Levine, 1987). Second, adults have different learning styles (Gordon, 2004). Third, although teachers who teach different content areas often can benefit from generic professional development, they also need to update content knowledge and develop pedagogical content knowledge (Shulman, 1987). This sometimes means different professional development for different content areas. Fourth, based on their personalities and personal philosophies, different teachers have different styles of teaching (Ornstein, 1990; Pajak, 2003), which might be more or less compatible with different types of professional development. Finally, teachers go through different stages of concern when learning how to apply educational innovations—from self-concerns to technical concerns, to concern about the impact of the innovation on students—and they progress through these stages of concern in different ways and at different times (Hall & Hord, 1987; Hord, Rutherford, & Huling-Austin, 1987). Addressing different levels of teacher concern, therefore, may well require different types of professional development, even when educators are focused on a single innovation.

One finding from the school improvement research is that in improving schools educators take collective action toward an agreed-upon purpose (Glickman, Gordon, & Ross-Gordon, 2004). But unity of purpose and action does not mean that different groups and individuals need to engage in professional development on the same day in the same way. Rather, variety of professional development frameworks and activities can be coordinated to move the school toward a common vision. I have described a variety of professional development frameworks in another work (Gordon, 2004). A few examples of alternative frameworks are

- training
- lesson study
- peer coaching
- dialogue groups
- collaborative work teams
- teacher leadership
- coteaching

- partnerships
- study groups
- networks
- action research
- teacher centers
- reflective writing
- self-directed professional development

Each of the above frameworks can be offered in a variety of forms, increasing the ways in which professional development can be differentiated. For example, a training program designed to develop common skills might involve different groups of teachers viewing demonstrations, making field trips, engaging in discussions, participating in simulations, or trying out new skills in their classrooms with peer assistance.

Coordinating differentiated professional development toward common goals is a complex undertaking. The school just beginning efforts to differentiate will wish to start with a limited number of frameworks and activities. However, in my own study of successful professional development programs across the nation, I found that over time these programs became more and more complex—and more and more differentiated (Gordon, 2000). The idea is to start small and build gradually toward an increasingly sophisticated program that takes into account teachers' career phases, learning styles, teaching responsibilities, and personal interests and concerns.

Standard 6: Successful Supervision Facilitates Self-Assessment and Self-Directed Development

Successful supervision facilitates teachers as they engage in self-assessment and personal reflection as a basis for self-directed professional development.

The need for collaboration around a common purpose is well established in the professional development literature. However, the need for collaborative work does not rule out self-directed professional development. Indeed, nearly all of the successful professional development programs I examined in the aforementioned study (Gordon, 2004) included self-directed development as part of a multifaceted professional development program. One requirement of these programs, however, was that the teacher link individual professional goals to school goals.

Effective self-directed professional development, like team and schoolwide professional development, is data-based. This means not only gathering data on one's professional performance and learning needs, but taking adequate time to reflect on that data, comparing desired professional performance to existing reality, and contemplating activities that will help to bridge the gap between personal vision and current reality. Successful self-directed development also involves continued data gathering and analysis to self-assess progress toward professional goals.

Self-directed professional development does not mean solitary professional development. It can—and usually should—involve collaboration with others as the teacher gathers data on her or his performance, assesses the data, designs an individualized plan, implements it, and self-assesses progress toward improvement goals. Supervisors and peers can assist the teacher with each of the steps in this self-directed process. The critical aspect that makes a plan self-directed is the teacher assuming responsibility for decisions at each step in the process, often with information, advice, and technical assistance from colleagues.

One tool that provides a structure for self-directed professional development is the teacher portfolio. The teacher can use the portfolio to display data, record reflections, document activities, and describe results of a self-directed project. Portfolios can be divided into sections, with each section including artifacts and reflections on a different phase of a self-directed project.

The sample professional development activity presented here is one designed to assist preservice and in-service supervisors with assessing their own professional development needs and learning styles and to plan self-directed professional development projects, thus experiencing the process they will later facilitate.

Professional Development Activity

This activity relates to the second standard listed above, which states "successful supervision facilitates educators as they engage in self-assessment and personal reflection as a basis for self-directed professional development." For instructional leaders to facilitate other's self-assessment and personal reflection, they must first engage in these processes themselves. This activity provides multiple opportunities for self-assessment and reflection. Although the activity is concerned with individual professional development, participants engage in the activity as part of a collegial support group.

In phase one of the activity, participants gather multiple types of data on their professional performance. Data sources might be students, teachers, supervisors, administrators, archival data, and so on. Data gathering methods could include surveys, interviews, systematic observation, videotaping, and so forth. The participants bring the data they have gathered to their collegial support group for assistance in data analysis and conclusion drawing. Each participant identifies a focus area for a long-term individual professional development plan.

In phase two, the participants complete several adult learning style inventories. A variety of inventories can be used for this phase. Possibilities include the Life Styles Inventory, Myers-Briggs Type Indicator, Kolb's Learning Style Inventory, Gregorc Style Delineator, and the Productivity Environmental Preference Survey. With assistance from the collegial group, participants compare the results of the chosen surveys, looking for themes about how they learn best. As the job-based data gathered earlier helps the participant to determine what professional growth she or he wishes to achieve, so the learning styles data helps the participant decide how to best achieve that professional growth.

In the phase three of the activity, the participants develop individualized professional development plans, including written reflection on the data they have gathered, objectives, learning activities, self-assessment activities, and a plan for using the results of their professional development to benefit other members of their school community. The planned professional development activities are not necessarily individual activities. They might include participating in group training, peer coaching, study groups, collaborative action research, and so on. The collegial group assists the participant throughout the planning process, asking critical questions, serving as a sounding board, and providing feedback. The activity culminates with the participant publicly sharing her or his plan.

Assessment Criteria

♦ Work-based data gathered by the participant is extensive enough and rich enough to provide a sound basis for identifying a focus area.

♦ The participant's written reflections on work-based data and adult learning inventories indicate in-depth self-reflection and critical-assessment.

♦ The participant's professional development objectives are consistent with the data, challenging, and achievable.

♦ Planned learning activities are well articulated, consistent with professional development objectives, and doable.

♦ Planned self-evaluation activities are well articulated, feasible, and appropriate for measuring the participant's progress toward professional development objectives.

♦ The participant's plan for sharing has the capacity to enhance colleagues' professional development.

♦ The participant's written plan and public sharing indicate a disposition toward facilitating others' self-assessment, personal reflection, and individual professional development.

References:

Allen, D., Fillion, S., Butters, J., Gordon, S. P., & Bently, K. C. (2004, April). *Considering national standards for instructional supervision: A review of the literature.* Paper presented at the annual meeting of the American Educational Research Association, San Diego, CA.

Brophy, J., & Evertson, C. (1976). *Learning from teaching: A developmental perspective.* Boston: Allyn & Bacon.

Cunningham, J. (2002). Building education professionals. *Leadership, 31*(4), 34–37.

Fetterman, D. M. (1996). Empowerment evaluation: An introduction to theory and practice. In D. M. Fetterman, S. J. Kaftarian, & A. Wandersman (Eds.), *Empowerment evaluation: Knowledge and tools for self-assessment & accountability* (pp. 3–46). Thousand Oaks, CA: Sage.

Gehrke, N. J. (1991). Seeing our way to better helping of beginning teachers. *Educational Forum 55*(3): 233–242.

Ginocchio, F. L. (1990). Teacher-clinicians put credibility into staff development. *Journal of Staff Development, 11*(2), 16–18.

Glickman, C. D., Gordon, S. P., & Ross-Gordon, J. M. (2004). *SuperVision and instructional leadership: A developmental approach,* (6th ed.). Boston: Pearson Education.

Gordon, S. P. (2000, November). *Professional development for teacher and school renewal: Alternative pathways, common characteristics.* Paper presented at the University Council for Educational Administration Annual Convention, Albuquerque, NM.

Gordon, S. P. (2004). *Professional development for school improvement: Empowering learning communities.* Boston: Pearson Allyn & Bacon.

Gordon, S. P., & Nicely, R. F. (1998). Supervision and staff development. In G. R. Firth & E. F. Pajak (Eds.), *Handbook of research on school supervision* (pp. 801–841). New York: Simon & Schuster Macmillan.

Hall, G. E., & Hord, S. M. (1987). *Change in schools: Facilitating the process.* Albany: State University of New York Press.

Heckman, P. E. (1993). School restructuring in practice: Reckoning with the culture of school. *International Journal of Educational Reform, 2*(3), 263–272.

Hord, S. M., Rutherford, W. L., Huling-Austin, L., & Hall, G. E. (1987). *Taking charge of change.* Alexandria, VA: Association for Supervision and Curriculum Development.

Krupp, J. (1987). Understanding and motivating personnel in the second half of life. *Journal of Education 169*(1): 20–47.

Levine, S. L. (1987). Understanding life cycle issues: A resource for school leaders. *Journal of Education 169*(1): 7–19.

National Staff Development Council. (2001). Standards for Staff Development. Retrieved on September 1, 2005 from http://www.nsdc.org/standards/index.cfm

Ornstein, A.C. (1990). A look at teacher effectiveness research: Theory and practice. *NASSP Bulletin, 74*(528): 78–88.

Pajak, E. (2003). *Honoring diverse teaching styles: A guide for supervisors.* Alexandria VA: Association for Supervision and Curriculum Development.

Senge, P. M. (1990). *The fifth discipline: The art and practice of the learning organization.* New York: Currency Doubleday.

Shulman, L. S. (1987). Knowledge and teaching: Foundations of the new reform. *Harvard Educational Review, 57*(1), 1–22.

Wu, P. C. (1987). Teachers as staff developers: Research, opinions, and cautions. *Journal of Staff Development, 8*(1), 4–6.

12

Standards for Supervision of Curriculum Development

Bernard Badiali

Meet the Author

Bernard J. Badiali

Bernard J. Badiali is an Associate Professor of Educational Leadership in the College of Education at the Pennsylvania State University. His main teaching and research activities have been in the areas of curriculum, staff development, school reform, supervision, and school/university relationships. Badiali is a former Chair of the Department of Educational Leadership at Miami University. He has served as a Leadership and Project Associate with the Institute for Educational Inquiry at the University of Washington. He has published numerous articles in a variety of educational journals and currently serves as Associate Editor of the Journal of Cases in Educational Leadership. He has recently developed a series of institutes for principals and instructional support teachers engaged in Scholastic RED, an on-line professional development program for teachers. His most recent book, *Teacher Leader* (with Thomas Poetter) was released by Eye on Education in 2000. Badiali also serves as a Professional Development Associate for the Central Pennsylvania Holmes Partnership Elementary Professional Development Schools.

Successful supervision:

- ◆ Assists in the identification of individual and collective plat-forms of beliefs about the aims of education, the nature of knowledge, the role of the teacher, and purposes of the curriculum

- ◆ Involves close collaboration with stakeholders in the processes of curriculum development, including setting goals, developing objectives, characterizing instruction, creating unit plans, speci-fying materials, and devising program assessments

- ◆ Renders curriculum policy and processes accessible and trans-parent to all stakeholders, including parent and community groups

- ◆ Fosters continuous deliberation on curriculum issues and prob-lems by connecting theory, research, and practice

- ◆ Ensures that curriculum planning leads to successful curricu-lum implementation by being knowledgeable of school im-provement and change process

- ◆ Ensures equitable access to knowledge for all students regard-less of race, gender, ethnicity, special needs, or social class

This chapter will focus on the supervision of curriculum development. It is intended for everyone who has or will have responsibilities for curriculum development and implementation beyond curriculum creation within a sin-gle classroom. The standards suggested in this chapter are intended as school-based standards. That is, they are standards that should be discussed, negotiated, adapted, or amended to fit the context of a particular school or school district. I strongly encourage all school leaders to make every attempt to come to consensus before creating policy for curriculum supervision. A school's curriculum belongs to an array of stakeholders. To maximize the probability that standards are implemented, there must be considerable de-liberation (McCutchen, 1995) and agreement about their nature.

At this point in the text you may have become comfortable with the no-tion that supervisory practices will benefit from an enumerated compilation of standards. However, to paraphrase Eisner (2002), "standardized supervision is an oxymoron." What good supervisors do is exercise good judgment. Of course, they should be well informed about the mechanics of curriculum design but, more importantly, they need to be knowledgeable and wise about the complexities of curriculum development. They should be keenly aware of the political nature of curriculum. They should understand the culture and values of their communities and how those values intersect with the demands and expectations of educational policy writ large. Curriculum supervisors should also understand their own values and biases with regard to the knowledge they believe to be of most worth. Standards then, like any governing policies, should not be considered rules, but rules of thumb tempered by good judgment.

Professional development standards are not new to the province of curriculum supervision. Almost every curriculum text used to prepare curriculum specialists includes a syllabus of recommended skills and knowledge necessary to design and maintain school curriculum. Although curriculum is a field of study unto itself, it shares a special relationship with the field of supervision. Those fields overlap and intertwine in the same way curriculum and instruction overlap and intertwine. The relationship between curriculum and supervision is tightly woven. Does this mean a curriculum supervisor must have expertise and intimate knowledge of every content area and every instructional practice? I think not. Of course, the more a supervisor knows about curriculum content and instruction the better. A critical attribute for curriculum supervision is that one understands the processes and principles involved in organizing and managing curriculum. This implies that all of the skills and dispositions that apply to supervision in general also apply to curriculum supervision, especially those skills that have to do with group dynamics, because good curriculum development is a group process.

The following recommended standards have been derived largely from examining well-respected texts within the fields of curriculum and supervision. Figure 12.1 illustrates what some prominent curriculum scholars consider to be essential knowledge, skills, and dispositions for curriculum supervision. I constructed it by analyzing tables of contents, relating direct suggestions from the authors, or making inferences based on author's commentary within the text.

It would misrepresent the current field of curriculum to suggest that a review of popular texts created mainly for the preparation of curriculum supervisors in schools describes all of the possibilities for curriculum supervision. We must acknowledge that many scholars in the curriculum field have redefined curriculum to include a much broader interpretation of the meaning of the term. To many scholars, curriculum is not simply a course to be run, or all of the experiences a child has under the aegis of the school. A growing number of curriculum scholars have distanced themselves from the world of practice. These scholars have been called curricularists or reconceptualists. They emphasize sociological and philosophical critiques of school curriculum decisions. Curricularists have created what some consider to be a new field, called curriculum studies, that emphasizes theory (Pinar, 2004).[1]

Because much of this discourse focuses on issues of social justice within the curriculum, any earnest student of curriculum, which includes the curriculum supervisor, would be remiss in not giving it serious consideration. The critical discourse in curriculum studies often gives perspective and insight into problems of curriculum practice.

Standards for Successful Curriculum Supervision

Standard 1: Successful Supervision Assists Identification of Individual and Collective Platforms of Beliefs

Successful supervision assists in the identification of individual and collective platforms of beliefs about the aims of education, the nature of knowledge, the role of the teacher, and purposes of the curriculum.

There are many essential and profound questions about school curriculum. Among the most interesting are these: What does it mean to be educated? What is the purpose for school? What knowledge is of most worth? I would like to think educators take time to consider and reconsider these questions fairly often. It might surprise you to learn what an array of responses one gets to these queries. Responses to these questions vary for a number of reasons. An educator's position on these questions may be contingent on the unique school experience: the grade level, subject area, school context, or school's culture. Every educator has a tacit, often unarticulated, set of values and beliefs that should be explored (Sergiovanni & Starratt, 2001). Curriculum development is a group process, so it is necessary to make beliefs and assumptions transparent. Consciously knowing one's educational orientation is essential. To better understand your own answers to these and other questions important to curriculum development, complete the Curriculum Platform Q-Sort (Poetter & Badiali, 2002) exercise, the sample professional development activity for this chapter.

---

1 For a complete discussion of the state of the field of curriculum, see Sears & Marshall (1990).

Figure 12.1. Comparison of Curriculum Supervision Responsibilities in Selected Texts

Authors	Text	Vision & Goals	Collaboration	Problem Solving
Tanner, D., & Tanner, L. (1995)	Curriculum Development: Theory Into Practice	Visioning and goal setting	Enhancing leadership capacity	Problem solving
Henderson (in Uhrmacker & Matthews, 2005)	Intricate Palette	Building a democratic platform	Building a work culture; establishing a network of leaders	Building inquiry capacity
Ornstein, A. C., & Hunkins, F. P. (1998)	Curriculum: Foundations, Principles, and Issues	Create mission or goal statement	Confer with parent, community, and professional groups	Problem solving
Armstrong, D. G. (2003)	Curriculum Today	Process of curriculum revision	Resource to curriculum teams	
Oliva (Supervision & Curriculum Development (1998)	Handbook of Research on School Supervision	Specification of curriculum goals & objectives	Specification of needs	
Wiles, J. & Bondi, J. (1998)	Curriculum Development	Long-range planning with stakeholders	Develop objectives with staff	Problem identification and solution
Harris, B. M. (1985)	Supervisory Behavior in Education	Work with committees to establish objectives	Work with committees to select personnel for curriculum projects	
Eisner, E. (2002)	The Educational Imagination	Curriculum ideologies, aims and objectives	Stimulate teacher ingenuity	Consider nonrational approaches to problems
Glickman, C. D., Gordon, S. P., & Ross-Gordon, J. M. (2004)	SuperVision and Instructional Leadership: A Developmental Approach	Sources of curriculum development	Reflective choice given to teachers	Enhancing collective thought and action

Evaluation	Building Capacity	Curriculum Development	Theory & Practice	Instruction
Needs assessment and summative evaluation	Creating conditions for improvement		Transform theory to practice	Design and Development
Comprehensive evaluation	Cultivating public understanding	Creative designing	Cultivating public understanding	Artistic, reflective teaching
Agree on a program for continuous evaluation	Develop tools for planning	Agree on program for continuous development, implementation and design	Balance demands of local, state, and national interests	
Processes of curriculum assessment	Process of curriculum implementation	Processes of curriculum development	Blend theory with practice	
Selection of evaluation techniques		Organization and implementation of curriculum		Selection of strategies
Needs assessment; evaluation of curriculum	Disseminate innovations	Development program for continuous curriculum development		
	Edit and publishes curriculum guides	Give demonstrations for using new approaches and materials		
Assessment should reflect the values of the intellectual community	Promote educational connoisseurship	Planning sequence is arbitrary	Theories provide generalizations to aid teacher reflection	Teaching as art
One of 14 components of program evaluation	Increase levels of teacher involvement	Deliberate sources of development	Match level of teacher development with level of curriculum development	Identify strategies that correspond to goals

Standard 2: Successful Supervision Involves Collaboration With Stakeholders

Successful supervision involves close collaboration with stakeholders in the processes of curriculum development, including setting goals, developing objectives, characterizing instruction, creating unit plans, specifying materials, and devising program assessments.

Before 1920, curriculum development was thought to be the exclusive purview of school administrators. It may be commonplace today, but until the Denver program in 1922, teachers did not participate in planning curriculum reform (Tanner & Tanner, 1987). Today's schools see supervision and curriculum development as interrelated processes; both are dependent on collaboration with classroom teachers. Collaborative teams have become the norm in schools that are striving to be professional learning communities (DuFour & Eaker, 1998). In learning communities, collaboration includes many stakeholders at many levels. Unfortunately, many of today's schools have to endure a period of legislated learning (Glickman, Gordon, & Ross-Gordon, 2004) where teachers and administrators seem practically powerless in the decision making process. High-stakes testing threatens to trump local decision making, taking much of the richness and texture from curriculum by limiting its focus. As a result of the testing movement, the task of the curriculum supervisor has become more difficult with regard to promoting collaboration and local decision making. This is the challenge that must be met to ensure that stakeholders at all levels remain vitally involved in curriculum development.

At the very least, curriculum can be thought of on four different levels beginning with the first and most important, the classroom level. At this level, the primary stakeholders are the teacher and the students. The size and number of stakeholders gets larger when we think of the curriculum at level two, the grade or department level. This level includes groups of teachers, students, and support personnel. At the third level, the number of stakeholders becomes larger because this level involves the entire school or district. At the fourth level, the curriculum stakeholders include the broader community, state policy makers, and possibly federal officials. Regardless of what level we are considering, the role of curriculum supervisor requires as much collaboration as is necessary to reach consensus. Figure 12.2 suggests aspects of curriculum development in which different stakeholders should collaborate.

Figure 12.2. Stakeholders in Collaboration

Level	Goals	Objectives	Instructional Approach	Materials	Program Assessment
1. Teachers and students	*	*	*	*	*
2. Groups of teachers, students, and support personnel	*	*	*	*	*
3. Representatives across the school district	*	*	*	*	*
4. Educators, community members, policy makers	*			*	*

* Identified stakeholders should collaborate in this aspect of curriculum development.

Standard 3: Successful Supervision Renders Clarity to Curriculum Policy and Processes

Successful supervision renders curriculum policy and processes accessible and transparent to all stakeholders, including parent and community groups.

Curriculum supervisors should work to create a process for making school curriculum open to all stakeholders. Stakeholders should be aware of curriculum policies and decisions and the reasons for them. This is not to suggest that an individual or interest group can demand changes in the curriculum. It is to ensure that all interested voices can be heard. When families, senior citizens, or educators have questions about the content or nature of the curriculum, they must have a process for voicing their concerns. Curricula, like public schools in general, are designed to serve the public good. In doing so, they invite input from all corners of a school's community. Curriculum supervisors should take lead responsibility for devising a process of public access to curriculum and for resolving the inevitable conflicts and disputes that naturally occur when differing viewpoints are aired.

Standard 4: Successful Supervision Fosters Curriculum Deliberation Using Theory, Research, and Practice

Successful supervision fosters continuous deliberation on curriculum issues and problems by connecting theory, research, and practice.

Sound decision making has always been a cornerstone of curriculum supervision. Although current federal and state mandates appear to be limiting local decision making, school-based curriculum teams still decide how curriculum should be designed and delivered. Curriculum supervisors take lead responsibility for seeing that decisions are made fairly and collaboratively. They are responsible for ensuring that all decisions about curriculum are well informed by research and scholarship in the field. Curriculum supervisors should stay current by reading and reflecting on how research and theory can inform curriculum in their school. It is incumbent on curriculum supervisors to keep decision makers apprised of any new information that has potential to inform their judgment. The gap between research and practice, and researchers and practitioners, has been well described (Eisner, 2002). The curriculum supervisor endeavors to narrow that gap by connecting ideas with practice.

Conventional research has not had the impact on practice that most educational scholars hoped for. Most practitioners do not read research journals. Those who do take the time to read professional journals have little faith that research other than their own will have relevance in their settings. There seems to be a general mistrust among practitioners that findings from national studies will generalize to local situations. Attitudes of practitioners notwithstanding, the curriculum supervisor should be well informed about current research and scholarship in the field, because part of the curriculum supervisor's function is to act as a resource to decision-making teams as they deliberate about what is in the best interests of the students they serve.

Another function in this regard is for curriculum supervisors to be knowledgeable about the practice and promise of classroom research, often called action research, teacher research, or teacher inquiry (Dana & Yendol-Silva, 2003; Glanz, 1998; Glickman et al., 2004; Nolan & Hoover, 2004). Adapted from a concept developed by Lewin (1951), action research suggests that teachers, principals, specialists, and other school-based personnel can take on the role of researchers in their own classrooms and school settings. Curriculum development, like teaching, involves a process of solving a complex set of problems. Action research is a systematic approach to addressing problems of importance to the teacher or curriculum development team. According to Nolan & Hoover (2004), a variety of questions can drive the action re-search process.[2] Curriculum can be the focus of questions ranging from the classroom level (How can I design a unit on fractions so it focuses more on a conceptual understanding rather than a procedural approach to equivalent fractions?) to the program level (How can we revise the middle school read-ing program so students become better critical readers of print and electronic texts alike?) to the district level (What is a fair and reasonable policy to address issues of censorship?).

There is little variation between action research and inquiry. The word "research" can conjure up visions of scientific data collection and statistical manipulation. Inquiry is less formal. The process still relies on formulating good questions from problems, but there are no fast rules about sampling, controlled environments, data, or hypothesis testing. Inquiry is, however, a systematic approach that includes specifying a question or questions, collect-ing data (often field notes, informal surveys, or interviews), interpreting the data, drawing conclusions, and formulating a plan of action to address the initial problem. This process fits well with curriculum development or curric-ulum improvement planning. The curriculum supervisor should not only take part in the inquiry process, but also be able to guide and model it for others.

Standard 5: Successful Supervision Ensures That Curriculum Planning Leads to Curriculum Implementation

Successful supervision ensures that curriculum planning leads to curric-ulum implementation by being knowledgeable of school improvement and change processes.

Supervision, especially curriculum supervision, implies taking part in the struggle for continuous improvement. As agents of change, supervisors have the responsibility for ensuring that the difficult work of curriculum develop-ment does not simply result in a written document that sits on a shelf. Unfor-tunately, that has been the fate of many well-planned curricula. A good rea-son for widespread involvement of the stakeholders is to ensure a sense of ownership. Ownership maximizes the chance that the curriculum that is planned together gets implemented. Keeping in mind that curriculum should be somewhat fluid and responsive to the changing needs of children, the curriculum supervisor has responsibility to monitor the curriculum's

---

2 For a comprehensive description of action research, see chapter 6 in Nolan and Hoover's *Teacher Supervision and Evaluation: Theory into practice.*

impact on students and convene groups for curriculum revisions as necessary.

Knowing the literature on school change can be indispensable to successful curriculum implementation. Despite what some outsiders may think, schools are very complicated places. They were created to prepare the young to participate responsibly in a democratic society. Democracy is dramatically dynamic and often perplexing. Anyone who has had brilliant ideas that never get implemented can tell you school change can be perplexing too. At this moment, you have some personal theories about how schools change. The Curriculum Q-Sort will help you access and articulate your position on the goals and aims of schooling. You should also try to articulate and clarify your personal theories of school change. I like to do this work by writing. I find writing helps me discover what I believe as I struggle to express my thoughts. You can do that by asking yourself a few simple questions. How has change come about in your school? What has changed during the last few years in your school and why? How was the change orchestrated? Why was it successful or unsuccessful? If the change was successful, what good did it serve? What could have been done differently?

The history of school reform and curriculum change is not filled with success stories. Sarason (1990) claimed that schools have been intractable with respect to school reform. I think we must include curriculum reform in that assertion. He says school reforms fail because reformers "have a superficial conception of how complicated settings are organized: their structure, their dynamics, their power relationships, and their underlying values and axioms" (p. 5). Fullan (1993) suggested there are eight basic lessons when considering school change.

1. You cannot mandate what matters.
2. Change is a journey, not a blueprint.
3. Problems must be seen as friends.
4. Vision and strategic planning come later.
5. Individualism and collectivism must have equal power.
6. Neither centralization nor decentralization works.
7. Connection with the wider environment is critical to success.
8. Every person is a change agent. (p. 22)

Another useful theory of school change is the Concerns Based Adoption Model (CBAM) (Hord, Rutherford, Huling-Austin, & Hall, 1987). CBAM became the inspiration for the simulation *Making change for school improvement* (Mundry & Herbert, 1988), a powerful tool for understanding the issues involved in curriculum implementation. The eight lessons built into the simulation are extremely relevant to the work of curriculum supervisors:

1. Change takes time and persistence.

2. Individuals go through stages in the change process and have different needs at different stages.

3. Change strategies are most effective when they are chosen to meet people's needs.

4. Administrative support and approval is needed for change to occur.

5. A critical mass of support is just as important as developing administrative support.

6. An individual or committee must take responsibility for organizing and managing change.

7. The objective of any change is to benefit students, not just "convert" staff.

8. Successful change is planned and managed. (Mundry & Hergert, 1988, p. 22)

The last axiom for change in Fullan's list is most relevant for curriculum supervisors as their role is to be in the thick of things. That does not mean curriculum supervisors must direct all of the activities around implementation. It means the curriculum supervisor shepherds the process. Implementation requires collaboration more than any other curriculum activity. Collaborative structures like team meetings, inquiry, workshops for stakeholders, and public engagement are critical to implementing a curriculum change.

Standard 6: Successful Supervision Insures Equitable Access to Knowledge for All Students

> *Successful supervision insures equitable access to knowledge for all students regardless of race, gender, ethnicity, special needs, or social class.*

In their edited text, *Access to Knowledge: The continuing agenda for our nation's schools*, Goodlad and Keating (1994) brought together experienced scholars to thoroughly explain the issues having a profound impact on school curriculum for decades. These issues are real. They are present, in varying degrees, in every school community. If schools are to live up to their promise for all children, then curriculum supervisors must become aware of and conversant about the impact of issues such as poverty, racial discrimination, unfair assessment, tracking, and gender equity. These issues are persistent not only because they are so difficult to address and resolve, but also because it takes more than a little courage to engage them. Even the best curriculum planning efforts can miss the mark if serious consideration is not given to equity. There is a heavy weight of responsibility on curriculum supervisors to make these issues known to all stakeholders and to try to get them to recognize and deal with such issues in their settings. According to Goodlad,

> deep-seated myths and prejudices about the distribution of ability to learn contribute significantly to differentiating students' access to the array of knowledge schools provide. The internal organization of schools, partly reflecting these myths and prejudices and partly designed to make the school's job easier, usually serves to create sharp differences in the educational opportunities enjoyed by students. (p. 3)

All of us have blind spots. Nowhere is that more evident than when considering issues of equity and privilege. My hope is that curriculum supervisors will help us all to discover our blind spots, not deny them. They have a moral obligation to invoke the highest ideals when working with individuals and groups on curriculum matters. That is a big task, but one well worth undertaking.

Professional Development Activity

The Q-Sort below can be completed individually, then discussed by pairs or small groups of preservice or in-service supervisors.

Curriculum Platform Q-Sort

Below you will find 20 statements describing our public system of education. These statements are arranged in four categories. They address the aims of education, the nature of knowledge, the role of the teacher, and the purpose of the curriculum. Your task is to prioritize these statements by numbering them from one to five in each category. Assign the number five to the statement you believe best represents your beliefs, four to the statement you believe represents your belief next, and so on until you have assigned a number to all five statements in each category. When you have completed this task, follow the directions in the rating guide to summarize your responses.

Aims

_____ A. To improve and reconstruct society; education for change

_____ B. To promote democratic, social living; to foster creative self-learning

_____ C. To educate the rational person; to cultivate the intellect through transmitting worthwhile knowledge that has been gathered, organized and systematized

_____ D. To provide for the construction of active citizens; to nourish civic literacy, citizen participation and political responsibility

_____ E. To promote the intellectual growth of the individual; to educate the competent person for the benefit of humanity

Knowledge

_____ A. Focus on skills and subjects needed to identify and ameliorate problems of society; active concern with contemporary and future society

_____ B. Focus on past and permanent studies, mastery of facts and universal truths

_____ C. Focus on reconstructing a visionary language and public philosophy that puts equality, liberty, and human life at the center of the notions of democracy and citizenship

_____ D. Focus on growth and development; a living–learning process; active and relevant learning

_____ E. Focus on essential skills and academic subjects; mastery of concepts and principals of subject matter

Teacher's Role

_____ A. Teachers are critical intellectuals who create democratic sites for social transformation. They empower students to question how knowledge is produced and distributed.

_____ B. Teachers serve as change agents for reform; they help students become aware of problems confronting humankind.

_____ C. Teachers should help students think rationally, based on the Socratic method and oral exposition; explicitly teach traditional values.

_____ D. Teachers are guides for problem solving and scientific inquiry.

_____ E. Teachers should act as authority figures who have expertise in subject field or content areas.

Curriculum

_____   A.   Curriculum centers on classical subjects and literary analysis. It is constant.

_____   B.   Curriculum centers on social critique and social change dedicated to both self- and social empowerment

_____   C.   Curriculum centers around essential skills (the three Rs) and major content subjects (English, Science, History, Math, and Foreign Language)

_____   D.   Curriculum centers on examining social, economic, and political problems, present and future, on a national as well as international level

_____   E.   Curriculum centers on student interests; involves the application of human problems; subject matter is interdisciplinary

Rating Guide for the Curriculum Platform Q-Sort

When you have completed the Q-Sort, go back and look at each category. Place the number that you assigned to each statement in the space provided in Figure 12.3. Add the columns to determine the educational philosophy with which you most agree. Grouped together, these statements represent the major tenants of each philosophy.

Figure 12.3. Rating Guide

	Perennialism	Essentialism	Progressivism	Reconstructionism	Critical Theory
Aims	C	E	B	A	D
Knowledge	B	E	D	A	C
Teacher's Role	C	E	D	B	A
Curriculum	A	C	E	D	B
Total					

Making Sense of Your Ratings

Figure 12.4 on the next page, will help you determine which philosophy your beliefs most closely align with. It is rare when ratings indicate a strong alignment with only one philosophy. Usually ratings indicate an eclectic mix with one or two ratings emerging as preferences. Compare your own preferences using Figure 12.4 to make sense of your ratings. Then compare your ratings with a partner. Discuss how your philosophies are different or similar and why.

The Q-Sort exercise can be helpful with members of any group working together on curriculum. It is useful to put a master chart of ratings on display so everyone can see the range of ratings. A group display will make it easy to compare and contrast ratings. As a supervisor, knowing your philosophical orientation and that of your coworkers can help you understand where conflicts may arise and why.

Figure 12.4. Characteristics of Philosophical Orientations

	Philosophical Base	Instructional Objective	Knowledge	Role of Teacher	Curriculum Focus	Related Curriculum Trends
Perennialism	Realism	To educate the rational person; to cultivate the intellect	Focus on past and permanent studies; mastery of facts and timeless knowledge	Teacher helps students think rationally; based on the Socratic method and oral exposition; explicit teaching of traditional values	Classical subject; literary analysis; constant curriculum	Great books; Paideia proposal (Hutchins, Adler)
Essentialism	Idealism; realism	To promote the intellectual growth of the individual; to educate the competent person	Essential skills and academic subjects; mastery of concepts and principles of subject matter	Teacher is authority in his or her field; explicit teaching of traditional values	Essential skills (the three Rs) and essential subjects (English, math, science, history, foreign language)	Back to basics; Excellence in education (Bagley, Bestor, Bennett)
Progressivism	Pragmatism	To promote democratic, social living	Knowledge leads to growth and development; a living–learning process; focus on active and interesting learning	Teacher is a guide for problem-solving and scientific inquiry	Based on students' interests; involves the application of human problems and affairs; interdisciplinary subject matter; activities and projects	Relevant curriculum; humanistic education; alternative and free schooling (Dewey, Beane)
Social Reconstructionism	Pragmatism	To improve and reconstruct society; education for change and social reform	Skills and subjects needed to identify and ameliorate problems of society; learning is active, concerned with contemporary and future society	Teacher serves as an agent of change and reform; acts as a project director and research leader; helps students become aware of problems confronting humanity	Emphasis on social sciences and social research; examining social, economic, and political problems; focus on present and future trends	Equality of education; cultural pluralism; international education; futurism (Counts, Grant, & Sleeter)
Critical Theory	Marxism	To challenge and deconstruct society, the status quo, powerful oppressors; to teach citizens to act politically for social justice	Focus on how the world works to privilege some and not others; awareness of race, class, gender, sexuality, and (dis)ability politics	Teacher acts with conscience and resolve as a social agent of change in the world with students	Teacher opens up societal norms to criticism and action	Some forms of service learning; socially active, alternative education programs (Freire, Apple, Giroux)

Assessment Criteria:

Using Figure 12.5, you can assess the results of the exercise.

12.5. Evaluation Rubric for Curriculum Orientation

	Excellent	*Good*	*Fair*	*Poor*
Identified Curriculum Orientation	Articulates how the curriculum orientation connects to my current practice	Describes several relationships between curriculum orientation and my practice.	Sees little relationship between curriculum orientation and my practice.	Sees no relationship between curriculum orientation and current practice.
Compares Curriculum Orientation to that of a colleague	Describes numerous similarities and differences in orientations using workplace examples.	Describes similarities and differences in orientations using workplace examples	Describes few similarities and differences in orientations.	Identifies no differences with colleague in orientation.
Compares Curriculum Orientation to that of the group	Describes numerous similarities and differences in orientations with group. Suggests implications.	Describes several similarities and differences in orientations with group.	Describes few similarities and differences in orientations with group.	Identifies no similarities or differences in orientations with group.
Sees Implications for Curriculum Development	Articulates numerous implications for curriculum development and for group processes.	Articulates several implications for curriculum development and for group processes	Articulates few implications for curriculum development and for group processes	Articulates no implications for curriculum development and for group processes

References

Armstrong, D. G. (2003). *Curriculum today.* Upper Saddle River, NJ: Pearson.

Dana, N. F., & Yendol-Silva, D. (2003). *The reflective educator's guide to classroom research.* Thousand Oaks, CA: Corwin Press.

DuFour, R., & Eaker, R. (1998). *Professional learning communities at work: Best practices for enhancing student achievement.* Bloomington, IN: National Educational Service.

Eisner, E., (2002) *The educational imagination* (3rd ed.). Upper Saddle River, NJ: Merrill Prentice Hall.

Fullan, M. (1993). *Change forces: Probing the depths of educational reform.* London: Falmer Press.

Glanz, J. (1998). *Action research: An educational leader's guide to school improvement.* Norwood, MA: Christopher-Gordon.

Glickman, C. D., Gordon, S. P., & Ross-Gordon, J. M. (2004). *SuperVision and instructional leadership: A developmental approach,* 6th ed. Needham Heights, MA: Pearson Education.

Goodlad, J. I., & Keating, P. (Eds.). (1994). *Access to knowledge: The continuing agenda for our nation's schools.* New York: The College Board.

Harris, B. M. (1985). *Supervisory behavior in education* (3rd ed.). Englewood Cliffs, NJ: Prentice Hall.

Henderson, J. (2005). Standing on Elliot Eisner's shoulders. In P. B. Uhrmacher & J. Matthews, (Eds.), I*ntricate palette: Working the ideas of Elliot Eisner* (pp. 53–62). Upper Saddle River, NJ: Pearson Education.

Hord, S., Rutherford, W., Huling-Austin, L.,& Hall, G. (1987). *Taking charge of change.* Alexandria, VA: Association for Supervision and Curriculum Development

Lewin, K. (1951) *Field theory in social science.* New York: Harper & Row.

McCutcheon, G. (1995). *Developing the curriculum: solo and group deliberation.* White Plains, NY: Longman.

Mundry, S. E., & Herbert, L. F. (1988). *Making change for school improvement.* Andover, MA: The Network Inc.

Nolan, J., Jr., & Hoover, L. A. (2004). *Teacher supervision and evaluation: Theory in to practice.* Hoboken, NJ: Wiley.

Ornstein, A. C., & Hunkins, F. P. (1998). *Curriculum, foundations, principles, and issues* (3rd ed.). Allyn & Bacon.

Pinar, W. F. (Ed.). (2004). *What is curriculum theory?* Mahwah, NJ: Erlbaum.

Poetter, T., & Badiali, B. (2002) *Teacher leader.* Larchmont, NY: Eye On Education.

Sarason, S., (1990). *The predictable failure of educational reform.* San Francisco, CA: Jossey-Bass.

Sears, J. T., & Marshall, J. D. (Eds.). (1990). *Teaching and thinking about curriculum: Critical inquiries.* New York: Teachers College Press.

Sergiovanni, T. J., & Starratt, R. J. (2001). *Supervision: A redefinition* (7th ed.). New York: McGraw-Hill.

Tanner, D., & Tanner, L. (1987). *Supervision in education.* New York: Macmillan.

Tanner, D., & Tanner, L. (1995). *Curriculum development: Theory into practice* (3rd ed.). Englewood Cliffs, NJ: Prentice Hall.

Wiles, J., & Bondi, J. (1998). *Curriculum development* (5th ed.). Upper Saddle River, NJ: Pearson.

13

Standards for Supervision of Action Research

Jeffrey Glanz

Meet the Author

Jeffrey Glanz

Jeffrey Glanz, Ed.D., currently serves as Dean of Graduate Programs and Chair of the Department of Education at Wagner College in Staten Island, New York. Dr. Glanz has authored, co-authored, and co-edited many books and peer-reviewed articles. His most recent publications include *What Every Principal Should Know About Leadership: The 7 Book Collection* published by Corwin Press. Consult his web site for additional information: http://www.wagner.edu/faculty/users/jglanz/web/.

Successful supervision:

♦ Employs action research as one of a variety of viable strategies to improve instruction

♦ Encourages the use of action research to create meaningful, ongoing, and nonevaluative instructional dialogue to improve teaching practice

♦ Promotes reflection and self-assessment throughout the action research process

♦ Employs action research to enhance decision making by identifying and solving critical problems

♦ Creates a systemwide mindset for school improvement by incorporating action research to instill a professional problem-solving ethos in the school

♦ Fosters action research as a means of promoting student achievement

Overview

In this chapter, I intend to lay the groundwork to support supervision as action research. Briefly explaining its emergence as a viable alternative to traditional supervision and its reliance on nonevaluative and collaborative strategies, the chapter then presents a case study and a professional development activity to support the standards outlined above.

The chapter offers these standards for action research as suggestions for practice, fully realizing the nature of supervision as action research is highly contextual. Readers should consider these standards, descriptions, and case studies as tentative, developmental, and idiosyncratic. Readers are encouraged to consider the extent to which supervision as action research makes sense in a given school or community.

Defining supervision has been a source of much debate for years (Bolin, 1987). Is supervision a function of administration, curriculum, staff development, action research, or a combination of these and other activities? Alfonso and Firth (1990) noted the study of supervision lacks focus largely because of the "lack of research and continuing disagreement on the definition and purposes of supervision" (p. 188). Traditional supervisory practice has received voluminous criticism (Glickman, 1992; Gordon, 1992; Sergiovanni, 1992; Starratt, 1992) for its lack of focus, reliance on noncollaborative and evaluative practices, and adherence to hierarchy and administrative fiat. The need for the creation and implementation of alternative approaches was recognized (Sullivan & Glanz, 2000). A wide range of options emerged, from forms of clinical and developmental supervision, to nonevaluative approaches of mentoring and peer coaching. More recently, action research has emerged as a popular way of involving practitioners, both teachers and principals, so that they better understand their work. Although originally developed primarily for the professional development of teachers, action research recently gained favor among principals as a way of improving schools by focusing on reflective practice for instructional improvement.

First popularized in the 1940s by Kurt Lewin (Adelman, 1993), action research was initially systematically applied in education by Stephen Corey, a professor at Teachers College, Columbia University. Corey encouraged teachers and supervisors to use action research to improve their own practice. Corey (1953) advocated that fundamental change could not occur without direct involvement of teachers and principals. He explained,

> The studies must be undertaken by those who may have to change the way they do things.... Our schools cannot keep up with the life they are supposed to sustain and improve unless teachers, pupils, supervisors, administrators, and school patrons continuously examine what they are doing. Singly and in groups, they must use their imaginations creatively and constructively to identify the practices that must be changed to meet the needs and demands of modern life, courageously try out those practices that give better promise, and methodically and systematically gather evidence to test their worth.... This is the process I call action research. (p. viii)

Action research gained further legitimacy when distinguished educators like Hilda Taba, curriculum specialist and also a professor of education at Teachers College, Columbia University, advocated action research in the late 1950s. She believed action research contributed much toward curriculum development. She saw two basic purposes for action research: to produce evidence needed to solve practical problems and to help those who are doing the action research to acquire more adequate perspective regarding their instructional problems (Taba & Noel, 1957, p. 2). For a more detailed description of this history, see Glanz (in press).

Recently, Sullivan and Glanz (2005) viewed supervision as the center for the improvement of instruction. They said supervision is the process of engaging teachers in instructional dialogue to improve teaching and increase student achievement. In this light, supervision uses an array of strategies or even alternatives to traditional supervision.

More recently, action research, building on past efforts to make supervision more collaborative and reflective, is viewed as a supervisory approach that not only engages teachers in reflection about their teaching, but also encourages teachers to examine the pedagogical practices that directly influence student achievement (Calhoun, 2002; Danielson, 2002; Marzano, Pickering, & Pollock, 2001). If supervision is a process that engages teachers in instructional dialogue to stimulate reflection and improve teaching and learning, then action research that aims to encourage reflection is a very important part of any instructional supervision program (Zepeda, 2003a). Action research is one of the neglected areas or instruments for instructional improvement. Once thought of as only a tool to collect data for teacher personal and professional development, action research today is employed by principals as a cutting-edge practice that encourages teachers, as thoughtful professionals, to reflect, refine, and improve teaching. Action research, then, becomes an integral component in any instructional supervision program.

In sum, supervision based on collaboration, participative decision making, and reflective practice is the hallmark of a viable school improvement program designed to promote teaching and learning. Action research has gradually emerged as an important form of instructional supervision to engage teachers in reflective practice about their teaching and as a means to examine factors that aim to promote student achievement. This chapter will now provide a case study and professional development activity that reflect the aforementioned standards. The case and activity reflect actual school experiences, although in some cases names and locations are fictionalized.

Case Study

This case study about one teacher is drawn from a larger study that examined alternatives to supervision (see Sullivan & Glanz, 2000). Doris Harrington is a tenured math teacher at Northern Valley Regional High School, a school that is comprised of 1,100 students. Having taught in the school for 18 years, Doris is excited about the new program that principal Bert Ammerman spearheaded to enhance professional development and instructional improvement. "I think it's neat that we now have a system in place in which we feel empowered. I mean, having an option, a choice in determining my professional development is certainly new and much appreciated," she said.

Doris selects an "action research" plan as a part of the supervisory program that teachers, supervisors, and administrators collaboratively developed. She said, "I've read so much about action research and am so excited that others now appreciate how important it is to provide time for teachers to reflect about what we do every day in the classroom." Doris's observations confirm many educators who maintain that encouraging effective teaching is one of the most important responsibilities of instructional supervisors (Schon, 1988).

Familiarizing herself with the literature on action research (Glanz, 2003; Mills, 2002), Doris reviews the four basic steps: (1) selecting a focus for study; (2) collecting data; (3) analyzing and interpreting the data; and (4) taking action. She wonders about her classroom. She asks herself a series of questions: What has been successful? How do I know these strategies are successful? What needs improvement? What mistakes have I made? In what ways can I improve my instructional program? Most importantly, which instructional strategies work best with my students in a given subject or topic? In collaborative conversations with her assistant principal, Jim McDonnell, Doris frames her project.

She wonders whether or not the time and energies expended on cooperative learning activities are worth the effort. Although familiar with the extensive research on the subject, Doris decides to compare her fourth period math class with her sixth period class in terms of how cooperative learning strategies will affect student achievement and attitudes towards problem solving in mathematics. She chooses these two classes because they are somewhat equivalent in mathematical problem solving ability. She selects a nonequivalent control group design commonly associated with ex post facto research because the study involves the use of intact classes.

She randomly assigns "cooperative learning" as the primary instructional strategy to be used with the fourth period class, while the other class will work on mathematical problem solving through the traditional textbook method. After six weeks of implementing this plan, she administers a posttest math exam and discovers, after applying a t-Test statistic, that the group exposed to cooperative learning attained significantly higher mathematical problem solving scores than the group taught math traditionally. Doris keeps an anecdotal record throughout the research project and also administers an attitude questionnaire to ascertain how students felt about learning math using cooperative learning groups as compared to learning math in the more traditional format.

Based on her findings, Doris decides to incorporate cooperative learning procedures with all her classes. In consultation with Jim McDonnell, she develops a plan to continue assessments throughout the year. Jim asks Doris to present her findings at both grade and faculty conferences.

Doris's enthusiasm for action research was emphatic: "Employing action research engenders greater feelings of competence in solving problems and making instructional decisions. In the past I never really thought about the efficacy of my teaching methods to any great extent. The time spent in this project directly impacts on my classroom practice. I'm much more skeptical of what really works and am certainly more reflective about what I do. Action research should, I believe, be an integral part of any instructional improvement effort. No one has to convince you to change an instructional strategy. Once you gather and analyze your own data, you'll be in a position to make your own judgements about what should or should not be done. Action research empowers teachers!"

Reflective Questions About Case Study

- How could Doris's experiences be replicated in your school or district?
- Would such a supervisory approach work for untenured teachers? Explain why or why not.
- What guidelines would you establish to implement action research as instructional supervision in your school or district?
- What are the benefits and limitations of such an approach to supervision?
- Explain why or why you wouldn't feel comfortable incorporating such a supervisory approach.
- What are other ways to incorporate supervision as action research?

Professional Development Activity

This activity relates most specifically to the sixth standard listed above, which states successful supervision fosters action research as a means of promoting student achievement. Although other standards come into play here, the activity seeks to engage participants in perhaps the most difficult or elusive standard, that of addressing the impact of action research on student achievement.

In the first phase of the activity, participants read the case study below.

Case Study

The International High School (IHS), a multicultural alternative educational environment for recent arrivals to the United States, serves students with varying degrees of English proficiency. The school's mission is to enable each student to develop the linguistic, cognitive, and cultural skills necessary for success in high school, college, and beyond.

IHS is a learning community in which professional development is not a separate initiative but, rather, is built into everything that is done. The faculty and the student body are organized into six interdisciplinary teams. On each team, four teachers (math, science, English, and social studies teachers) and a support services coordinator are jointly responsible for a heterogeneous group of about 75 students, 9th through 12th graders. The faculty works with the same group of students for a full year providing a complete academic program organized around themes like motion, conflict and resolution, or the American dream. Teams also provide affective and academic counseling.

The interdisciplinary teams provide an ideal infrastructure for professional development. Significant decision-making power over curriculum and even supervision is delegated to the teams. Team members engage in action research as not only an alternative to traditional supervision, but also, more importantly, a means to support faculty professional development and ultimately, student learning.

Maria Rodriguez, Bill Evans, Fred Alvaro, and Martha Cunningham are working together on a team. Integral to professional development at IHS is to brainstorm ideas on a wide variety of topics. Any team member can raise a problem or concern for group reaction. During one of these reflective sessions, Maria expressed concern about students' test scores in writing. Other members shared her concern. Statewide examinations in writing were mandated two years ago, and the team was concerned that preliminary data indicated students were significantly deficient in this area, especially because under the former administration little attention had been paid to writing. Team members met over the summer to decide on a curriculum plan for teaching writing, eschewing prepackaged writing programs all too common in other schools in the city. After much research, and in consultation with a prominent local university, the team decided to implement a rather well-known writing program sponsored by the university, although with significant modifications. Infusing writing in all content areas together with individual and small group writing consults, the team set out to make writing a priority in the fall semester. The team decided to field test the new program with a randomly selected group of students in 10th grade and identified a comparable group of 10th graders not in the program.

Eric Nadelstern, the principal at the time, supported the team and provided targeted professional development. He encouraged teams to use action research to demonstrate the impact of teaching on student writing achievement. As part of the program, students kept detailed writing portfolios that contained writing samples over time illustrating writing maturity. Writing assessments were continuously administered. Detailed monitoring of student progress along with constructive feedback were hallmarks of the program. After the administration of the statewide writing examination in May of that academic year, team members met to assess the impact of the program on student achievement, student writing motivation, and on the effectiveness of the teaching strategies employed by the teachers. Figure 13.1 summarizes their findings.

Figure 13.1 Summary of Findings

Instrument	Standard	Percentage Meeting	Conclusion
Standardized Writing Achievement Test	50% above 50th percentile	65% above 50th percentile (25% improvement over previous year); only 35% of girls scored above norm	Expectation met; examine achievement of girls (interviews, etc.)
Writing Portfolios	At least 50% scoring " acceptable" on portfolio rubric	55% scored acceptable but only 15% for girls	Expectation met overall but examine achievement for girls
Monthly Teacher-Made Exams	At least 50% scoring " acceptable" on writing rubric for idea development, sentence structure, and grammar	80% scored acceptable, but significantly less for girls	Expectation met overall but examine achievement for girls
Student Surveys	At least 80% registered satisfaction with new approach to writing	70% approval rating, but only 10% for girls	Expectation not met; further study needed

The second phase of the activity involves breaking into groups of no more than three individuals to undertake the following task: Based on the data collected in phase one as indicated above in the chart, plan phase two of the action research for the following school year. Answer the following questions:

- What conclusions can we draw from the data?
- What surprises, if any, are evident?
- What steps might we take to address these concerns?
- How might we share findings with others?
- What additional action research strategies might we employ?
- How might we better encourage high achievement for all students?

The third phase of the activity involves helping participants develop an "action plan" to address concerns expressed during the second phase. It is unlikely that participants will come up with a systematic action plan to address their concerns without guidance. At best, a number of viable suggestions might be offered. During this phase, participants are provided a set of guidelines for developing an action plan that might include, among others, a framework for conducting additional action research that includes, but is not limited to, a group leader to guide the plan, a group-developed goal statement, an objective or focus, additional research questions, a division of labor among participants of the study, an instructional plan to address stated concerns in phase two, a process for additional data collection, analysis, interpretation, built-in time for reflection and discussion, and a written document summarizing findings and recommendations.

Assessment Criteria

- Extent to which participants identify an action research project aimed to promote student achievement that is practical and feasible to carry out within the context of a school setting
- Extent to which participants identify at least three leadership behaviors that directly relate to promoting student achievement via use of action research
- Extent to which each of the aforementioned behaviors includes measurable indicators of success
- Extent to which participants develop a practical plan (written and shared with others) to promote student achievement via use of action research that includes assessment instruments to chart progress

Conclusion

I have described supervision based on collaboration, participative decision making, and reflective practice as the hallmark of a viable school improvement program designed to promote teaching and learning. Action research has gradually emerged as an important form of instructional supervision to engage teachers in reflective practice about their teaching and as a means to examine factors that aim to promote student achievement.

If supervision as action research is to make a meaningful and sustained impact in this standards-based era, influenced by national currents to standardize curriculum and emphasize greater accountability via high-stakes testing, then supervision standards need to be articulated, discussed, shared, implemented, and assessed. In this chapter, supervision as action research has been framed with six suggested standards.

References

Adelman, C. (1993). Kurt Lewin and the origins of action research. *Educational Action Research, 1*(1), 7–24.

alfonso, R. J., & Firth, G. R. (1990). Supervision: Needed research. *Journal of Curriculum and Supervision, 5*, 181–188.

Bobbitt, F. (1913). Some general principles of management applied to the problems of city school systems. *In Twelfth Yearbook of the National Society for the Study of Education, Part I, The supervision of city schools* (pp. 7–96). Chicago: The University of Chicago Press.

Bolin, F. (1987). On defining supervision. *Journal of Curriculum and Supervision, 2*, 368–380.

Calhoun, E. J. (2002). Action research for school improvement. *Educational Leadership, 59*(1), 18–24.

Corey, S. M. (1953). *Action research to improve school practices.* New York: Teachers College Press.

Danielson, C. (2002). *Enhancing student achievement: A framework for school improvement.* Alexandria, VA: Association for Supervision and Curriculum Development.

Glanz, J. (1991). *Bureaucracy and professionalism: The evolution of public school supervision.* New Jersey: Fairleigh Dickinson University Press.

Glanz, J. (2003). *Action research: An educational leader's guide to school improvement.* Norwood, MA: Christopher-Gordon.

Glanz, J. (2005). Actin research as instructional leadership: Suggestions for principals. *National Association of Secondary School Principals Bulletin* (NASSP Bulletin), 89 (643), 17–27.

Glickman, C. D. (1992). Introduction: Postmodernism and supervision. In C. D. Glickman (Ed.), Supervision in transition (pp. 1–3). Alexandria, VA: Association for Supervision and Curriculum Development.

Gordon, S.P. (1992). Paradigms, transitions, and the new supervision. *Journal of Curriculum and Supervision, 8*, 62–76.

Marzano, R. J., Pickering, D. J., & Pollock, J. E. (2001). *Classroom instruction that works: Research-based strategies for increasing student achievement.* Alexandria, VA: Association for Supervision and Curriculum Development.

Mills, G. E. (2002). *Action research: A guide for the teacher researcher* (2nd ed.). Englewood Cliffs, NJ: Prentice Hall.

Northern Valley Regional High School District. (2000). *Differentiated supervision.* Damerest, NJ: Northern Valley Regional High School.

Schon, D. A. (1988). Coaching reflective teaching. In P. P. Grimmett & G. F. Erickson (Eds.), *Reflection in teacher education* (pp. 19–30). New York: Teachers College Press.

Sergiovanni, T. J. (1992). Moral authority and the regeneration of supervision. In C. D. Glickman (Ed.), *Supervision in transition* (pp. 30–43). Alexandria, VA: Association for Supervision and Curriculum Development.

Starratt, R. J. (1992). After supervision. *Journal of Curriculum and Supervision, 8*, 77–86.

Sullivan, S., & Glanz, J. (2000). Alternative approaches to supervision: Cases from the field. *The Journal of Curriculum and Supervision 15*(3), 212–235.

Taba, H., & Noel, E. (1957). *Action research: A case study.* Washington, DC: Association for Supervision and Curriculum Development.

Zepeda, S. (2003a). *Instructional supervision: Applying tools and concepts.* Larchmont, NY: Eye On Education.

14

Standards for Program Evaluation

James F. Nolan, Jr.

Meet the Author

James F. Nolan Jr.

Dr. Nolan is currently the Henry J. Hermanowicz Professor of Education and Director of the Elementary Professional Development School Partnership at Penn State University. He is the co-author of three books: *Teacher Supervision and Evaluation: Theory into Practice* (Wiley/Jossey-Bass); *Classroom Management: A Professional Decision-Making Approach* (Allyn & Bacon); and *Teachers and Educational Change: The Lived Experience of Secondary School Restructuring* (SUNY Press). The professional Development School Collaborative that he directs was named the Distinguished Program in Teacher Education in 2002 by the Association of Teacher Educators and the Outstanding School University Partnership in 2004 by the Holmes Partnership.

Successful supervision:

◆ Identifies specific goals, objectives, questions, and evaluation standards that will guide program evaluation efforts by involving key stakeholders in the evaluation effort

◆ Collects a wide variety of data types that are matched to the goals and purpose of program evaluation efforts

◆ Ensures data-gathering procedures result in valid and reliable types of information that are useful in addressing the goals and objectives of the program evaluation process (Joint Committee on Standards for Program Evaluation, 1994)

◆ Carefully describes the perspectives, procedures, and rationale used to interpret findings of program evaluation efforts to make the basis for value judgments clear (Joint Committee on Standards for Program Evaluation, 1994)

◆ Ensures the program evaluation report is fair and complete in addressing both strengths and weaknesses of the program, to build upon strengths and improve weaknesses (Joint Committee on Standards for Program Evaluation, 1994)

◆ Ensures that program evaluations are both formative and summative, enabling ongoing adjustments to programs, leading to a summative determination of program effectiveness

Differences Between Evaluation and Research

"The supervisory process, whether exercised by a superintendent, a district supervisor, a principal, or a department chairperson [or teacher] inescapably involves program evaluation" (Sergiovanni & Starratt, 1993, p.164). These words, written 12 years ago, have been made prophetic over the last decade by the growth in high-stakes educational accountability mandates at both federal and state levels. Program evaluation, though focused most often on the evaluation of curricular and instructional programs for students, should also include evaluation of supervision and professional development programs designed for professional educators. Ongoing program evaluation is the responsibility of all of the professionals within the organization; however, those in supervisory roles have a special role to play. "A supervisor cannot be personally involved in every evaluation but should be responsible for seeing that the evaluation of special projects and of the overall instructional program is ongoing. The supervisor—whether school principal, department head, lead or master teacher, district director, or assistant superintendent—should constantly remind himself or herself of the standards for evaluation of educational programs" (Glickman, Gordon, & Ross-Gordon, 2004, p. 309). The purpose of this chapter is to explicate a set of standards by which the evaluation of instructional and curricular programs, as well as supervision and professional development programs, can be judged.

Many authors who write about instructional supervision link research and evaluation skills when discussing program evaluation. On the one hand, this linkage makes complete sense because the knowledge and skills necessary to carry out effective program evaluation are quite similar to those needed by researchers. On the other hand, this linkage can be problematic if the supervisor is not aware of some of the fundamental differences between evaluation and research. Before addressing the specific standards for program evaluation, we will turn our attention to pointing out how evaluation and research differ.

Fitzpatrick, Sanders, and Worthen (2004) said

> Evaluation uses inquiry and judgment methods including: (1) determining standards for judging quality and deciding whether those standards should be relative or absolute, (2) collecting relevant information, (3) applying the standards to determine value, quality, utility, effectiveness, or significance" (p. 5).

Evaluation differs from research in several important respects. The motivation of the evaluator is to provide information that will aid stakeholders in this specific instance, as opposed to adding knowledge to the field in general. The intent of the evaluator is to make judgments and decisions about the quality or effectiveness of a program, whereas the intent of the researcher is to draw conclusions about a phenomenon. The agenda for the evaluation is set through involvement and dialogue with key stakeholders, whereas researchers typically sets their own agenda. The criteria used to assess evaluations are accuracy, credibility, usefulness, and integrity, whereas research is assessed in terms of internal validity, reliability, and ability to be generalized. Finally evaluation is typically time-bound, that is, focused on a very short period of time, whereas the best research often accumulates over a long period of time (Fitzpatrick et al., 2004; Guskey, 2000). These distinctions between evaluation and research point out that even those supervisors who have developed skills as researchers still need to develop an understanding of program evaluation specifics to successfully carry out their roles.

A wide variety of approaches can be employed in any program evaluation, including objectives-oriented, management-oriented, consumer-oriented, expertise-oriented, and participant-oriented evaluation (Fitzpatrick et al., 2004). Regardless of the evaluation paradigm employed, the six standards for program evaluation articulated at the beginning of this chapter should be used as the basis for effective program evaluation. Our attention now turns to those specific individual standards.

Evaluation Goals, Objectives, and Questions

The first standard for program evaluation asserts the necessity for involving key stakeholders in identifying the purpose and goals for the program evaluation as well as the questions and standards that will drive the evaluation process. Sergiovanni and Starratt (1993) explained this further:

> An evaluation report can be prepared for different audiences. The evaluation of an experimental program, when prepared for a research community, might be unintelligible to a citizens' oversight committee. A self-study report prepared by a schoolwide faculty-parent committee would differ from a student report card. A faculty report on new textbooks prepared for the school board would differ from a psychologist's evaluation of the match between student developmental stages and a new textbook for a publishing house. Recent research on the politics of evaluation reporting suggests that not only what is evaluated but also the way the conclusions are drawn from the evaluation depends greatly on the audience for whom the evaluation is prepared. (p. 165)

It is important the supervisor begin the evaluation process by engaging the key stakeholders in a discussion about the purposes for the evaluation, the specific questions that need to be addressed by the evaluation, and the standards by which the program in question will be judged. Though many state evaluation systems, heavily influenced by the No Child Left Behind Act of 2001, lay out very narrowly defined questions and standards for school evaluation, local education agencies still have latitude in developing other standards and evaluation methods that can be used to assess program quality at the local level. For example, the local school or school district might choose to place heavy emphasis on a variety of outcomes that are typically ignored or under-valued by state assessment systems, such as higher level thinking and problem-solving skills, teamwork and social skills, citizenship behavior of students, student interest in school and learning, school or classroom climate, and student affective outcomes.

When the supervisor fails to engage fellow administrators, teachers, school board members, parents, and other community stakeholders in discussions concerning those program outcomes that are highly valued and should be assessed, the district becomes a prisoner to the single mandates of the state assessment system. An ongoing dialogue needs to be maintained across stakeholders that continually asks three questions:

1. What educational goals or outcomes for students are most important to us?

2. What evaluation questions should we be asking to assess these outcomes?

3. What standards of quality will we use in deciding if the goals are being met?

The answers to these three questions drive the entire process of program evaluation. These same three questions can be used to address not only educational programs for students, but also professional development and supervision programs for teachers. Too often, these fundamental evaluation questions are not asked about teacher supervision and professional development. As a result, supervision and professional development programs do not benefit from ongoing, rigorous evaluation efforts.

Identifying Data Collection Methods

Although the process of identifying the purposes of evaluation, the key questions, and the standards used will help identify the types of data needed to complete the evaluation, developing a plan for data collection is still a complicated process. The evaluation of an instructional program could include the collection of a wide variety of data types, such as student scores on state and national standardized tests; student scores on specialty standardized tests like the ACT, SAT, or Advanced Placement Examinations; teacher-made tests; student portfolios; student performances; student work samples; follow-up studies of former students in postsecondary institutions or on the job; surveys and/or interviews of parents, students, former students, teachers, and administrators; and case studies of individual students or groups of students over time. The supervisor must play a leading role in determining which of these data sources are most germane to the local school curricular and instructional program evaluations.

In addition to identifying the various data types to be collected, the program evaluator must consider the sampling procedures that should be used in collecting the data. Even though some types of state assessment data must be collected concerning the performance of every student in the school, collecting every type of data for every student is a tremendously costly exercise in both financial and human costs. Thus, some sort of stratified sampling procedure in which representatives of the various subgroups within the school are included seems to be a program evaluation necessity.

There are also numerous decisions to be made concerning data collection when evaluating professional development or supervision programs for professional educators. Guskey (2000) suggested that data concerning professional development effects may be collected at five different levels of interest, depending on the evaluation purpose, and questions: (1) the reactions of participants, (2) the learning of participants, (3) the level of support for participant learning within the organization, (4) participant's use of new knowledge and skills, and (5) student learning outcomes. A comprehensive professional development and supervision evaluation includes looking at the impact at all five levels, as well as multiple types of data from multiple participants or groups of participants at each level.

To aid the program evaluator in making decisions concerning the general types of data that might be collected for any program evaluation effort, Fitzpatrick et al. (2004) suggested the following possible data collection methods: documents and records, systematic observation of the program learning activities, telephone interviews; face–to-face interviews, written or electronic surveys, focus groups, tests, and alternative assessments to paper–and-pencil tests. In making decisions concerning program evaluation design, it is wise to consider the contribution that each of these data types could make to answering the evaluation questions developed through interaction with stakeholders. It is also advisable for program evaluation to use triangulation as a key aspect of data collection (Fitzpatrick, et al., 2004; Popham, 1988). Triangulation refers to the process of using multiple data sources to capture the same phenomenon. For example, using teacher interviews, systematic observation, and student surveys to examine changes in teacher behavior after participating in professional development or using standardized test items, teacher-made tests, and student work samples to examine student learning of a particular concept.

Ensure Validity and Reliability

It is possible to collect a wide variety of data concerning an educational program but fail to capture data that meet accepted standards for validity and reliability. Most educators define validity as the question of whether a test or other data collection tool measures what it is supposed to measure, but the issue is a bit more complex.

Validity asks the question of whether the inferences or interpretations drawn from the data collected are really appropriate (Popham, 1988). Validity resides not in the data collection tool itself, but in how the data are used. Validity really refers to the match among the data that were collected, the individuals from whom the data were collected, and the interpretations or inferences drawn from the data. For example, a test of student achievement may be a valid measure of learning for native speakers of English, but the same test might not be a valid measure of learning for a group of students whose native language was not English. The appropriate interpretation that might be drawn from the test for the nonnative speakers probably would center on their English comprehension skills rather than on their subject matter achievement. It is critical that the supervisor understand the various data types used in program evaluation and shepherd the process of data interpretation to make sure that valid uses are made of the data.

Reliability is the other measurement issue involved in data collection and interpretation. Reliability refers to the consistency of a data collection tool. What evidence is there that this same data collection tool applied in the same context to the same population will yield essentially the same results? Unlike validity, which resides in the uses and interpretations of data, reliability is a property of the data collection strategy itself. The reliability of paper–and-pencil measures, such as tests and surveys, can be calculated numerically through a variety of strategies (for example, use of alternate forms, split-half reliability, repeated measures, etc.). The reliability of other strategies, such as interviews and focus groups, depends to a large degree on the quality of the interview schedules that are developed and the fidelity with which interviewers adhere to the interview protocol. The use of multiple data sources like triangulation to capture the same data can help the supervisor gain a general sense of the reliability of the collected data. If the various data types yield essentially similar results, then the supervisor can feel confident that reliability is generally high. When the results differ widely across data types, the wise supervisor understands that reliability is in serious question. In such cases, it is important to examine the various data collection tools to see where the differences arise as well as to consider collecting more data before making any decisions or determinations about program quality.

Making the Basis for Value Judgments Clear

As noted earlier and as the word itself implies, the fundamental intent of a program evaluation is to make decisions concerning the value of the program. These value decisions should be made on the basis of clearly stated standards and criteria. Some program evaluation decisions have to be made on the basis of absolute criteria. For example, the state assessment systems

developed as a result of the No Child Left Behind Act of 2001 are based on absolute criteria. A certain percentage of students as a whole, and also of student subpopulations, must meet proficiency levels in reading and math each
year until 2014, when all students must be proficient. These standards, once
set by the state and approved by the federal government, are absolute.

However, most standards and criteria for school district program evaluation are relative and more open-ended. There are typically multiple standards and criteria that might be used to judge program quality, including impact on student learning, costs of the program, parental satisfaction and interest in the program, impact of the program on professional educators,
service to particular subgroups of students afforded by the program, space
requirements, etc. The supervisor's task is to encourage the key stakeholders
to clearly articulate the standards and criteria that will be used as the basis for
judgments concerning program quality early in the process. Establishing the
criteria early in the process has multiple benefits: it requires key stakeholders
to come to some common understandings concerning their shared values; it
provides an opportunity to check the data collection plan to make sure the
data collected will provide a clear basis for making quality judgments; and it
should help to prevent any powerful individuals or groups from dominating
the judgment-making process later on.

Although the important standards and criteria for judgment-making
should be articulated early in the process, it is worthwhile to allow space for
additional important standards and criteria to emerge during the process of
data collection. Sometimes, the data collection process will yield either benefits or drawbacks to a program not anticipated by the stakeholders who
helped to design the evaluation process. When unanticipated benefits or
drawbacks are identified, they should be brought to the attention of key
stakeholders for discussion concerning their inclusion as additional standards and criteria for making judgments concerning program quality.

In addition to those standards and criteria identified by stakeholders as
useful for assessing the quality of a particular program, Sergiovanni and
Starratt (1993) have identified a generic set of standards that can be applied to
the evaluation of most educational programs for both students and professional staff. These generic standards include:

- ♦ Equity: Does the program treat all groups equitably or favor
  some groups?
- ♦ Multicultural perspective: Does the program honor multicultural realities?
- ♦ Connectedness: Is the program linked to other programs and
  initiatives or does it divert resources from other programs?
- ♦ Schoolwide goals: Does the program intentionally and explicitly attend to schoolwide goals?

Evaluation Addresses Both Strengths and Weaknesses

There are very few program efforts, either for students or for professional educators, that are either totally successful or completely unsuccessful. The vast majority of programs have areas of both strength and weakness. Let's take, for example, a differentiated supervision program that allows teachers to make choices concerning how they will be supervised and grow professionally. Teachers who are self-motivated and seeking new ways to learn may benefit tremendously from the freedom that allows them to stretch and take risks. On the other hand, teachers who are less interested in continuous growth might find the new system allows them to take the path of least resistance and maintain the status quo. It is critical that a program evaluation of the new differentiated supervision plan addresses the consequences for both of these subgroups of teachers. The same is true with the evaluation of the instructional program. One of the major benefits of the No Child Left Behind Act of 2001 is the focus on various subpopulations of students within the school. The result is a renewed understanding on the part of key stakeholders concerning the differential impact of instruction on different students. By the same token, it is important the stakeholders be made aware of how the increased attention being paid to math and reading (the tested subjects) impacts learning in other subject areas that are not tested, such as social studies, fine and performing arts, physical education, etc. Effective evaluation, even summative evaluation, should leave stakeholders with a deep understanding of what the strengths of a particular program are, what the weaknesses are, and what steps might be taken to improve the weaknesses.

Formative and Summative Evaluation

Closely related to the notion of identifying both strengths and weaknesses through program evaluation is the belief that program evaluation should start very early in the program implementation process, enabling evaluation to be both formative and summative. Formative evaluation occurs while a program is in operation with the goal of providing ongoing information concerning strengths and weaknesses so the program can be improved. Summative evaluation, on the other hand, is conducted at the completion of a program with the goal of providing key stakeholders with information concerning the overall merit or worth of a program (Guskey, 2000). Although some externally funded programs in school districts require strong summative evaluation components, it seems the vast majority of program evaluation efforts in schools are formative in nature. Except for programs that are targeted at a particular temporary situation, most school districts do not begin programs with the intention of having the program go away.

It can also be argued that no evaluation effort is completely summative in nature because the results of a summative evaluation can often be used to improve programs that will be designed in the future and/or programs that are in existence in other locations. Thus, all evaluations should be designed with a formative use in mind. That is, they should be designed to benefit the program being evaluated or other similar programs.

On the other hand, I would argue every program also benefits periodically from evaluations that are somewhat summative in nature. By that I mean an evaluation that not only looks at how to improve the program, but also takes a look at the overall worth of the program. Too often programs are piloted with a formative evaluation design used to improve the program early in its existence and the evaluation process ends there. No effort is ever undertaken to assess the impact and worth of the program after it has been fully implemented. One might argue that many school programs, for both students and professional educators, have outlived their usefulness but have been allowed to go on living because no summative evaluation effort was ever mounted. Effective evaluation begins early in the implementation process, using formative evaluation strategies to improve the program, and continues after the program has been fully implemented in a summative effort to assess the overall impact and worth of the program.

Conclusion

Program evaluation is an important task for all of those who play a role in instructional supervision, including central office administrators, district supervisors, curriculum directors, principals, and teachers. Evaluation is a complex undertaking. There is much to know and be learned. Books, professional journals, workshops, and graduate courses are devoted to this complex task. Although supervisors need not be experts in educational evaluation, it is important that they be aware of general standards that can be applied to design evaluations and also can be used to judge the quality of any program evaluation. Such standards will be useful in evaluating curricular and instructional programs as well as in evaluating supervision and professional development programs intended for professional staff. The increased focus on evaluation and mandated accountability have made it imperative that all those engaged in supervision understand the process of program evaluation and have the knowledge and skills necessary to oversee evaluation efforts.

Professional Development Activity

This activity relates to the second standard listed above, which states that successful supervision collects a wide variety of data types that are matched to the goals and purposes of program evaluation efforts. This activity presents you with a real-life scenario and asks you to develop a plan for data collection to evaluate the impact of a specific instructional supervision program.

The school district in which you are hoping to become a building principal has recently decided to move from a traditional teacher evaluation system to a differentiated supervision process designed to enhance teacher growth. As part of the process of moving to differentiated supervision, the district decided that it would be useful to prepare a pilot group of teachers and administrators to engage in the process of clinical supervision (as defined by Cogan and Goldhammer). A group of 10 administrators volunteered to participate in the pilot program. There are three elementary principals, two middle-school principals, two high-school principals and one vocational education director. Each of these administrators will be supervising two teachers in their building using clinical supervision. In addition, the assistant superintendent and superintendent will each supervise one teacher at the elementary level. The 18 teachers who will be supervised will participate with the administrators in a five-day training program in clinical supervision next October. Each administrator and teacher dyad has agreed to complete five or six clinical supervision cycles during the remainder of the school year. The intent of the pilot is to prepare the principals to do clinical supervision on a larger scale and to prepare the teachers to eventually become peer coaches.

The district supervision and evaluation committee responsible for planning, implementing, and evaluating the move to differentiated supervision has recognized the need to evaluate this pilot program. The committee has identified the following evaluation questions as most pertinent:

♦ To what degree do the participants posses the knowledge and skills necessary to engage in the process of clinical supervision?

♦ Are administrators able to abandon the role of traditional evaluator and engage in a collaborative supervision process?

♦ Does the clinical supervision process result in changes in teacher thinking and/or behavior?

♦ What factors or variables inhibit or facilitate the implementation of clinical supervision?

Your task is to develop a plan for collecting evaluation data during the upcoming school year to address the evaluation questions developed by the supervision and evaluation committee. Your plan should include types of data to be collected; data sources (i.e., from whom the data will be collected);

and a timeline for data collection. Finally, you should write a two to three page rationale justifying the data collection plan you have developed.

Assessment Criteria

♦ Each of the four evaluation questions is addressed through multiple data collection strategies.

♦ Each of the data collection strategies included in the plan is germane to the evaluation question being addressed.

♦ Data collection strategies include plans for collecting data from the participants as a whole as well as from each of the important subgroups (i.e., teachers, principals, central office administrators; elementary, middle- and high-school levels).

♦ The timeline for the data collection plan is reasonable,

♦ The rationale for the data collection plan points out the congruence between the evaluation questions and data collection strategies.

♦ The rationale for the data collection plan draws on accepted standards of program evaluation.

References

Fitzpatrick, J. J., Sanders, J. R., & Worthen, B. R. (2004). *Program evaluation: Alternative approaches and practical guidelines* (3rd ed.). Boston, MA: Pearson.

Glickman, C. D., Gordon, S. P., & Ross-Gordon, J. M. (2004). *Supervision and instructional leadership: A developmental approach.* Boston, MA: Pearson.

Guskey, T. R. (2000). *Evaluating professional development.* Thousand Oaks, CA: Sage.

Joint Committee On Standards for Educational Evaluation. (1994). *Standards for evaluation of educational programs, projects, and materials.* New York: McGraw-Hill.

Popham, W. J. (1988). *Educational evaluation* (2nd ed.). Englewood Cliffs, NJ: Prentice Hall.

Sergiovanni, T. J., & Starratt, R. J. (1993). *Supervision: A redefinition* (5th ed.). New York: McGraw-Hill.

Appendix

List of All
Proposed Standards

Standards of Democratic Supervision

Successful supervision:

1.1   Promotes and facilitates students and teachers coming to know themselves and to be themselves

1.2   Helps students and teachers become more self-directed, both individually and collectively

1.3   Promotes and facilitates everyone's transpersonal development

1.4   Promotes and facilitates a voice in policies, practices, and procedures for everyone

1.5   Encourages various types of discourse and communication events

1.6   Promotes and facilitates critical inquiry—of self, context(s), and practices—and fosters critique

1.7   Acts on critical input

1.8   Promotes and facilitates the elimination of coercion and intimidation

1.9   Fosters different kinds of association, in classrooms and throughout the organization

1.10   Buffers the organization and its individuals from undemocratic or antidemocratic forces

1.11   Calls on supervisors to adopt a role as "first among equals"

Standards of Ethical Learning and Teaching

Successful supervision:

2.1   Establishes good working relationships with teachers and support staff based on respecting and trusting their professional and moral competence and based on genuinely caring for them in their intrinsic goodness

2.2   Encourages teachers to establish good working relationships with each student, based on understanding the student's cultural and immediate social environment and respecting all students' present talents and interests and their huge potential

2.3   Identifies and articulates personal and civic values and meanings in the curriculum being taught by teachers with whom supervisors work

2.4   Encourages teachers as they plan their curriculum to articulate the personal and civic value of the material under study

2.5   Encourages teachers to translate various units of the curriculum they are teaching into personally and publicly meaningful learnings that foster student's sense of identity, membership, and participation in the natural, cultural, and social worlds

2.6   Encourages teachers and learners to develop a sense of responsible participation in the world, reflected in the material under study in the classroom

2.7   Encourages teachers to develop rubrics with learners for personally authentic learning

Standards of Collegiality and Collaboration

Successful supervision:

3.1   Creates and sustains a learning community that supports teaches as both learners and leaders

3.2   Reduces isolation by encouraging teachers and other school personnel to collaborate by engaging in critical discussions about instructional practices that transcend individual classrooms

3.3   Promotes a culture of cooperative work and risk taking among teachers

3.4   Promotes a can-do attitude and a safety net as teachers face uncertainties associated with high-stakes learning and work environments

3.5   Pays attention to affective domains, including developing professional relationships, promoting openness to individual and collective improvement, and caring for teachers by nurturing relational trust, respect, personal regard, and integrity

3.6   Provides momentum for the development of differentiated forms of supervision (e.g., action research, portfolio development, peer coaching) where teachers are the major actors setting the course for expanded learning opportunities

Standards of Reflective Practice

Successful supervision:

4.1   Reviews actions and accepts feedback about actions and perceptions of those actions in conversations with others

4.2   Plans actions, describes plans, and checks plans with others

4.3   Interprets and constructs meaning in conversations, and inquires about interpretations of others

4.4   Invites feedback and asks questions about assumptions, perspectives, and beliefs about self and others

4.5   Openly accepts criticisms for actions and decisions and does not become defensive when questioned by others

4.6   Accepts responsibility for decisions or actions taken. Does not rationalize behaviors, blame policy, others, or practices for actions or decisions.

4.7   Asks questions about the effects of actions or decisions on others (e.g., colleagues, employees, clients, students, on policy and/or future practice)

4.8   Asks questions about the extent to which the actions or decisions are moral or ethical

4.9   Asks questions about the results of actions or decisions on disenfranchised, underrepresented, and/or marginalized populations

Standards of Critical Inquiry

Successful supervision:

5.1   Asks whose interests are being served through teaching and schooling

5.2   Facilitates effective teaching for the least advantaged in the school and its community

5.3   Provides the opportunity for students to have ownership and voice in their learning

5.4   Assists educators to develop, enhance, and promote school–community relations in teaching

5.5   Pursues questions about why teaching is enacted the way it is, what sustains particular practices, and how to pursue alternatives

5.6   Examines learning in terms other than "deficit" terms and focuses instead on the wider forces that interfere with teaching and learning

5.7   Has a paramount concern with ensuring the advancement of a socially just curriculum

Standards of Diversity

Successful supervision:

6.1   Provides a variety of opportunities for teachers and students to develop and disseminate desirable public and private visions, values, knowledge, and skills about diversity in U.S. history, life, culture, and education

6.2   Provides systematic assessment and constructive feedback to teachers and students about building their emerging competencies in ethnic and cultural diversity

6.3   Makes necessary resources available and facilitates their use, ensuring that ethnic and cultural diversity are woven into all aspects of the educational enterprise in ways that are appropriate to task, domain, context, and audience

6.4   Determines if multiple ethnic, cultural, social, and experiential perspectives are used in analyzing challenges and providing opportunities for learning about and responding to diversity

6.5   Monitors teaching and learning activities for and about cultural diversity to ensure that they are always multiethnic, multiracial, multidisciplinary, and multidimensional

6.6   Helps classroom teachers and other educators develop a deep knowledge and critical consciousness of how cultural diversity influences the educational opportunities, programs, practices, and outcomes for students from different ethnic groups, and develop skills to make these processes more multicultural

6.7   Ensures that comprehensive approaches are used to teach and learn about ethnic, racial, cultural, and social diversity on a regular basis throughout the educational process

6.8   Helps teachers and students determine and continually improve the quality of their teaching and learning about ethnic and cultural diversity with respect to relevance, accuracy, and significance

6.9   Assists teachers to systematize their decision making, problem solving, implementation actions, and progress monitoring for making all aspects of the educational enterprise more inclusive of and responsive to ethnic, racial, cultural, social, and linguistic diversity

Standards for Clinical Supervision

Successful supervision:

7.1   Is grounded in a thorough understanding of the students and the context in which the teacher works

7.2   Is grounded in a comprehensive understanding of pedagogy and encourages a deliberate and articulate connection between classroom activities and the instructional goals of the teacher for the students

7.3   Elicits from each teacher, a meaningful discussion of student learning progress and consideration of how adaptive teaching strategies contribute to present and future learning of diverse and individual students

7.4   Provides a framework in which many learning and communicative styles are possible, given the instructional needs of the students, and refrains from imposing any one style upon the teacher

7.5   Models that learning to teach is a developmental process, and thus modifies feedback to make it accessible to the teacher and to address the most important dimensions of teaching or areas of immediate need

7.6   Helps teachers (and supervisors) articulate and document how seemingly small episodes of teaching relate to a larger vision for educating students and promotes supportive collegial relationships among educators to develop a collaborative learning community in a school

7.7   Models qualities of tactful and skilled communication, goal clarity, data-based performance assessment, and guided self-evaluation

7.8   Seeks to help teachers build their professional identity through thoughtful connections among clear goals for students, documentation of student accomplishment, a personal mission or platform for teaching, and careful analysis of personal teaching performance

Standards for Teacher Evaluation

Successful supervision:

8.1   Employs differentiated procedures for teacher evaluation. These procedures are appropriate to respective levels of teachers' professional development

8.2   Requires that teachers and administrators to work as collaborative partners to identify teachers' professional development goals, appropriately assess those goals, analyze data collected as evidence of effort toward and accomplishment of the goals, and to interpret the implications of such evidence for the improvement of teaching and learning

8.3   Evaluates teachers using data derived from multiple sources and points in time. Ideally, data are also provided by multiple evaluators.

8.4   Recognizes that evaluation of teaching is both formative and summative; however, the majority of evaluation resources are used for formative evaluation processes

8.5   Ties evaluation of teaching both to individual teachers' professional development goals and to school and/or program improvement goals

8.6   Ensures that evaluation policies and the goals and outcomes that are the basis for evaluation of teaching are well defined, plainly articulated, and clearly communicated. Administrators and teachers are well informed about these policies and goals.

Standards for Supervision of Professional Development

Successful supervision:

9.1   Involves participants in the planning, delivery, and evaluation of professional development programs

9.2   Facilitates job-embedded professional development

9.3   Assists teachers with gathering and analyzing data on student learning as part of professional development

9.4   Offers opportunities for dialogue on curriculum, teaching, and learning as part of the professional development process

9.5   Differentiates professional development activities to address differences in career phase, adult learning style, teaching assignment, teaching style, interests, and concerns

9.6   Assists teachers as they engage in self-assessment and personal reflection as a basis for self-directed professional development.

Standards for Supervision
of Curriculum Development

Successful supervision:

10.1 Assists in the identification of individual and collective platforms of beliefs about the aims of education, the nature of knowledge, the role of the teacher, and purposes of the curriculum

10.2 Involves close collaboration with stakeholders in the processes of curriculum development, including setting goals, developing objectives, characterizing instruction, creating unit plans, specifying materials, and devising program assessments

10.3 Renders curriculum policy and processes accessible and transparent to all stakeholders, including parent and community groups

10.4 Fosters continuous deliberation on curriculum issues and problems by connecting theory, research, and practice

10.5 Ensures that curriculum planning leads to successful curriculum implementation by being knowledgeable of school improvement and change process

10.6 Ensures equitable access to knowledge for all students regardless of race, gender, ethnicity, special needs, or social class

Standards for Supervision
of Action Research

Successful supervision:

11.1 Employs action research as one of a variety of viable strategies to improve instruction

11.2 Encourages the use of action research to create meaningful, ongoing, and nonevaluative instructional dialogue to improve teaching practice

11.3 Promotes reflection and self-assessment throughout the action research process

11.4 Employs action research to enhance decision making by identifying and solving critical problems

11.5 Creates a systemwide mindset for school improvement by incorporating action research to instill a professional problem-solving ethos in the school

11.6 Fosters action research as a means of promoting student achievement

Standards for Program Evaluation

Successful supervision:

12.1   Identifies specific goals, objectives, and evaluation standards that will guide program evaluation efforts by involving key stakeholders in the evaluation effort

12.2   Collects a wide variety of data types that are matched to the goals and purpose of program evaluation efforts

12.3   Ensures data-gathering procedures result in valid and reliable types of information that are useful in addressing the goals and objectives of the program evaluation process

12.4   Carefully describes the perspectives, procedures, and rationale used to interpret findings of program evaluation efforts to make the basis for value judgments clear

12.5   Ensures that the program evaluation report is fair and complete in addressing both strengths and weaknesses of the program, to build upon strengths and improve weaknesses

12.6   Ensures that program evaluations are both formative and summative, enabling ongoing adjustments to programs, leading to a summative determination of program effectiveness